Studies in Computational Intelligence

Volume 1254

The series "Studies in Computational Intelligence" (SCI) publishes new developments and advances in the various areas of computational intelligence—quickly and with a high quality. The intent is to cover the theory, applications, and design methods of computational intelligence, as embedded in the fields of engineering, computer science, physics and life sciences, as well as the methodologies behind them. The series contains monographs, lecture notes and edited volumes in computational intelligence spanning the areas of neural networks, connectionist systems, genetic algorithms, evolutionary computation, artificial intelligence, cellular automata, self-organizing systems, soft computing, fuzzy systems, and hybrid intelligent systems. Of particular value to both the contributors and the readership are the short publication timeframe and the world-wide distribution, which enable both wide and rapid dissemination of research output.

Indexed by SCOPUS, DBLP, WTI AG (Switzerland), zbMATH, SCImago.

All books published in the series are submitted for consideration in Web of Science.

Soumi Majumder • Bitan Misra

AI-Empowered Industrial Relations

Springer

Soumi Majumder
Future Institute of Engineering and Management
Future Business School
Kolkata, West Bengal, India

Bitan Misra
Computer Science and Engineering
Techno International New Town
Kolkata, West Bengal, India

ISSN 1860-949X ISSN 1860-9503 (electronic)
Studies in Computational Intelligence
ISBN 978-3-032-14556-7 ISBN 978-3-032-14557-4 (eBook)
https://doi.org/10.1007/978-3-032-14557-4

This Springer imprint is published by the registered company Springer Nature Switzerland AG
The registered company address is: Gewerbestrasse 11, 6330 Cham, Switzerland

Preface

Artificial intelligence (AI) has become a revolutionary force in many societal and economic areas in the quickly changing twenty-first century. It can completely transform labour and industrial relations, presenting both difficult obstacles and never-before-seen opportunities. This book examines how artificial intelligence (AI) will impact labour negotiations, future of employment, and larger dynamics of industrial relations. AI's incorporation into labour and industrial relations has several potential advantages for companies and workers alike. Among the principal benefits are increased productivity and efficiency: AI can automate repetitive jobs, freeing up human labour to concentrate on more intricate, imaginative, and strategic duties.

There are two sides to the coin regarding AI integration with labour and industrial relations. On the one hand, it presents the possibility of greater production, better decision-making, and more efficiency. AI-powered solutions may automate repetitive operations, analyse large data sets for patterns and trends, and give companies and employees insightful information. However, the development of AI also brings with it worries about privacy, loss of jobs, and possibility of a worsening of already-existing workplace disparities.

The book covers the following topics: introduction to AI-driven industrial relations, importance and benefits of incorporating AI in industrial relations, AI and its applications in different industries, harnessing the power of industrial AI for optimizing operations and productivity, impact of AI on work and workers, automation and job displacement, rise of new jobs and skills, algorithmic management and employee monitoring, future of work: human–AI collaboration, collective bargaining and dispute resolution, AI facilitating more efficient negotiations, role of unions in an AI-powered workplace, AI-assisted dispute resolution mechanisms, legal and ethical considerations in AI-driven industrial relations, importance of ethical development and use of AI, shaping the future of work through collaboration, future trends and opportunities in AI-driven industrial relation, exploring emerging trends and advancements in AI for industrial relations, opportunities for collaboration between humans and machines in industrial settings, case studies and success stories, and real-world examples of organizations implementing AI in industrial relations.

Kolkata, West Bengal, India Soumi Majumder
Kolkata, West Bengal, India Bitan Misra

Contents

About the Authors

Soumi Majumder is a Research Scholar in the Department of Business and Management at Lincoln University College, Malaysia, and an Assistant Professor at the Future Business School, Future Institute of Engineering and Management, Kolkata, India. She has over 10 years of academic and 2 years of industry experience and has previously served at institutions such as Sister Nivedita University, Techno India College of Technology, and NSHM College of Management and Technology. She has authored five books, including titles published by Springer Nature, Taylor & Francis, and Emerald, along with two edited volumes. Her research focuses on quality of work life, stress management, employee engagement, leadership, and entrepreneurship, with over 25 papers in reputed national and international journals and conferences. She holds one patent and four copyrights from the Government of India and serves as a reviewer for journals by Elsevier, Springer, Emerald, and Sage.

Bitan Misra is currently working as an Assistant Professor in the Department of Computer Science and Engineering at Techno International New Town, Kolkata, West Bengal, India. She has published more than 30 research papers in various international journals, book chapters, and conferences. She has written five books published by Springer Nature, Taylor & Francis, and Elsevier. She has served as a reviewer in many peer-reviewed journals and conferences. She holds multiple patents and copyrights from the Government of India. She has also worked as Associate Editor in the International Journal of Ambient Computing and Intelligence (IJACI). Her main research interests include optimization techniques, deep learning, evolutionary algorithms, and soft computing techniques. She is a member of IEEE and Internet Society.

About the Authors

Chapter 1
Introduction to AI-Driven Industrial Relations

1.1 Introduction

"Industrial Relations" encompass interactions between employers and employees at various levels, including the national, regional, and company. It also addresses social and economic issues such as wage determination, working hours, and working conditions. Every country's industrial relations system is shaped by its unique historical, economic, and political background, leading to differences between nations. Within industrial relations, social dialogue is essential for communicating and sharing information, preventing and resolving conflicts, and addressing work-related issues [1]. Social dialogue is effective as a tool for democratic governance and participation, as well as a factor for economic stability and growth and a method for promoting peaceful workplace relationships. Industrial relations play a crucial role in businesses, as they impact the work environment, as well as the production and delivery of goods and services [2]. Before setting up operations in a specific country, companies must thoroughly research and comprehend how industrial relations function due to the variations between systems. For example, individuals might be interested in determining if collective bargaining takes place within a scenario involving multiple employers if collective agreements are expanded to include all employees and employers (regardless of union or organization membership), whether numerous unions are permitted within a specific company and if they all can enter into collective agreements, or if unions typically have contentious relationships and participate in group conflicts. In addition, owing to globalization, new approaches, such as international framework agreements (IFAs) between a multinational corporation and a global union, have been developed to expand industrial relationships internationally [3]. Six primary parties are actively connected to every industrial relations system (Fig. 1.1). The individuals mentioned include workers, companies, employer groups, governments, labor unions, legal system participants, and dispute resolution forums. Artificial intelligence comprises various

S. Majumder, B. Misra, *AI-Empowered Industrial Relations*, Studies in Computational Intelligence 1254, https://doi.org/10.1007/978-3-032-14557-4_1

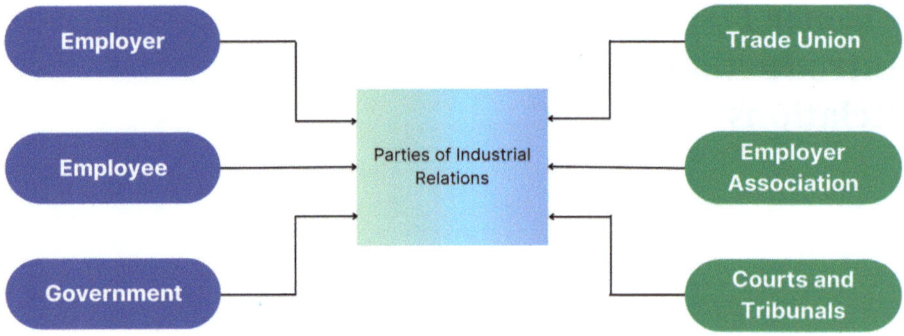

Fig. 1.1 Parties of industrial relations

technologies that work together to allow machines to perceive, understand, take action, and learn with intelligence similar to that of humans. Perhaps this is why there is variation in people's understanding of artificial intelligence, AI is not a singular entity. Machine learning and natural language processing are included in the AI field. Every individual is progressing in their way and, when used alongside data, analytics, and automation, can assist companies in reaching their objectives, whether it is enhancing customer service or streamlining the supply chain.

Industrial relations also encompass the methods by which these connections are manifested (such as collective bargaining, workers' involvement in decision-making, and resolving grievances and disputes), as well as the handling of conflicts between employers, employees, and labor unions when they occur [4]. Therefore, it can be inferred that industrial relations are the interactions between individuals and their companies within the workplace that determine employment terms and conditions. The goals of IR are discussed in this section. The interests of both labor and management should be protected by fostering strong mutual understanding and goodwill among all industry participants to prevent conflicts and promote productive and harmonious relationships. The goal is to increase productivity during times of full employment by reducing turnover and absenteeism; minimizing strikes, lockouts, and other disruptions through fair wages and improved living and working conditions; and enhancing economic conditions for workers within existing industrial and political frameworks, with state oversight to regulate production and support positive industrial relations. In the fast-changing environment of the twenty-first century, artificial intelligence (AI) has become a game-changing factor in diverse areas of society and the economy. Its capacity to transform labor and industrial relations is notably important, providing new possibilities and intricate hurdles. This artefact investigates the diverse impacts of AI on the future of work, labor talks, and wider aspects of industrial relations [5, 6].

In recent years, there have been significant advancements in the field of artificial intelligence, which involves creating computer systems capable of completing tasks that usually need human intelligence. AI technologies are becoming more advanced and widespread, ranging from machine learning algorithms that handle large datasets to natural language processing systems that comprehend and produce human-like text. As these advancements in technology further develop, their influence on the workplace and labor relations intensifies. Both positive and negative aspects of incorporating AI into labor and industrial relations exist. On the other hand, it provides the possibility of higher efficiency, better decision-making, and increased productivity [7]. AI-driven systems can examine intricate data collections to detect patterns and trends, streamline repetitive duties, and offer valuable information to both employers and employees. However, the increase in AI has raised concerns about job loss, privacy, and the possible worsening of current inequalities in the workforce. Before delving into the specific uses of AI in labor and industrial relations, it is crucial to first establish a fundamental grasp of AI and its importance in this field.

Artificial intelligence includes a variety of technologies and methods. Machine learning involves algorithms that can analyze data and then make predictions or decisions. NLP refers to computers' ability to comprehend, analyze, and produce human language [8]. Computer vision refers to systems that can analyze and comprehend visual data in the environment. Robotics is the creation and control of machines capable of carrying out manual activities. Expert systems are artificial intelligence programs that imitate the decision-making skills of a human expert. AI can be utilized in different areas of workforce management, negotiations, dispute resolution, and policymaking within labor and industrial relations. It's possible uses vary from automating administrative tasks to offering advanced analytics for strategic decision-making.

1.2 Importance of AI-Driven Industrial Relations

The goal of artificial intelligence is to integrate human cognition into the functioning of machines. The reason for the emergence is to minimize human involvement in the operation of machinery and enhance productivity [9]. The application of automation is expanding to various sectors, including industry e-services and personal devices, to replace human effort and enhance job quality in areas previously managed by humans. For example, in a factory where human involvement increases the likelihood of errors in work processes, the use of robots can eliminate the possibility of human error [10]. Hence, the utilization of air has increased over time because of its strong algorithm and ability to perform intricate tasks flawlessly. The rapid implementation of automation in industry and businesses represents the digital transformation and technological advancement of the business environment. Additionally, the fourth industrial revolution has hastened the process of converting analog data into digital formats, providing insight into both business and no business operations. AI has the ability to manage data processing, utilization, and handling, highlighting the importance of AI adoption in business settings. Improving decision-making in businesses by using AI to predict data related to the business. It can also offer round-the-clock services to customers with no interference from intermediaries. Hence, the utilization of artificial intelligence as a means to oversee operations is advantageous for businesses, leading to the advancement of artificial intelligence [11]. The common characteristics of AI, as recognized by numerous global businesses, include intricate problem-solving abilities, rapid reaction times, and efficiency in completing tasks. This explains why integrating automated technologies into a business is increasingly essential, as it offers cost savings and provides a competitive edge within the industry. Nonetheless, implementing it is becoming more expensive for a company because of the presence of multiple intricate algorithms and cutting-edge technologies [12]. Furthermore, an AI-powered machine cannot generate creative outputs, as it is unable to generate innovative ideas for a product or service. Creativity is essential for businesses to offer valuable services to customers and keep them back. Furthermore, the occurrence of unemployment and ethical concerns in the operation of AI present challenges for policymakers and strategy developers.

Even though AI offers many advantages in the business world, there are also significant drawbacks that must be taken into account when developing strategies. AI plays a vital role in today's business world, necessitating a well-trained workforce for its operation and significantly affecting the traditional workforce. Nevertheless, it also generates new employment possibilities for skilled individuals adept at crafting automated technologies. Therefore, the increase in AI has both direct and indirect effects on the industrial relationships of companies. With the rise of Industry 4.0, various issues, such as cybersecurity and data protection, have become major concerns [13]. Technologies are affected by cybersecurity threats. By promptly responding, automated technologies and devices are utilized to minimize the adverse effects of data security breaches and cyberattacks. Artificial intelligence has the ability to prevent cyber security attacks and protect business data. It enhances the flexibility of digital technologies and AI. Nevertheless, AI has also been noted to lack ethics, as it fails to distinguish between ethical and unethical work processes. Cyber attackers also utilize AI to target digital devices and pilfer data and information [14]. Therefore, human thinking and processing cannot be replaced by AI. The introduction of AI in organizational management has brought about changes in both the internal and work environments, which in turn influence a company's performance and productivity (Fig. 1.2). The results of these changes are listed below.

1.2.1 Shift in Power

Integrating artificial intelligence into a business organization represents a swift shift in overseeing business operations. Prior to the implementation of artificial intelligence, humans were responsible for controlling and monitoring processes, but artificial intelligence can now oversee and manage all organizational activities independently [15]. Hence, control and oversight move from people to machines,

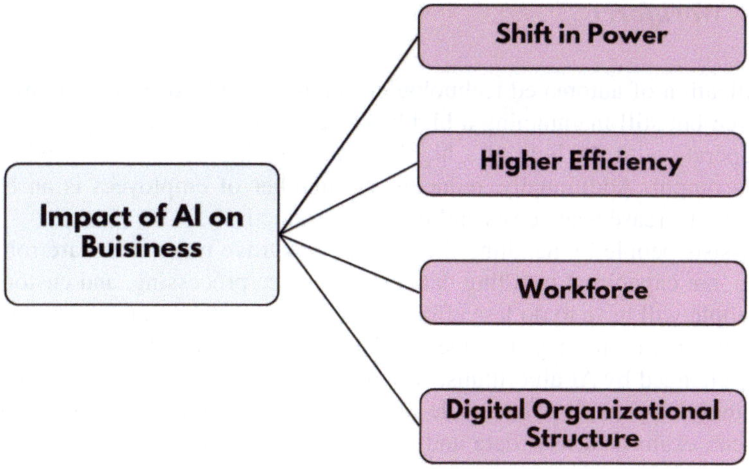

Fig. 1.2 Impact of AI on business

marking a significant shift in a company's operations and work environment. AI forces us to reevaluate the concept of power itself, moving the emphasis from individual control to networked systems and from dominance to cooperation. In the AI age, governance—the development of structures that guarantee openness, responsibility, and inclusivity—is essential to the future of power [16]. Moreover, AI operates without the need for human involvement, resulting in a decrease in the need for human–machine interaction and a reduction in the workforce. In this case, AI will be more than simply your phone's helpful assistant or the chatbot that responds to customer service inquiries. It will develop into something far more potent—an unseen, all-knowing force that directs the most important facets of existence, such as public policy, healthcare, and education [17].

1.2.2 Higher Efficiency

Human involvement in production and manufacturing processes carries the risk of errors in business operations, whereas AI operations are characterized by greater accuracy and fewer mistakes [18]. As a result, artificial intelligence is more efficient than human labor. Additionally, AI-operated vehicles can function nonstop around the clock, demonstrating the efficiency of AI-driven technologies. Many of them have been able to scale their daily operations at an ever-increasing rate and automate their laborious, manual processes thanks to this data-driven technology. Furthermore, they are not in any way compromising quality for number; AI has made it feasible for safer and more dependable procedures in ways that were previously believed to be unachievable. As businesses employ AI to make more educated business decisions, its real-world applications are expanding [19, 20].

1.2.3 Workforce

The utilization of automated technologies is reducing the size of the conventional workforce but still maintaining a highly skilled workforce. A company can effectively operate with the help of a highly skilled workforce that can produce more valuable output. Additionally, reducing the number of employees is an effective strategy to decrease wage costs and increase productivity.

AI assists people by handling the tedious, repetitive tasks. Software robots, for instance, are capable of handling data entry, invoice processing, and customer service. People will have to do less effort, make fewer mistakes, and get better results as a result. Operations may stop due to a defective system or a broken machine. This is being changed by AI algorithms, which can now anticipate equipment problems before they happen [21]. To decide on and carry out predictive maintenance, AI agents can examine sensor data and previous maintenance logs. The success of a company and the smooth and effective operation of each department are largely dependent on its business processes. Natural language processing (NLP), machine learning (ML) models, and artificial intelligence (AI) are some of the technologies used in AI process optimization [22].

1.2.4 Digital Organizational Structure

The way organizations are structured is changing due to the implementation of artificial intelligence. AI advancements are enabling the distribution of shared responsibility. Furthermore, it enables decentralized decision-making and workflows through the use of AI to offer relevant data on business areas such as product demand. The skillset required for management is changing due to the adoption of AI technologies, and businesses are restructuring to better utilize these technologies [23]. The implementation of AI has made the strategic management of business operations simpler for the organization. The strategic management of business processes with AI involves gathering business data and analysing it to obtain information and insights into the organization's position and status. Examining data connected to the business entity reveals various findings about the operational procedure, highlighting weaknesses and issues impacting the business while also offering information to improve decision-making practices more effectively. The strategic management process involves analysing the internal and external factors of a business to provide important insights. AI effectively analyses organizations' market position by providing the best realistic reflection of data. Hence, examining business data allows for enhancements in the strategic management process of a company to reach long-term goals and objectives via its activities. AI-powered technologies also enhance a company's strategy for various activities, such as marketing, production, and distribution. For example, data analysis offers precise forecasts for upcoming business trends such as consumer needs, necessary resources, and seasonal variations. Improving the efficiency of business in production, inventory management, distribution channels, and other areas is beneficial. Additionally, AI can operate independently without any human involvement [24]. This indicates a rise in business efficiency, which also drives alterations in marketing distribution as well as other channels. Furthermore, advancements in intelligent technology services such as "smart warehouse management systems" and automated devices are enhancing operations and maximizing the use of allocated resources. It allows for efficient management of business operations and minimizes unnecessary expenses. Hence, it is efficient in lowering operational expenses for a business entity and strategic activities. Adopting AI in business also has negative effects on workforce skills and other aspects of the business. The effect on employees is a result of the implementation of technology in a company. Nonetheless, employees in companies lack the necessary skills to operate AI equipment effectively [25]. The deficiency in skills affects both the performance of the workforce and the use of automated devices. Furthermore, it affects the employment of manual workers and lowers the expenses of salaries. This occurrence has a detrimental effect on both the workforce and the company. Furthermore, the lack of communication between employees and management causes interruptions in upskilling processes, further hindering the AI adoption process. The limited ability of AI to generate creative ideas for products or services harms product differentiation. If the business does not have a distinct identity and innovative ideas, it may not reach its ultimate objective [26]. A decrease in creativity could impact the dependability of AI technologies. AI technologies are efficient in mechanically manufacturing products. Ethical AI has been integrated into companies to oversee operations such as production and customer service [26]. There is inadequate ethics in the implementation of AI in the workplace. AI must adhere to both ethical and legal guidelines regarding collecting data, even when it involves breaching privacy policies. Businesses are encountering many obstacles regarding incorporating AI technologies due to this problem.

AI technology is becoming increasingly crucial in the fields of HR and employee relations. AI-powered tools provide HR professionals with valuable benefits, enabling them to save time, increase productivity, and make better informed choices. AI allows HR professionals to concentrate on the welfare and happiness of their employees by granting swift access to pertinent information, ensuring their safety, and promoting reconciliation when needed. AI simplifies tasks, enabling HR professionals to spend additional time and focus on creating valuable personal relationships [27]. Technology is undoubtedly essential for HR and employee relations to function, with AI helping to improve these functions and leading to a more productive and efficient workplace setting.

1.3 Ways to Influence AI in HR and Employee Relations

AI transforms HR and employee relations by providing innovative solutions that boost productivity, precision, and employee contentment. AI enables ER professionals to prioritize strategic and people-oriented aspects of their roles by automating tasks, analysing data, and offering actionable insights. The incorporation of AI in ER not only streamlines processes but also greatly enhances participation and adherence across organizations, improving decision-making and customizing employee experiences. The use of AI in HR and employee relations offers numerous advantages that greatly improve the efficiency and promptness of these essential roles. This is how artificial intelligence has an impact. The benefits of AI in HR and employee relations are as follows:

1.3.1 Developed Efficiency and Productivity

AI is responsible for automating manual tasks, allowing HR and ER professionals to focus on strategic responsibilities. This change not only increases efficiency but also improves work quality, enabling teams to concentrate on aspects needing human intelligence and skill.

1.3.2 Improved Scalability

With workplace problems becoming increasingly intricate and teams frequently working with scarce resources, artificial intelligence intervenes to enhance processes. This enables a company to manage increased workloads efficiently without sacrificing quality or responsiveness [28].

1.3.3 Superior Data-Driven Decision-Making

AI enables easy analysis of enormous datasets. This technology offers a profound understanding of trends and patterns, enabling the team to make well-informed decisions and introduce ongoing enhancements in all areas [29].

1.3.4 Cost Savings

AI reduces costs related to handling employee relations by automating common tasks. This involves reducing time, resources, and possible legal costs, making it an economical choice for companies [30].

1.3.5 Fewer Monotonous Duties

AI frees HR and ER professionals from monotonous, routine duties. AI takes care of these routine tasks, freeing one's team to focus on more meaningful and satisfying work, leading to increased job satisfaction and productivity [31].

1.3.6 Managing Financial Duties

AI is also being used more frequently by employers to handle employee payments and financial tracking. AI helps with payroll processing and detects irregularities in financial transactions, thus preventing financial losses [30].

1.3.7 Customization

The idea of mass personalization in employee training and development can be facilitated by AI. With AI, a company can determine the unique needs of both individuals and groups of employees and tailor training to meet those needs [30].

1.3.8 Experience in Real-Time

Large datasets, both structured and unstructured, may be analyzed in real time by AI systems, which can then identify patterns and designs. Costs are decreased by the efficient use of resources and services made possible by real-time interactions [29].

1.3.9 Calculating Capacity and Power

Modern organizations deal with vast amounts of data and information, and they need to use technologies such as artificial intelligence to become cleverer and more creative. AI was purposefully created to be extremely powerful, and profitable, and assisting humans in minimizing their tedious tasks [32].

1.3.10 Analysis

Employee relation's visibility is being transformed into workforce data by AI-driven analytics. By looking at patterns in employee engagement, performance, and behavior, these technologies help emergency room professionals make better judgments. AI can identify trends that could indicate problems like excessive employee turnover or inefficiency within a department, allowing for the implementation of preventative measures [33].

1.3.11 Individualized Education and Training

AI can detect skill gaps and customize learning experiences to meet the needs of each learner, promoting ongoing development and assisting staff members in retraining or upskilling.

1.3.12 Availability

By providing information in a variety of languages and formats, AI greatly enhances accessibility in employee relations, catering to a diverse workforce. Chatbots and virtual assistants driven by AI may instantly respond to employee inquiries at any time, facilitating more inclusive employee interactions [31, 33]. By making it simpler for employees to get the information and assistance they require whenever they need it, regardless of time or location restrictions, this improved accessibility enhances the experience of workers.

1.3.13 Heightened Attention on Strategic Projects

HR professionals may devote more time to workforce development, talent management, and developing initiatives that support corporate objectives when they are not burdened with manual, repetitive duties.

1.3.14 Better Employee Onboarding

Having a well-organized employee onboarding process is crucial for anyone working in human resources. It's essential for keeping top personnel and ensuring they succeed in their new position right away. It can be difficult to create an onboarding procedure that positions your company and new personnel for success [34]. Your team can receive the training they require at the appropriate time by utilizing customized AI-powered training modules. With AI-powered coaching and training, you can give constant encouragement, and guarantee that new hires receive adequate assistance and incorporated into the team.

1.3.15 Offboarding

AI offboarding solutions can efficiently expedite and enhance the offboarding process for the company and the departing employee. HR departments, for instance, can automate a number of offboarding procedures, including monitoring knowledge transfer, tracking exit interviews, and gathering employee feedback [35]. Some businesses use chatbots to respond to inquiries from departing staff members or offer assistance as needed.

1.4 Challenges of AI in HR and Employee Relations

While AI has numerous advantages for HR and employee engagements, it also presents significant obstacles that must be carefully addressed to ensure its ethical and responsible application. Organizations must cautiously integrate AI into their HR procedures to prevent potential negative consequences that could impact trust and productivity.

1.4.1 Lack of Information in Hiring Decisions

AI tools may not have the same level of understanding as human HR professionals do. This shallowness could lead conclusions to ignore the intricacies of human behaviors and situations, which may lead to unjust or unsuitable employment choices.

1.4.2 Introduction to Unintentional Bias

Although AI is intended to be objective, biases from historical data can be unintentionally perpetuated in algorithms. This problem can undermine the fairness and neutrality of HR procedures, impacting all aspects, from hiring to staff assessments and advancements. Trust can erode when there is too much dependence on AI for sensitive interactions in HR, diminishing crucial human aspects. Employees may sense that an impersonal system is dealing with their concerns instead of being handled with empathy and understanding, potentially decreasing both trust and satisfaction levels among employees [13].

1.4.3 Data Privacy and Confidentiality Concerns

The incorporation of AI in HR processes poses significant dangers to confidentiality and safety. AI systems must be structured with caution to comply with data privacy laws and safeguard employee data privacy and security to prevent data breaches and unauthorized access.

1.4.4 Absence of Empathy and Compassion

The field of human resources necessitates emotional intelligence, empathy, and comprehension. AI is capable of performing repetitive tasks and analyzing large volumes of data efficiently, but it is unable to understand the subtleties of human emotions and behavior. When working with AI-driven systems, workers may feel alienated or disengaged, which could lower their job satisfaction and make conflict resolution less successful.

1.4.5 Pressure of AI Adoption

AI is currently being pushed everywhere in the IT industry, and HR directors may begin implementing AI or be pressured to do so by other company executives without considering whether it is the best way to solve an issue. The effectiveness of AI systems depends greatly on the accuracy and correct interpretation of the data they are analyzing. Inaccurate data or faulty algorithm design can lead to mistakes in analysis and decision-making, impacting employee evaluations and strategic HR planning [36]. Errors such as these can lead to faulty strategies that may damage the organization. These obstacles highlight the need for a well-rounded method of incorporating AI in HR, guaranteeing that technology aids rather than weakens the human side of employee interactions.

1.4.6 Information Errors and Incorrect Interpretations

The caliber of the data that AI systems process determines how effective they are. Everything from strategic HR planning to employee evaluations can be impacted by errors in analysis and decision-making caused by inaccurate data or badly designed algorithms. These mistakes may result in misdirected tactics that have a negative impact on the company [34].

1.4.7 Interoperability with Current Systems

Human resource management systems are already in place in many firms. Assessing how AI technologies work with current systems, preventing interruptions, and maximizing the effectiveness of the entire HR infrastructure are all part of ensuring interoperability.

1.4.8 Corporate Culture Shift

Organizations must undergo a cultural transformation in order to implement AI. This entails fostering an environment where workers welcome technology as a tool to improve their work and encourage cooperation between AI-driven and human operations.

1.4.9 Opposition to Change

Because they are uncomfortable with new technology or fear losing their jobs, workers may oppose the adoption of AI. Effective communication, emphasizing the advantages of AI, and proving that it enhances rather than replaces human labor are all necessary to overcome this obstacle.

1.4.10 Complexity of the Learning Curve

As HR experts adjust to new technologies, a learning curve is introduced by the incorporation of AI. Training materials and programs are necessary to guarantee that employees know how to use AI tools efficiently in their day-to-day work.

1.5 Future of AI in Employee Relations

In HR, everyone agrees that the people are company's top asset now and will continue to be in the future. If companies want their businesses to thrive, they must provide our people with support, development, training, promotion, and recognition. Each employee requires someone to listen and offer assistance. This will remain the same. Unfortunately, problems of harassment and discrimination are unlikely to continue shortly. There will always be a need for a respectful employee relations professional to listen to someone's story and conduct a thorough investigation. Technology can help us in this effort. Chatbots can receive information but are unable to make decisions [37].

According to Accenture's report, AI: Built to Scale, 84% of corporate leaders feel that AI is necessary to meet their growth goals. Nevertheless, 76% admitted to facing challenges in implementing AI throughout their companies. To date, there has been no guiding plan for moving from proof of concept to production and scale, a shift that many find challenging. At this turning point, businesses must take the required actions to grow effectively. During Industry 5.0, AI is crucial in customizing products and services for specific customer requirements. AI algorithms process large amounts of data to enable unparalleled levels of personalization, guaranteeing that products perfectly match individual preferences [4]. However, there are obstacles involved in this integration. Ethical issues arise as privacy and biases are impacted by AI-powered decisions. The impact of AI is significant as we transition from Industry 4.0 to Industry 5.0, driving a change in perspective toward interconnected, human-focused systems. As artificial intelligence enhances job roles, changes in workforce dynamics occur, leading to a change in the required skills. Even with its restrictions, AI facilitates enhanced teamwork between humans and machines, creating opportunities for increased productivity and innovation.

Balaji Viswanathan, MD & CEO of Expleo India, discussed the customization and personalization of products and services in Industry 5.0, highlighting that AI transforms these processes through advanced data analytics. AI algorithms examine large sets of data, deducing valuable information about personal preferences, actions, and requirements. This allows companies to customize products and services with unparalleled accuracy, fulfilling individual customer needs. AI enhances the complete product and service lifecycle, from personalized recommendations in e-commerce to tailored manufacturing processes. Its ability to adapt allows sectors to develop tailored solutions, improving customer happiness and promoting a dynamic, customer-focused environment in Industry 5.0. He also mentioned the difficulties and moral aspects that come with the expanding use of AI in Industry 5.0, as it becomes more essential. Ensuring the privacy of data, mitigating algorithmic bias, and addressing job displacement are crucial challenges. Depending heavily on large datasets raises concerns about data security and the possibility of improper use. Ethical considerations include identifying who is responsible for AI decisions and avoiding biased results. To maintain a balance between technological progress and societal welfare, stringent regulations and transparent AI development methods are necessary [38]. Finding this balance is crucial for encouraging the incorporation of responsible AI in Industry 5.0, supporting creativity while protecting ethical standards and societal values.

Aditya Joshi, the CEO and MD of OpalForce, mentioned that AI is crucial in the shift from Industry 4.0 to Industry 5.0, influencing different areas. Industry 5.0 adopts a people-focused strategy, employing artificial intelligence to promote customization, eco-friendliness, and financial development. AI allows for personalized mass production, improves resource efficiency for sustainability purposes, and enhances decision-making with data analysis. Collaboration is enhanced through the use of AI technologies, encouraging creativity and cooperation on a worldwide scale [39]. The resilience of supply chains increases, worker safety levels rise, and quality control improves. In Industry 5.0, it is crucial to prioritize ethical AI usage to ensure that technological progress is in line with human values and societal norms, representing a significant change from Industry 4.0.

Bhuvan Desai, the VP of Client Operation at Uplers, emphasized that AI is fundamentally transforming the dynamics of the workforce and the skills needed, signalling a major change in the worldwide job market [40]. AI-powered automation takes over simple tasks, allowing humans to focus on more intricate and imaginative pursuits. While this results in higher efficiency and productivity, it also requires a change in skill sets. There is a growing need for workers to learn and improve their skills in digital literacy, data analysis, and AI as the demand for these abilities increases. Industry 5.0 focuses on teamwork between humans and machines, necessitating skills such as adaptability, problem-solving, and critical thinking. Furthermore, AI enhances the decision-making process, requiring a workforce that can understand and utilize insights generated by AI. As smart technologies are adopted by organizations, a remote workforce is formed, which includes both humans and AI systems. Effectively managing this transformation requires taking a proactive stance on education and training, developing a workforce that can leverage the mutual connection between humans and AI in the constantly changing future work environment. In line with this goal, Uplers is currently conducting a campaign on AI that covers four stages: awareness, exploration, experience, and applicability. In the upcoming months, the goal is to raise awareness within the Uplers community and enable them to eliminate unnecessary tasks via AI tools.

Dr. Sandeep Reddy, HoD, Artificial Intelligence and Data Science, KLH Hyderabad Campus stated that AI enhances human-machine collaboration in Industry 5.0. In the realm of Industry 5.0, artificial intelligence serves as the linchpin for transformative human-machine collaboration. AI seamlessly integrates into the industrial landscape, increasing their capacity for complex decision-making and problem-solving. By working alongside humans, AI has become a stalwart ally in enhancing productivity and efficiency. The interconnectedness fostered by IoT devices amplifies this collaboration, creating a cohesive and intelligent manufacturing ecosystem [41]. Industry 5.0 heralds an era where AI augments human capabilities, ushering in a symbiotic relationship that propels industries toward unprecedented levels of innovation and success. AI is the key driver of Industry 5.0, transforming the way companies function and creating new ideas. AI facilitates the smooth blending of technology and human teamwork by analyzing large datasets, improving decision-making, and automating processes. Industry 5.0 signifies a significant change towards prioritizing humans, with AI enhancing human skills to promote creativity, productivity, and long-term development. Adopting AI in Industry 5.0 not only drives technological progress but also fosters a balanced partnership between machines and humans, creating a future where innovation knows no limits and industries flourish through the combined knowledge of both people and technology.

In today's globally connected society, artificial intelligence and data science are seen as two key influences driving significant changes in technology advancements. Their mutually beneficial partnership revolutionizes sectors and impacts our perceptions of and interactions with the world. The combination of AI's replication of human intelligence and Data Science's ability to extract insights from big data creates new chances for innovation and progress. The United States creates the foundation of contemporary technological environments. This continues to drive innovation in various industries such as healthcare, finance, transportation, education, and others.

Additionally, as mentioned in our top artificial intelligence course, a key result of this merging is evident in automation [42]. Artificial intelligence systems quickly and accurately analyse extensive data, enabling the automation of repetitive tasks in various fields. This enhances both effectiveness and output while also freeing up human resources to focus on strategic and creative pursuits. Moreover, customized interactions driven by artificial intelligence and data analysis have revolutionized customer involvement and contentment [43]. These technologies utilize data insights to customize product recommendations and educational experiences for individual preferences and needs, fostering stronger connections and loyalty.

Therefore, AI and Data Science reach beyond specific industries to address larger societal issues such as environmental sustainability and public safety. By assessing environmental information and forecasting natural calamities, AI and Data Science contribute to disaster readiness and mitigation activities, showcasing their capacity to address worldwide problems. Simply put, the merging of AI and data science represents a fundamental change in our approach to problem-solving, decision-making, and innovation [44]. As these technologies continue to evolve and progress, their innovative impact in various industries will continue to increase. This moulds the future of mankind in creative and groundbreaking manners.

1.6 The Scope of Artificial Intelligence (AI) in Industrial Relation

Automation in various industries is made possible by AI technologies, leading to increased efficiency and productivity through the completion of repetitive tasks. Automation simplifies processes and reduces operational costs across various sectors, including manufacturing, logistics, customer service, and finance.

1.6.1 Customization

AI algorithms analyze extensive data to tailor user experiences. AI enhances customer interaction and satisfaction through product recommendations, content curation, and marketing campaign creation [8]. AI eliminates the need for guessing when determining what each unique client wants. Through AI personalization, each touchpoint in the consumer journey is optimized. Each user may have their personalized marketing, support, suggestions, etc. Artificial intelligence changes how companies engage with their customers, reshaping what consumers find valuable in products, services, and brand interactions. AI, through the utilization of machine learning and deep neural networks, allows for a level of personalization and customization that was previously unthinkable only 10 years ago. Businesses that do not adjust may lose clients to competitors who are more skilled in technology. Those who adopt AI have an exceptional chance to create stronger connections with each person they assist.

1.6.2 Health

In the healthcare field, artificial intelligence enables early disease identification, analysis of medical images, drug development, and customized treatment strategies. AI-powered advancements improve patient results, streamline clinical processes, and revolutionize healthcare services. Self-driving vehicles utilize artificial intelligence algorithms to understand their surroundings, make choices, and navigate without the need for human input [45]. This technology has the potential to transform transportation, enhance road safety, and reduce traffic congestion. Digital transformation in healthcare, particularly through AI integration, has the potential to greatly enhance healthcare systems and patient outcomes. AI-powered algorithms can examine large datasets to assist in the early detection of diseases and provide more precise diagnoses. Machine learning algorithms can forecast the likelihood of developing a disease by analyzing patient information. Artificial intelligence allows for tailoring treatment plans according to the patient's genetic information and health background. This method of precision medicine can improve the effectiveness of treatment and decrease negative impacts [46].

1.6.3 Finance

AI algorithms examine financial data to identify fraud, predict market trends, and enhance investment portfolios. AI-driven financial services improve risk management, automate trading strategies, and enhance decision-making procedures [47]. The financial industry utilizes artificial intelligence to support data analytics, performance evaluation, forecasts and projections, real-time computations, customer support, intelligent data retrieval, and other operations. Financial services companies can utilize this array of technologies to gain a deeper understanding of customers and markets, analyze and derive insights from digital journeys, and engage in interactions that mimic human intelligence and behaviors at a significant volume. By utilizing neural networks and deep learning, machine learning (ML), a branch of artificial intelligence, enables a system to autonomously learn and develop without direct programming through the analysis of massive amounts of data. It enables financial organizations to utilize data to train models that employ machine learning techniques to address certain problems and offer suggestions for future improvements.

1.6.4 Education

AI-driven education platforms provide custom learning experiences tailored to the unique needs of each student [48, 49]. Adaptive learning algorithms enhance curriculum design, assess student performance, and enhance educational results. AI technologies play a role in promoting environmental sustainability by analysing data to improve resource management, predict natural disasters, and combat climate change. AI-powered solutions support the conservation of energy, reduction of waste, and efforts to preserve resources

1.6.5 AI in the Manufacturing Industry

Intricacy, unpredictability and dynamic nature are some of the challenges that come with creating engineering and industrial processes and systems. The way that many technicians and industrial professionals approach their work has altered recently due to big data, rapid processing, cloud computing, and artificial intelligence techniques (such as machine learning and deep learning). These innovations offer manufacturers and experts innovative and thought-provoking answers to difficult real-world issues [50, 51].

1.7 Conclusions

In summary, artificial intelligence (AI) and data science are not just advancements in technology; they are drivers of significant shifts in the way businesses, communities, and people engage with their surroundings. The possibility of revolutionizing businesses exists through their integration, from streamlining operations with automation to offering personalized experiences for customers. Moreover, AI and data science have greatly influenced areas such as healthcare and environmental sustainability. These advancements offer unmatched opportunities for detecting diseases early, tailoring treatments to individuals, and preserving the environment. Organizations can leverage AI algorithms and advanced analytics to improve decision-making, optimize resource allocation, and mitigate risks. As we further discover the vast possibilities of AI and Data Science, the potential for innovation and expansion knows no bounds. Therefore, adopting new technologies is not just a strategic necessity for companies; it is also an ethical obligation to quicken advancement towards a wiser, more effective, and environmentally friendly future. Therefore, the use of data and AI-driven technologies enables us to create a path for revolutionary transformation that transcends industry boundaries and speeds up the advancement of society toward a more promising future.

References

1. Connolly, H. (2023). How the field of industrial relations remains relevant for understanding the global political economy of work. In *Handbook of research on the global political economy of work* (pp. 266–278). Edward Elgar Publishing.
2. Majumder, S., Chowdhury, S., & Chakraborty, S. (2023). Interactive web-interface for competency-based classroom assessment. *International Journal of Education and Management Engineering, 13*(1), 18.
3. Dobbins, T., Johnstone, S., Kahancová, M., Lamare, J. R., & Wilkinson, A. (2023). Comparative impacts of the COVID-19 pandemic on work and employment—why industrial relations institutions matter. *Industrial Relations: A Journal of Economy and Society, 62*(2), 115–125.

4. Wright, C. F. (2023). Addressing problems for labour not problems of labour: The need for a paradigm shift in work and industrial relations policy. *Labour and Industry: A Journal of the Social and Economic Relations of Work, 33*(1), 11–21.
5. Carstensen, M. B., Ibsen, C. L., & Schmidt, V. A. (2022). Ideas and power in employment relations studies. *Industrial Relations, 61*(1), 3–21.
6. Girigiri, B. W., & Badom, P. M. (2021). Industrial harmony and work discontent: Employer and employee relations perspective. *International Journal of Research Publications, 80*(1), 209–219.
7. Roy, G. K., & Dubey, A. (2022). A note on industrial relations code, 2020. *The Indian Journal of Labour Economics, 65*(2), 533–543.
8. Nowak, J. (2021). From industrial relations research to global labour studies: Moving labour research beyond Eurocentrism. *Globalizations, 18*(8), 1335–1348.
9. Boumans, S. (2022). Neoliberalisation of industrial relations: The ideational development of Dutch employers' organisations between 1976 and 2019. *Economic and Industrial Democracy, 43*(4), 1610–1631.
10. Clibborn, S. (2021). Australian industrial relations in 2020: COVID-19, crisis and opportunity. *Journal of Industrial Relations, 63*(3), 291–302.
11. Gasparri, S., & Tassinari, A. (2020). 'Smart' industrial relations in the making? Insights from analysis of union responses to digitalization in Italy. *Relations industrielles/Industrial Relations, 75*(4), 796–817.
12. Dobbins, T., Hughes, E., & Dundon, T. (2021). 'Zones of contention' in industrial relations: Framing pluralism as praxis. *Journal of Industrial Relations, 63*(2), 149–176.
13. Doellgast, V., & Wagner, I. (2022). Collective regulation and the future of work in the digital economy: Insights from comparative employment relations. *Journal of Industrial Relations, 64*(3), 438–460.
14. Bondy, A. S. (2022). Conflictual complementarity: New labour actors in corporatist industrial relations. *Work, Employment and Society, 36*(4), 683–700.
15. Poole, M. (2021). *Theories of trade unionism: A sociology of industrial relations*. Routledge.
16. Horowitz, M. C. (2018). Artificial intelligence, international competition, and the balance of power. *Texas National Security Review, 1*(3), 36–57.
17. Radanliev, P. (2024). Artificial intelligence: Reflecting on the past and looking towards the next paradigm shift. *Journal of Experimental & Theoretical Artificial Intelligence, 37*(7), 1–18.
18. Varghese, S. (2022). The industrial relations code, 2020: Legislative commentary. *International Journal of Law Management & Humanities, 5*(1), 1924–1928.
19. Vinichenko, M. V., Melnichuk, A. V., & Karácsony, P. (2020). Technologies of improving the university efficiency by using artificial intelligence: Motivational aspect. *Entrepreneurship and Sustainability Issues, 7*(4), 2696.
20. Waltersmann, L., Kiemel, S., Stuhlsatz, J., Sauer, A., & Miehe, R. (2021). Artificial intelligence applications for increasing resource efficiency in manufacturing companies—A comprehensive review. *Sustainability, 13*(12), 6689.
21. Eubanks, B. (2022). *Artificial intelligence for HR: Use AI to support and develop a successful workforce*. Kogan Page Publishers.
22. Farrow, E. (2022). Determining the human to AI workforce ratio–exploring future organisational scenarios and the implications for anticipatory workforce planning. *Technology in Society, 68*, 101879.
23. Majumder, S., & Dey, N. (2022). Artificial intelligence and knowledge management. In *AI-empowered knowledge management* (pp. 85–100). Springer Singapore.
24. Williams, S. (2024). Expanding the boundaries of industrial relations as a field of study: The role of 'New Actors'. In *The value of industrial relations* (pp. 65–75). Bristol University Press.
25. LeCounte, J. F. (2024). HRM solutions: A framework for small business owners to manage industrial relations while facilitating labour unionisation mitigation. *International Journal of Organizational Analysis, 32*(1), 1–16.

26. Majumder, S., Chowdhury, S., Dey, N., & Santosh, K. C. (2022). Balance your work-life: Personal interactive web-interface. *International Journal of Interactive Multimedia and Artificial Intelligence, 7*(7), 90–96.
27. Ghani, F. A., Razali, N. A., & Rasli, M. A. M. (2021). Unfair dismissal under the industrial relations (amendment) act 2020: A legal review. *Global Business and Management Research, 13*(4s), 973–982.
28. Bosch, G. (2021). Industrial relations and inequality in the EU. In *Europe's income, wealth, consumption, and inequality* (pp. 452–485). Oxford Academic.
29. Berg, J., Green, F., Nurski, L., & Spencer, D. A. (2023). Risks to job quality from digital technologies: Are industrial relations in Europe ready for the challenge? *European Journal of Industrial Relations, 29*(4), 347–365.
30. Malik, A., Budhwar, P., Mohan, H., & NR, S. (2023). Employee experience–the missing link for engaging employees: Insights from an MNE's AI-based HR ecosystem. *Human Resource Management, 62*(1), 97–115.
31. Chukwuka, E. J., & Dibie, K. E. (2024). Strategic role of artificial intelligence (AI) on human resource management (HR) employee performance evaluation function. *International Journal of Entrepreneurship and Business Innovation, 7*(2), 269–282.
32. Singh, A., & Pandey, J. (2024). AI driven HR automation-a boon for industrial relations: Empirical evidence. *Indian Journal of Industrial Relations, 59*(3), 411–425.
33. Priya, M. S., Khan, S., Siddiqui, S., Sharma, M. S., & Verma, S. (2024). The role of AI in shaping the future of employee engagement: Insights from human resource management. *Library Progress, 44*(3), 15213–15223.
34. Yanamala, K. K. R. (2020). Ethical challenges and employee reactions to AI adoption in human resource management. *International Journal of Responsible Artificial Intelligence, 10*(8), 1–13.
35. Thakur, R. A., Talukdar, M., Iyer, S., Liu, L. C., Chen, C. L., & Singh, A. (2025). AI and employee well-being: Assessing the ethical implications of AI-driven human resource practices in Indian universities. *Journal of Ecohumanism, 4*(1), 2338–2351.
36. Asri Wijayanti, C. (2022). The utilization of information and communication technology in industrial relations disputes resolution in Indonesia. *Journal of Positive School Psychology, 6*(2), 5862–5866.
37. Arancibia, P., & Torres, R. (2021). The future of employment and industrial relations. In *New directions in the future of work* (pp. 143–161). Emerald Publishing Limited.
38. Gligor, D. M., Pillai, K. G., & Golgeci, I. (2021). Theorizing the dark side of business-to-business relationships in the era of AI, big data, and blockchain. *Journal of Business Research, 133*, 79–88.
39. Parmenas, N. H., & Samosir, R. S. (2023). Industrial relations dispute simulation system prototype with artificial intelligence approach. *Buletin Ilmiah Sarjana Teknik Elektro, 5*(2), 291–302.
40. Liu, H. Y. (2023). The role of the state in influencing work conditions in China's internet industry: Policy, evidence, and implications for industrial relations. *Journal of Industrial Relations, 65*(1), 3–21.
41. Ghosh, S., Majumder, S., & Peng, S. L. (2023). An empirical study on adoption of artificial intelligence in human resource management. In *Artificial Intelligence techniques in human resource management* (pp. 29–85). Apple Academic Press.
42. Youn, S., & Jin, S. V. (2021). "In AI we trust?" The effects of parasocial interaction and technopian versus luddite ideological views on chatbot-based customer relationship management in the emerging "feeling economy". *Computers in Human Behavior, 119*, 106721.
43. Kaur, M., AG, R., & Vikas, S. (2021). Adoption of Artificial Intelligence in human resource management. *Indian Journal of Industrial Relations, 57*(2), 331–342.
44. Hantal, B., & Hantal, B. (2021). Globalization, emerging technologies & future industrial relations. *Indian Journal of Industrial Relations, 56*(3), 438–449.

45. Balkanyi, L., & Cornet, R. (2019). The interplay of knowledge representation with various fields of artificial intelligence in medicine. *Yearbook of Medical Informatics, 28*(01), 027–034.
46. Pakdemirli, E., & Wegner, U. (2020). Artificial intelligence in various medical fields with emphasis on radiology: Statistical evaluation of the literature. *Cureus, 12*(10), e10961.
47. Xu, Y., Liu, X., Cao, X., Huang, C., Liu, E., Qian, S., et al. (2021). Artificial intelligence: A powerful paradigm for scientific research. *The Innovation, 2*(4), 100179.
48. Zhang, C., & Lu, Y. (2021). Study on artificial intelligence: The state of the art and future prospects. *Journal of Industrial Information Integration, 23*, 100224.
49. Zheng, L., Zhang, S., Huang, H., Liu, R., Cai, M., Bian, Y., et al. (2023). Artificial intelligence-driven rechargeable batteries in multiple fields of development and application towards energy storage. *Journal of Energy Storage, 73*, 108926.
50. Arinez, J. F., Chang, Q., Gao, R. X., Xu, C., & Zhang, J. (2020). Artificial intelligence in advanced manufacturing: Current status and future outlook. *Journal of Manufacturing Science and Engineering, 142*(11), 110804.
51. Kim, S. W., Kong, J. H., Lee, S. W., & Lee, S. (2022). Recent advances of artificial intelligence in manufacturing industrial sectors: A review. *International Journal of Precision Engineering and Manufacturing, 23*, 111–129.

Chapter 2
The Merging of Fourth Industrial Revolution and Fifth Industrial Revolution

2.1 Introduction

The Fourth Industrial Revolution represents the current and developing environment in which cutting-edge technologies such as the Internet of Things (IoT), robotics, virtual reality (VR), and artificial intelligence (AI) are transforming the lifestyles and work approaches of modern society. The first Industrial Revolution, taking place in the eighteenth and nineteenth centuries, marked the shift from mainly agricultural societies to greater industrialization driven by innovations such as the steam engine. The Second Industrial Revolution, driven by electricity, witnessed advancements in industries, large-scale production, and technological development. Technologies associated with the Fourth Industrial Revolution include artificial intelligence, the Internet of Things, robotics, virtual reality, mobile devices, 3D printing, smart sensors, big data/analytics, augmented reality (AR), data visualization, cognitive computing, geolocation, customer profiling, blockchain, quantum computing, and cloud computing [1].

The Industrial Revolution transformed economies dependent on agriculture and handcrafted items into those focused on large-scale industry, mechanized manufacturing, and factory systems (Fig. 2.1). Established industries saw increased productivity and efficiency due to the implementation of new machinery, energy sources, and approaches to work organization. The Fourth Industrial Revolution (4IR) [1–3] marks an era of technological progress that is blurring the lines between the physical, digital, and biological domains. It is characterized by the integration of smart systems and cutting-edge manufacturing techniques, powered by data, artificial intelligence (AI), and various other technologies. The Fourth Industrial Revolution (4IR) includes robotics, 3D printing, the Internet of Things (IoT), blockchain technology, quantum computing, and genetic modification. The Fourth Industrial Revolution (4IR) significantly impacts multiple dimensions of life, including

S. Majumder, B. Misra, *AI-Empowered Industrial Relations*, Studies in Computational Intelligence 1254, https://doi.org/10.1007/978-3-032-14557-4_2

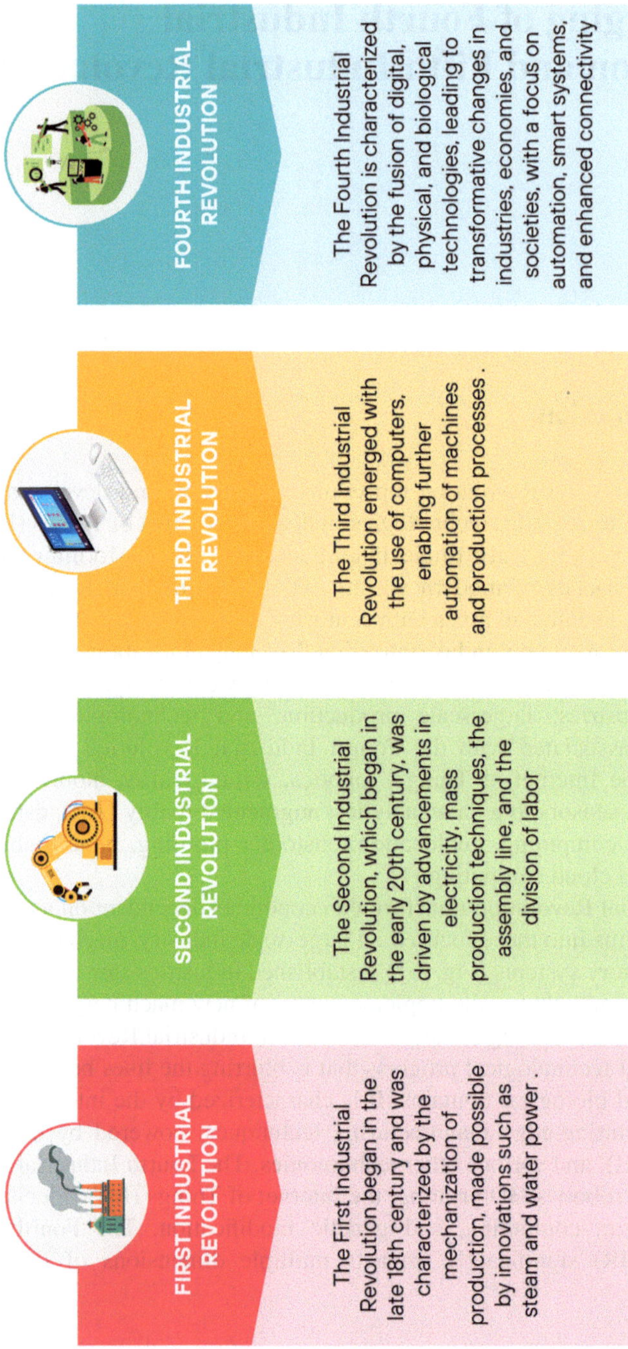

Fig. 2.1 Industrial revolution and its societal impact

healthcare, transportation, and agriculture. It is also bringing about transformative changes in our ways of living and disrupting many sectors.

Specific advantages of the fourth industrial revolution include: (i) An increase in productivity, efficiency, and quality, (ii) Greater safety for workers, (iii) Better decision-making, (iv) Heightened competitiveness. The Fifth Industrial Revolution (5IR) represents a new phase of industrialization that focuses on collaboration between humans and machines to improve societal well-being. Rooted in the Fourth Industrial Revolution (4IR), the 5IR is characterized by its Human-centered approach: It prioritizes the well-being of diverse stakeholders, including businesses, staff, clients, and the community. The Fifth Industrial Revolution emphasizes sustainability and resilience, encompassing ecosystems. Integration of technology: The fifth industrial revolution merges IT and AI with robotics and biotechnology to create an "ultra-smart society." Collaboration between humans and machines in the 5IR entails combining human creativity and skills with the effectiveness, output, and consistency of robots. Emerging technologies: The fifth industrial revolution (5IR) integrates artificial intelligence, automation, big data analysis, the Internet of Things (IoT), machine learning, robotics, intelligent systems, and virtualization. The Fifth Industrial Revolution is set to transform society and human life. It challenges long-standing philosophical views on the uniqueness of human perception. The notion of 5IR highlights collaborative connections between humans and machines, focusing on the interests of diverse stakeholders including society, companies, employees, and consumers. Industry 5.0, known as the fifth industrial revolution, is characterized by advanced technologies like artificial intelligence (AI), the Internet of Things (IoT), and robotics. The incorporation of these technologies into manufacturing processes is creating production systems that are exceptionally connected and smart.

2.2 The Fourth and Fifth Industrial Revolution and Its Impact on Industrial Relation

Both challenges and opportunities for industrial relations are being presented by the transformations of the industrial landscape due to the Fourth and Fifth Industrial Revolutions. Adjusting to these alterations will necessitate teamwork among employers, workers, and policymakers to guarantee a seamless shift and the establishment of a more sustainable and fairer industrial environment. Emphasizing sustainability and placing humans at the core may result in the establishment of fresh labor policies and methods that give importance to the welfare of workers and environmental accountability. The teamwork involving humans and machines might generate new job positions and require the workforce to undergo reskilling and upskilling. Enhanced automation and utilization of advanced technologies such as artificial intelligence, robotics, and the Internet of Things. Enhanced connectivity and data sharing among machines, devices, and systems. Streamlined product design and manufacturing processes aided by technologies like 3D printing. Industry 4.0, also referred to as the Fourth Industrial Revolution, is distinguished by the merging of digital, physical, and biological technologies.

2.2.1 *The Fourth Industrial Revolution and Its Impact on Industrial Relation*

Industry 4.0, also known as the Fourth Industrial Revolution, is defined by the incorporation of digital technologies, artificial intelligence, and the Internet of Things (IoT) into various industries, including manufacturing [4, 5]. This revolution has brought about major changes in the way businesses operate and in the dynamics of labor. Industry 4.0 is transforming industrial relations in numerous important ways. Here are a few of the main effects:

(i) **Technological Unemployment:** a significant worry is the possibility of technological unemployment, where automation and AI may take over specific roles, causing shifts in employment structures.
(ii) **Upskilling and Reskilling:** to adjust to these changes, businesses are placing more emphasis on upskilling and reskilling their employees. This is crucial to ensure that employees can continue to work effectively with modern technologies and stay competitive in the job market.
(iii) **Changing Worker Expectations:** the revolution has changed worker expectations about job responsibilities, flexibility, and work-life balance, leading to a need for organizations to change how they manage their human resources.
(iv) **Technological Unemployment**: one of the primary issues linked to Industry 4.0 is the problem of technological unemployment. With the rise of automation and artificial intelligence, numerous traditional jobs are in danger of being substituted. This transition may result in changes in job structure, posing new obstacles for labor relations when workers face displacement or have to switch to different positions.
(v) **Changing Nature of Work**: The incorporation of cutting-edge technologies like robotics and the Internet of Things (IoT) is changing the very essence of work. Employment is becoming increasingly specialized, demanding fresh abilities and expertise. This change requires an emphasis on training and retraining employees so they can adjust to new technologies and stay competitive in the job market.
(vi) **Worker Expectations and Engagement:** worker expectations are evolving along with the increasing presence of digital technologies. Workers are more and more looking for flexibility, independence, and improved balance between work and personal life. Organizations need to adjust their approaches to industrial relations in order to meet changing expectations, resulting in a more content and involved staff.

(vii) **Collaboration Between Humans and Machines**: Industry 4.0 focuses on a cooperative method in which humans and machines collaborate. This change may result in different types of teamwork and cooperation, necessitating a revision of labor relationships to enable successful interactions between humans and machines. Organizations must establish supportive environments for collaboration while also prioritizing the feelings of value and security among workers.

(viii) **Impact on Labor Unions and Collective Bargaining**: as the labor force changes, labor unions and collective bargaining also adapt. Unions might have to adjust their tactics in order to tackle the obstacles presented by automation and the gig economy. This involves supporting policies that safeguard the rights of workers in a more automated environment and making sure that workers have a say in conversations regarding technological advancements impacting their roles.

(ix) **Market Expansion and the Creation of New Markets**: New services, goods, and software are required to support the organizational shift that comes with any technological revolution. New product categories, employment, and other things will be created as a result.

(x) **Enhancement of Operational Efficiency:** By allowing companies to create more with the identical quantity of resources, Industry 4.0 is anticipated to further increase their profitability.

(xi) **Better Products and Infrastructure:** Regardless of the item's quality, reliability, or user interface, Industry 4.0 will boost operations' visibility and throughput, allowing them to continue offering value to customers and retaining their business.

(xii) **Improved Safety and Supply Chain Management:** Industry 4.0 methods, procedures, and technology will improve your supply chain's overall visibility. Additionally, your supply chain will be more interconnected, allowing for real-time monitoring along with improved cooperation and communication. For instance, this can enable the detection of supply chain issues such as bottlenecks before they affect the output of the production line.

(xiii) **Reduced Obstacles to Start a New Business:** One can already observe that the boundaries between inventors and markets are being lowered by new technologies like 3D printing for prototyping. Without the time and expense limits that come with traditional prototype methods, entrepreneurs may now launch their businesses and test different concepts with cheaper start-up costs. The entrepreneurial equation eliminates the usual obstacles to entry.

(xiv) **Facilitating Improved Cooperation:** As employees are one of manufacturing company's biggest assets, and they can use Industry 4.0 technology to enhance their productivity and interactions with one another. Cloud computing, real-time data, and collaborative platforms are examples of digital tools that can assist in dismantling organizational silos. Your staff will be able to collaborate considerably more effectively as a result, even across departments. Better cooperation, however, is not limited to internal teams; it can also be leveraged to improve a company's standing with suppliers, customers, and even stakeholders.

(xv) **Adaptability and Quickness:** Improved flexibility and agility are two further benefits of Industry 4.0. A Smart Factory, for example, makes it easier to increase or decrease performance. It also opens up opportunities for high-mix manufacturing, one-off manufacturing runs, and other procedures and makes it easier to introduce new products to the manufacturing line.

(xvi) **Improved Customer Service:** Industry 4.0 offers chances to improve customer service and improve the customer experience. For instance, you can solve issues fast with automated track and trace capabilities. Additionally, you will be able to provide clients with additional options, improve product quality, and experience fewer problems with product availability (see the point about greater profitability below).

(xvii) **Expediting Time to Market (TTM):** Industry 4.0 is the most effective approach to accelerating the process from concept to product launch. For ultimate operational perfection, more sophisticated technologies like artificial intelligence (AI) and real-time data analytics optimize each stage of the development process.

(xviii) **Increased Income:** Your production plant may see an increase in revenue as a result of many of the previously mentioned points. To meet an increase in demand or compete for a new contract, for instance, you may add a new shift with low staffing costs by completely automating your manufacturing line and integrating other Industry 4.0 technology.

The Fourth Industrial Revolution is changing industrial relations by bringing challenges like technological unemployment, shifting worker expectations, and the demand for new skills. Organizations need to carefully manage these changes in order to cultivate an efficient and committed workforce, and to ensure that labor relations adapt to the requirements of this emerging industrial period.

2.2.2 The Fifth Industrial Revolution and Key Impacts on Industrial Relations

Industry 5.0, also known as the Fifth Industrial Revolution, expands on the progress made in Industry 4.0 by focusing on promoting a more balanced partnership between humans and machines. This stage is dedicated to improving the quality of life and sustainability at work. The Industry 5.0 signifies a major change in industrial operations by merging cutting-edge technologies with a focus on human well-being, sustainability, and working together closely [3, 5, 6]. This revolution seeks to establish a more equitable connection between humans and machines, improving work satisfaction and tackling societal problems. The impacts are:

(i) **Human-Centric Approach:** industry 5.0 emphasizes putting workers' well-being on the same level of importance as productivity, taking a human-centric approach to technology. This change has the potential to increase job happiness and create a more involved group of employees.

(ii) **Collaborative Work Environments:** the focus on working together with machines could result in different types of work setups and labor relationships, promoting a spirit of teamwork and mutual objectives.

(iii) **Sustainability and Ethical Considerations**: as businesses implement more environmentally friendly measures, industrial relations must evolve to encompass ethical concerns and corporate social responsibilities.

(iv) **Human-Centric Work Environments:** in Industry 5.0, the focus is on ensuring the welfare of workers, creating settings that appreciate human creativity and emotional intelligence as much as technological progress. This change motivates companies to implement strategies that improve employee happiness and involvement, resulting in improved industrial relationships. By prioritizing humans in innovation, companies can establish work environments that are both effective and satisfying for employees.

(v) **Sustainability and Ethical Practices:** industry 5.0 emphasizes sustainability and ethical business practices as a fundamental principle. Businesses are more and more required to embrace "profit with purpose" models that combine financial objectives with social and environmental obligations. This change affects labor relations by requiring talks on corporate social responsibility (CSR) and the involvement of employees in advancing sustainable practices within their companies.

(vi) **Collaborative Human-Machine Interactions:** the Fifth Industrial Revolution focuses on promoting a peaceful partnership between humans and machines. This partnership boosts efficiency and necessitates fresh labor relations frameworks. As organizations integrate workers and machines more closely, it is important to properly train and support employees for their new roles, promoting teamwork and common goals.

(vii) **Adaptation of Labor Policies and Union Roles**: as work changes, labor policies and unions must also adjust. Unions might prioritize advocating for workers' rights within the framework of new technologies and sustainable methods. This involves bargaining for equitable pay, job stability, and educational chances that correspond to the requirements of Industry 5.0. Increased focus on ethical behavior could result in unions and management working together more closely to achieve common objectives concerning sustainability and worker welfare.

(viii) **Innovation and Creativity in the Workplace**: industry 5.0 promotes a culture of creativity and innovation, empowering employees to offer ideas and solutions. This change has the potential to create a livelier work environment with industrial relations based on transparency and teamwork. Companies that cultivate a culture of innovation can expect better staff morale and retention because employees feel appreciated and involved in their positions. The focus on human-centered practices, sustainability, and collaboration between humans and machines is transforming industrial relations in the Fifth Industrial Revolution. As companies adjust to these shifts, they must prioritize establishing encouraging work atmospheres, revising labor regulations, and promoting a culture of innovation to guarantee the success of both employees and businesses in this modern age.

(ix) **Resilience:** Production procedures in a resilient industry are very robust, protecting against interruptions and sustaining vital infrastructure in times of emergency. The pandemic's vulnerabilities highlight the need for supply chains and manufacturing components to be more resilient and agile. The resilience of businesses is being tested in light of the current climate catastrophe as well as other uncertainties related to wars and pandemics. An organization's total performance can be enhanced by resilience to provide it a competitive edge. Additionally, it strengthens an organization's standing in the market, lowering the chance of business collapse.

(x) **Industrial Environmental Management:** Real-time and forecast climate, humidity, temperature, and energy usage overviews are provided by smart, networked sensors and specially designed software. This is particularly useful for farms that rely heavily on the weather. Production can be increased and significant losses can be avoided by being aware of what to anticipate and where to step in.

(xi) **Efficiency in Manufacturing Forecasting:** Using tailored software, machine learning, and automation in factories, smart, networked machines can predict production efficiency based on ongoing operations. Processes can be modified based on parameters to prevent losses, which is what gives them flexibility.

(xii) **Extreme Personalization:** Customers are calling for more individualized and distinctive goods and services. The fifth industrial revolution is centered on new manufacturing technology, where businesses exploit the newest advancements to meet human requirements. In industry 5.0, hyper-customization refers to the capacity to boost client involvement. Offering a personalized experience can greatly increase conversion rates in a world when the average person's attention span has decreased to less than 8 s. By enabling businesses to provide the appropriate goods or services to the appropriate audience at the appropriate moment, hyper-customization can boost conversions.

(xiii) **An Adaptable Supply Chain:** A responsive supply chain is an adaptable business strategy made to satisfy the needs of many types of businesses. A supply chain that is responsive can swiftly adapt to variations in volume, demand, or weather. In the context of industrial revolution 5.0, a responsive supply chain entails working with new partners, like retailers and logistics service providers, to boost flexibility and cut costs across the board. Third-party consultation is another step in this process. The goal is to establish a culture of continual improvement while promptly meeting consumer demands. Based on their capacity to satisfy client demands, businesses might gain a competitive edge from a responsive supply chain.

(xiv) **Talent Recruitment and Retention:** Businesses are finding it more and more difficult to draw in and keep brilliant employees. Industry 5.0 helps by offering a more innovative and stimulating work environment. Compared to positions that are only concerned with machine operations, which ignore challenge and innovation, this promotes greater employee happiness and loyalty.

(xv) **Contribution to Society:** A new business model known as "industry 5.0" centers the production process around the needs of people. This industrial strategy aims to reduce waste and pollution while implementing circular production methods. In industrial 5.0, societal value is a crucial idea to take into account while creating and putting strategies into action. For businesses, achieving societal value can lead to a number of advantages, such as higher consumer demand, innovation, and economic expansion.

Both the implications for industrial relations are significant in both the Fourth and Fifth Industrial Revolutions. Although Industry 4.0 brings about challenges like technological unemployment and the requirement for ongoing education, Industry 5.0 presents chances to establish more inclusive and sustainable work settings. As these revolutions progress, it will be important to concentrate on human welfare and teamwork in order to shape the future of work and labor relations.

2.3 Introduction to Industrial AI and Its Application on Various Industries

Industrial AI merges Domain and Data, connected through Discipline, focusing on Industry-focused Research, Methodological Innovation and Education, in addition to Fundamental Research employing Systematic Thinking. Industrial AI fosters a more cohesive understanding and application of AI technologies in industries by integrating these key components. This cohesive approach enables businesses to address complex issues with innovative solutions, leveraging the interplay of knowledge, trustworthy data, and organized methods. Industrial AI [3, 7, 8] propels the field forward by introducing innovative methods and enhancing education, while also emphasizing fundamental research and strategic thinking to connect theoretical frameworks with industry needs, achieving new milestones. A Data-Centric Approach highlights the significance of both the amount and quality of data, guaranteeing the selection of suitable methods to address issues. By concentrating on the precision and significance of the data, it enables a more precise analysis and decision-making tailored to specific challenges. Industrial AI excels in numerous key domains by recognizing the unique challenges of each sector and employing specialized knowledge and data to develop tailored solutions that address specific requirements, delivering unparalleled precision and efficiency across diverse industrial applications. Industrial artificial intelligence, commonly referred to as industrial AI, entails the application of AI for industrial objectives like logistics, supply chain management, data analysis, and automation and robotics within the manufacturing industry. Industrial AI is typically set apart from other types of AI because it focuses on utilizing AI technologies instead of developing human or human-like systems. The datasets employed in industrial AI are usually larger, but may not be as high in quality as those utilized in general AI. Industrial AI also exhibits zero tolerance for inaccurate outcomes, delayed insights, or untrustworthy predictions.

Industrial AI is particularly effective for process plants because it can handle the complexity of managing substantial data volumes and swiftly evolving scenarios, which are too difficult for manual or digital approaches. The Industrial AI Data Foundry is a data hub that will contain more than 100 varied datasets from real industrial challenges, assisting engineers in understanding how to apply AI to address issues systematically. The datasets cover multiple sectors including automotive, aerospace, healthcare, semiconductors, energy, transportation, mining, construction, and industrial automation. The Industrial AI Data Foundry [9] is expected to be a major investment that will establish connections to the broader AI community as well as the research and innovation ecosystem. Its goal is to advance research and educational objectives in AI for applied data or AI for scientific and engineering research. Students will learn to utilize Industrial AI to uncover the concealed relationships between operational conditions and subsequently use this understanding to enhance the uptime, productivity, and efficiency of their operations. Industrial AI for predictive maintenance can detect early system variations, project the remaining useful lifespan, and refine maintenance activities to avert operational interruptions.

The goal of the industrial AI Data Foundry is to supply data to researchers, analysts, developers, and various stakeholders (including industry and government entities) to facilitate research, innovation, and discovery. AI aim to collect and share 100 datasets centered on four key AI sectors (manufacturing, renewable energy, transportation, and healthcare) to support researchers in understanding different industrial AI uses in manufacturing, such as virtual metrology, digital twins, cyber-physical systems, intelligent maintenance for mechanical parts, and sensory systems. Furthermore, the industrial AI center provides training materials for engineers to acquire and improve their expertise in developing industrial technology. Trends in the AI industry are transforming various sectors, bringing forth a new age of opportunities for business advancement. AI has emerged as the foundation of innovation across diverse sectors, ranging from healthcare to finance, logistics to manufacturing, revolutionizing operations and establishing new standards. In the contemporary interconnected business environment, organizations with substantial employee bases and resources face numerous challenges such as operational inefficiencies and complex decision-making processes. These companies need to consistently adapt to emerging technologies, market demands, and rivals to succeed. Consistently tackling these obstacles is a continual endeavor to enhance performance and sustain growth. Artificial intelligence is now more than a popular buzzword; it has become an essential instrument for businesses seeking innovative solutions to their vital challenges.

Businesses frequently require assistance with issues including massive data sets, uneven decision-making procedures, ineffective resource allocation, and the requirement for quick insights. These kinds of discomfort can obstruct development, reduce productivity, and jeopardize an organization's overall success. However, the use of AI helps to mitigate these difficulties and drives companies to previously unheard-of levels of success. The rise of AI industry trends marks a significant transformation across various sectors, bringing in a new age of opportunities for business growth. AI has become the foundation of innovation in numerous industries, including healthcare, finance, logistics, and manufacturing, by optimizing processes and establishing new benchmarks. In this time of swift digital progress, artificial intelligence serves as a vital ally, delivering tailored applications for important industries. AI is transforming conventional models in sectors such as healthcare, finance, manufacturing, and retail. Employing ML algorithms, predictive analytics, and sophisticated automation enables companies to leverage AI for enhancing operations, optimizing resource use, and acquiring insights into customer behavior and market trends. A report by Grand View Research forecasts that the global AI market will expand to $1811.8 billion by 2030, rising from $136.6 billion in 2022, indicating a 38.1% CAGR.

2.3.1 Role of AI in Business Operations

John McCarthy, an American computer scientist and cognitive scientist, introduced the term artificial intelligence in 1956, defining it as "the discipline and craft of developing intelligent machines." Artificial Intelligence (AI) is the capacity of a computer or computer-controlled robot to carry out tasks ordinarily performed by intelligent people, usually humans. Consequently, it exhibits exceptional abilities including reasoning, meaning comprehension, and experience-based learning. Through work automation, data analysis, and improved decision-making, artificial intelligence revolutionizes business procedures. AI significantly boosts operational efficiency [10] by automating routine tasks, streamlining supply chains, forecasting maintenance needs, and delivering tailored customer engagements. It serves a vital purpose in delivering data-informed decision-making assistance, enhancing cybersecurity, and facilitating talent recruitment, fostering innovation across different industries [10–12]. The capability of AI to continuously learn enables it to adapt to evolving business landscapes, positioning it as a formidable asset for boosting productivity, cutting expenses, and achieving a competitive edge for firms confronting the hurdles of today's corporate environment. The adaptability of AI is evident across various industries, allowing customized retail experiences, proactive maintenance in manufacturing, and sophisticated healthcare assessments. The ways in which artificial intelligence is applied across various significant sectors are discussed in the following section.

2.3.2 *AI Use and Applications in Major Industries: Case Studies*

2.3.2.1 Healthcare

The applications of AI in healthcare [13–16] are following:

Medical Imaging

The use of sophisticated algorithms and software to simulate human cognition in the analysis, interpretation, and understanding of medical data is known as artificial intelligence (AI) in healthcare. AI can swiftly evaluate enormous volumes of data, finding trends and forecasting outcomes that might improve decision-making in a range of healthcare contexts. To put it briefly, medical imaging refers to a range of technologies that monitor the human body in order to identify, monitor, or treat medical conditions. Non-invasive visualization techniques are mostly used by medical experts to identify damage and diagnose illnesses or chronic conditions. AI has shown exceptional sensitivity and accuracy in detecting imaging abnormalities and promises to enhance tissue-based detection and characterisation. AI quickly and accurately diagnoses diseases like pneumonia and tuberculosis by effectively analyzing X-rays and CT scans. It helps identify osteoporosis in X-rays, detect lung nodules, and lower the chance of overlooking malignant tumors. AI provides a comprehensive picture of patient health by fusing imaging data with electronic medical records. Medical professionals can identify problems or features that the human eye might miss by using AI analysis in medical imaging. Workflow, picture acquisition, and reconstruction are already areas where AI is being utilized. We can obtain more precise data with AI's assistance, which is crucial for subsequent diagnosis. AI in health care imaging is an essential part of contemporary healthcare since it improves patient outcomes and streamlines clinical operations.

Personalized Treatment

Traditional medical practices sometimes assumed that there was a one-size-fits-all approach to therapy. But it's becoming more and more obvious that a person's response to treatment is greatly influenced by their unique genetic, lifestyle, and environmental differences. This integration is based on personalized medicine, which takes into account each person's distinct biological, physiological, ecological, and behavioral traits. By using AI and machine learning to analyze the large and complex information generated by pharmacogenomics, medical professionals may predict drug reactions and tailor treatment plans based on each patient's distinct genetic makeup. Artificial intelligence makes it easier to develop customized treatment plans that maximize effectiveness and reduce adverse consequences by evaluating genetic data, combining patient data, and using predictive analytics. In order to choose the best therapies, precisely modify dosages, and anticipate prospective health problems, this method takes into account an individual's distinct genetic characteristics, behavioral patterns, and medical records. The complexity of gene-drug interactions highlights the need for advanced tools to predict and understand individual drug responses; in this sense, the application of artificial intelligence (AI) and machine learning can be essential in addressing these problems and creating customized healthcare.

Preventive care could also be improved by AI-powered tailored medicine. AI algorithms can determine which people are more likely to develop specific diseases by examining their genetic predispositions, lifestyle choices, and environmental circumstances. Early detection enables medical practitioners to carry out interventions and preventative actions, lowering the burden of disease and enhancing public health in general. The capacity for ongoing learning and adaptation is a key benefit of integrating AI into customized medicine. Treatment plans can be improved and optimized thanks to AI algorithms' real-time analysis of how patients react and treatment results. Over time, improved patient outcomes will result from therapies that are continuously refined and evolving thanks to this iterative approach.

EHR Analysis

When compared to old paper-based systems, Electronic Health Records (EHRs) have drastically changed the way health data is kept and accessible, but their development is far from finished. In essence, electronic health records (EHRs) are digital representations of a patient's medical history, records of treatments, and other health-related data. All of these types of documents are stored and managed electronically so that treating doctors, the patients themselves, and those involved can easily access them. Traditional paper-based medical records are being replaced with digitalized versions, which bring numerous advantages to the health industry. AI uses data from electronic health records to find patterns and trends, forecast the possibility of disease, and support individualized preventative measures. In order to predict the likelihood of conditions like diabetes or heart disease, it looks at historical medical records, individual lifestyle choices, and genetic data. It also finds trends in medicine use to avoid negative reactions. EHRs can also be used as a thorough digital software platform that oversees the multidisciplinary tasks required to provide high-quality, cost-effective patient care while enhancing caregiver efficacy and situations, provided that they are implemented properly and take operational workflows into full account.

Fraud Identification

AI looks at large healthcare databases to spot odd trends, stopping fraud by spotting practices like overcharging or unnecessary procedures. In order to make sure that resources are used for legitimate patient care, it examines billing information to identify questionable claims.

Remote Patient Care

As hospitals turned into high-risk areas and vulnerable people needed critical care in the comfort of their own homes, the pandemic accelerated the transition to telehealth. At-home care has accelerated thanks to remote patient monitoring (RPM), which gives physicians real-time information about their patients' health. By identifying minute changes in patients' health, AI-enabled RPM makes early intervention easier. This prompt action can lower the risk of complications and stop health problems from getting worse. AI-powered remote healthcare delivers medical services without geographical restrictions. Patients receive prompt care and can communicate their health details remotely, while AI assists healthcare professionals in identifying patterns, thereby enhancing preventative measures. For instance, people with diabetes can utilize wearables to continuously monitor their glucose levels, enabling rapid adjustments to their treatment strategies from afar. An AI-powered remote monitoring tool is used by a heart failure patient to continuously check their blood pressure, heart rate, and respiration rate. An imminent aggravation of heart failure may be indicated by the AI algorithm's detection of anomalous patterns in the patient's vital signs. In this case, an alarm is sent to a competent healthcare provider. The doctor can then swiftly avoid hospitalization by modifying the patient's medication. Beyond daily comforts, RPM with AI offers even more advantages. By reducing needless ER visits and simplifying the monitoring of high-risk patients, certain AI-powered RPM systems can aid in the reduction of hospital readmissions. AI has the ability to completely transform remote patient monitoring as it develops, breaking down barriers and guaranteeing that everyone has access to effective, patient-centered healthcare.

Efficient Medical Documentation

Healthcare practitioners can automate the assessment of structured dictation by using AI algorithms to expedite the medical documentation process. Physicians' spoken communications are transformed into structured electronic health records (EHRs) using natural language processing (NLP) and machine learning, improving accuracy and saving time. AI-based systems ensure accurate transcription of patient medical histories and conditions by comprehending medical terminology and context. Healthcare providers can concentrate more on patient care and less on administrative duties thanks to these tools, which can automatically update records, make diagnosis suggestions, and streamline the billing process.

Improved Medical Record Administration

By automating data entry, classification, and review, artificial intelligence (AI) improves medical record management. Healthcare professionals can find relevant information more quickly thanks to sophisticated algorithms that spot patterns in patient data. These AI-powered technologies improve organizational and retrieval procedures while lowering administrative tasks by guaranteeing correct documentation, safe data storage, and adherence to privacy regulations.

Assistance for Clinical Decision-Making

By evaluating large patient data collections and assisting with accurate diagnosis, AI supports clinical decision-making. AI helps healthcare professionals by combining data from imaging devices, test results, and medical records to find trends and treatment outcomes, ultimately improving the quality of patient care. Over time, these AI-driven choices change to reflect new research and enhance clinical results by developing individualized treatment plans based on each patient's unique health requirements.

Better Treatment of Patients

AI-driven medical facilities include a number of cutting-edge features, including automated diagnosis, medication evaluation, immediate priority, and patient-specific medication. Healthcare professionals can enhance patient outcomes, reduce errors, and optimize resource allocation by utilizing machine learning and prescriptive analytics. AI-powered platforms evaluate patient data to produce useful suggestions, allowing for customized treatment regimens and efficient population health management.

2.3.2.2 Retail and E-Commerce

Applications of AI in retail and e-commerce [17–19] industry are following:

Personalized Shopping Experience

AI analyzes customer behavior, preferences, and purchase history, offering tailored suggestions based on individual insights. Providing tailored product recommendations enhances the shopping experience, boosts customer engagement, and increases sales.

Dynamic Pricing Optimization

Dynamic pricing enables businesses to adjust prices in response to evolving consumer preferences. It is sometimes referred to as demand pricing, surge pricing, or time-dependent pricing. By evaluating enormous datasets, AI improves this approach by forecasting changes in demand, comprehending customer price sensitivity, and determining the ideal price point to optimize revenues or market dominance. Retailers employ AI algorithms to assess existing market conditions, competitors' pricing strategies, and consumer preferences. This enables dynamic adjustments to pricing, ensuring competitive pricing strategies, enhancing profits, and effectively responding to market fluctuations.

The development of algorithms, data collecting and analysis, and integration with current pricing systems are the fundamental elements involved in creating an AI-powered dynamic pricing solution. To guarantee responsible and long-lasting implementation, other factors like ethical ramifications and regulatory compliance must be taken into account. AI-powered systems employ algorithms and machine learning to evaluate massive datasets and identify the best price point for a good or service, in contrast to static pricing models where prices stay fixed for long periods of time. Businesses can now go beyond conventional pricing methods that depend on human tweaks or sweeping assumptions thanks to this technique. Rather, by continuously examining sales trends, rival price, customer willingness to pay, and outside variables like the weather or local events, AI-based dynamic pricing enables more thorough, data-driven assessment. Businesses may make sure that their pricing plans stay lucrative, dynamic, and in line with customer expectations by utilizing this capacity. Businesses can maximize customer willingness to pay during moments of high demand and modify prices to sustain sales during off-peak periods by optimizing prices. AI dynamic pricing makes guarantee that a business's products are always reasonably priced and can respond to market shifts more quickly than its rivals.

Demand Estimation and Inventory Administration

AI helps merchants maximize inventory effectiveness by forecasting developments, seasonal variations, and demand patterns. This reduces shortages and excess inventory, lowers storage costs, and boosts the supply chain's overall effectiveness.

Retailers may ensure product availability and meet customer expectations by precisely estimating demand.

Customer Service

AI-powered chatbots are used to respond to consumer inquiries, offer immediate assistance, and assist with order status monitoring. By providing quick responses, resolving common problems, and increasing overall customer happiness, virtual assistants are crucial for improving customer service and building a positive company image.

Image Recognition and Visual Navigation

AI image recognition has become a ground-breaking technology that is transforming how we perceive and evaluate visual data. Machines can now comprehend images and make deft decisions based on visual input thanks to the development of deep learning algorithms and neural networks. By seamlessly merging the digital and physical worlds, AI-enabled visual search technology completely transforms our perception of buying. Additionally, this new method of searching may become the standard as e-commerce develops. Customers can search for commodities using photos instead of text thanks to retailers' use of AI-driven visual search technologies. This improves the search process by making it easier and more effective. Additionally, picture recognition technology can be used for tasks including enhancing search accuracy, streamlining catalog management, and automatically tagging objects.

The value of visual search resides in its capacity to satisfy the demands of contemporary consumers who seek solutions that are quick, easy to use, and visually appealing. AI-powered visual search is transforming industries, from streamlining online shopping to improving healthcare diagnostic tools. In a manner that text-based approaches could never match, it facilitates smooth interactions and helps people locate exactly what they need. Artificial intelligence (AI) automatically increases search predictions and recognition accuracy through the usage of neural networks. By providing instant visual matches and tailored recommendations, this technology boosts user engagement. Businesses may improve consumer satisfaction and conversion rates by offering a simple and easy buying experience.

Customer Churn Prediction

Artificial intelligence allows online retail businesses to examine customer interaction data across various platforms, providing valuable insights for enhancing performance and identifying trends. Businesses can employ machine learning algorithms to forecast client attrition by examining factors like bounce rates and abandoned baskets on their website. By predicting future demands, companies can employ proactive strategies such as automated emails and tailored promotions to maintain customer interest and boost sales, resulting in reduced churn rates and higher profits.

Automated Product Tagging and Attribute Extraction

AI transforms the way e-commerce brands improve their catalogs by automatically labeling products and retrieving attributes. AI uses image recognition techniques to efficiently and accurately analyze product photos and determine key characteristics like color, style, and brand. This automated method helps customers find products more quickly and improves their shopping experience by streamlining catalog administration, minimizing manual labor, and guaranteeing uniformity in product categorization. The key is having accurate and comprehensive product catalog data. A key but often overlooked feature that aids in attaining this precision and completeness in product catalog data is efficient product attribute tagging. While scalability, uniformity, precision, and efficiency have long been problems for conventional techniques of identifying item qualities, fresh ideas and essentially novel approaches to overcoming these obstacles are emerging. Next-generation feature tagging remedies, driven by state-of-the-art Generative AI and RLMs, are revolutionizing the way online retailers optimize their selection, maintain product catalog data, and provide exceptional customer service.

Customer Segmentation

Leveraging AI-powered data analysis, customer segmentation allows retailers to categorize customers according to behaviors, preferences, and demographics. Using artificial intelligence algorithms based on common characteristics and behaviors, it divides a large market into more manageable, discrete consumer categories. This approach uses machine learning and data analytics to provide deeper insights into customer preferences. As a result, businesses may create highly targeted and personalized marketing strategies. The capacity of AI services to process enormous volumes of data more quickly and accurately than humans is one of their primary benefits. Large-scale data analysis by AI can reveal hidden ideas that human marketers might miss. This enables companies to spot worthwhile chances for individualization and customization that can boost engagement and conversions.

Simply said, geographic customer segmentation is based on the user's location. There are several methods to put this into practice. You can organize by zip code, city, state, or nation. The size, composition, and temporal and spatial movements of consumers are all factors in demographic segmentation. Gender disparities are used by several businesses to develop and promote their products. Parental status is yet another crucial aspect. This kind of information can be found in customer surveys. The foundation of behavioral consumer segmentation is historical customer behavior observations that can be utilized to forecast future behavior. For instance, the brands that consumers buy or the times when they make the most purchases. The behavioral component of consumer segmentation looks at both the reasons for purchases and how they evolve over time. Consumer psychological segmentation typically addresses issues such as opinions, views, and personality attributes. Customer sentiment can be measured using this data, which is gathered through customer surveys.

Stock Management

All procedures related to the production, storage, and delivery of commodities are included in inventory management. Making sure the correct products are available at the right time and location is its main objective. This entails keeping an eye on sales, orders, deliveries, inventory levels, and the movement of goods from manufacturers to the point of sale. Increased accuracy, lower costs, and happier customers are some advantages of AI inventory management. It is an essential part of contemporary supply chain strategy because of these benefits. By evaluating large data sets to find recurring patterns and trends in consumer behavior, artificial intelligence (AI) significantly contributes to better inventory management for businesses. Retailers can ensure optimal availability of goods at the appropriate times and levels by using artificial intelligence to leverage data to inform decisions about inventory, product assortment, and distribution tactics. Additionally, by proactively resolving problems and adjusting to market shifts, AI helps shops reduce risks like stock shortages and processing returns, which improves operational effectiveness and consumer happiness.

Improved and immediate forecasts generated by real-time data are made possible by artificial intelligence inventory management. This can be gathered from both internal and external sources, including social media, review sites and suggestions, statistics, and climate. By predicting anticipated demand by analyzing historical data and present market situations, AI also exhibits mastery of predictive analytics. Businesses may make well-informed judgments regarding price strategy, product promotions, and inventory replenishment by accurately forecasting future trends. This proactive strategy lowers inventory, increases operational effectiveness, and lessens stockouts.

Fraud Detection

A technologically driven method called artificial intelligence (AI) fraud detection uses machine learning to find fraudulent activity in big datasets. It involves training computers to spot patterns and anomalies that might point to fraud. AI empowers online retail sites to combat evolving fraud strategies while providing a seamless shopping experience for consumers. AI can identify fraudulent activities and accurately locate high-risk transactions by examining extensive amounts of transaction data in real-time. AI enhances security protocols by rapidly recognizing genuine and dubious transactions, safeguarding e-commerce platforms from financial damage and reputational harm while still focusing on customer satisfaction. There are more and more ways that financial fraud is being committed, such as leveraging generative AI to phish personal information, extracting compromised data from the dark web for credit card theft, and laundering money across fiat currencies, digital wallets, and crypto currencies. The internet underworld harbours numerous such financial schemes. AI can spot and draw attention to anomalies in real-time payment techniques, application usage, bank transactions, and other financial activities. This expedites AI-based fraud detection in banking and aids in preventing maleficence and fraud. AI in financial systems not only successfully detects anomalies but also lowers false positives. This is necessary to safeguard customer satisfaction without compromising security. To spot fakes, computer vision examines photo documents like passports and driver's licenses. While the AI examines the documents to search for fake records, NLP reads the documents to assess the accuracy of the data on them. Businesses are able to employ AI to avoid fraud because to technologies like NLP, Captcha, and GNNs. Businesses can identify fraud concerns before they materialize and avoid the catastrophic financial repercussions by utilizing dynamic rules and real-time reporting features.

Cross-Selling and Upselling

Merchants can effectively execute cross-selling and upselling tactics by leveraging AI to assess customer information, such as buying history, preferences, and upcoming purchases. Retailers may increase the mean value of orders and improve the overall shopping experience by using AI to suggest complementary goods or more expensive alternatives that match the needs of customers. This tailored approach to recommending products results in higher profits while also boosting customer satisfaction and loyalty, ultimately contributing to ongoing business success.

2.3.2.3 Banking and Financial Services

AI uses in the banking and finance sectors [20–22] encompass:

Fraud Detection and Prevention

AI is utilized in the banking and finance industry to identify fraud by analyzing transaction patterns, recognizing anomalies, and alerting to potential fraudulent activities. The integrity of monetary transactions is improved by machine learning algorithms that adjust to changing fraud tendencies.

Evaluation of Risks and Credit Assessment

AI-powered credit scoring makes use of non-traditional data and machine learning techniques to improve the precision of determining an individual's or business's creditworthiness. As a result, risk management is enhanced, enabling financial organizations to make informed decisions regarding loans.

Better Customer Assistance

AI-powered chatbots enhance customer assistance by providing quick answers to questions, helping with account problems, and giving tailored financial guidance. This process decreases delay in responding, increases customer happiness, and enhances the effectiveness of client interactions.

Anti-Money Laundering (AML) Compliance

AI is used to improve AML compliance by automating the examination of large volumes of transaction data. Machine learning algorithms can recognize atypical patterns and pinpoint possible instances of money laundering, assisting financial institutions in fulfilling regulatory obligations and effectively reducing risks.

Process Automation

AI-driven automation improves financial management by leveraging technology like voice-activated apps and optical character recognition (OCR) to boost precision and productivity. By streamlining processes like document scanning, data extraction, and information about clients access, these advances help businesses allocate resources intelligently and increase efficiency. Financial institutions may enhance compliance efforts, provide clients with excellent services through cutting-edge technological advances, and adjust to evolving regulatory needs by utilizing AI technologies.

Simplified Adherence to Regulations

AI assists financial organizations in efficiently and effectively managing intricate compliance obligations. AI systems employ deep learning and NLP to assess regulatory changes, enhancing decision-making and ensuring adherence to evolving standards. In the end, AI promotes confidence and transparency in the financial sector by speeding up compliance processes, decreasing labor-intensive tasks, and lowering the risks connected with non-compliance.

Advanced Documentation Handling

AI-driven processing of paperwork improves workflow efficiency and decision-making by revolutionizing how financial firms extract, comprehend, and analyze data. By automating processes like statement evaluation, contractual appraisal, and report production, AI systems increase operational effectiveness, accuracy, and compliance. By extracting crucial insights from complicated financial data, these tools lessen human labor and error, help businesses allocate resources more effectively, and promote smart expansion initiatives.

Debt Management

To improve collection efficiency and customer happiness, AI systems evaluate consumer data and payment patterns to create efficient collection tactics, rank accounts, and renegotiate payback conditions. These options help lending organizations minimize late payments, lower credit risks, and promote long-term financial stability for both lenders and borrowers.

Agreement Evaluation

By independently reviewing and analyzing legal papers in the financial services sector, AI-driven agreement analysis revolutionizes the legal document management procedure. AI systems use natural language processing (NLP) algorithms to extract important terms, risks, and obligations from complicated agreements, thereby improving compliance and risk administration procedures' precision as well as effectiveness. AI improves financial institutions by streamlining contract evaluations, enabling superior risk management, ensuring compliance with regulations, and supporting informed decision-making, ultimately fostering operational efficiency and regulatory adherence across the organization.

Computerized Financial Statement Compilation

AI-driven automation revolutionizes the production of financial reports by efficiently obtaining, analyzing, and organizing data from various sources to create thorough and accurate reports. AI simplifies data management, from rapid financial analysis to regulatory reporting, empowering businesses to confidently make data-driven, well-informed decisions. AI increases productivity and accuracy in financial reporting by automating repetitive operations and minimizing labor intensive tasks, which improves operational effectiveness and helps financial institutions and banks make better decisions regarding strategy.

2.3.2.4 Travel

Amid the ways AI is being used in the travel [23, 24] sector are:

Personalized Itineraries

Generative AI is revolutionizing personalized travel plans by analyzing vast amounts of data, such as finances, tastes, and social media activity. It creates personalized experiences using machine learning and natural language processing, and it interfaces with booking platforms with ease. The technology offers travelers the chance to customize their itineraries using user-friendly interfaces, offering a sneak peek at the future of customized travel. Beyond customer preferences, AI is also capable of analyzing an infinite amount of travel data, including changes in hotel and flight prices as well as well-known tourist sites across different locations. AI planners can find useful insights, like inexpensive vacations, with the aid of this subset of machine learning. Another branch of machine learning called natural language processing (NLP) enables AI travel itinerary planners to process input data and provide conversational, human-like responses. NLP is frequently used in customer service chatbots and virtual assistants, which can offer 24/7 assistance with itinerary issues and precise responses to inquiries from travelers.

Real-Time Travel Updates and Recommendations

AI enables travel agencies to provide real-time information and tailored suggestions according to user preferences and location. Serving as a virtual tour guide, it offers insightful recommendations for hidden treasures like quaint cafes, obscure art galleries, or picturesque vistas, enriching the journey.

Booking Assistance

Travelers frequently have questions and seek assistance when planning their trips, whether they are booking flights, vacation packages, hotels, or rental vehicles. AI chatbots are crucial for timely and precise help in these situations. Travelers can assess costs and make well-informed decisions by using Generative AI Tools to provide pricing information. Travelers are empowered to select options that fit their preferences, schedules, and budgets because current data is readily available. Chatbots with AI capabilities are essential for answering questions from passengers when they are making reservations. These chatbots offer prompt and accurate assistance, providing pricing information, assisting with option comparison, and enabling passengers to reach sensible choices that suit their preferences, time frames, and finances.

Planning a Vacation

AI serves as a customized travel companion, providing guidance based on the traveler's past travel experiences and personal interests. For travelers with limited time, AI may help create itineraries that maximize time for a more efficient and pleasurable trip by recommending well-liked restaurants, activities, and landmarks.

Smart Shopping

By incorporating hotel comparison features, generative AI-powered apps improve the user experience by enabling travelers to quickly compare important aspects like price, rating, and facilities. These applications optimize choices and provide the best rate possibilities by offering tailored suggestions based on the makeup of the group, the destination, and the length of stay. In order to guarantee a unique and unforgettable experience, guests can also add extras to their stay.

Customer Service

By providing round-the-clock support and guaranteeing that passengers receive timely answers to their questions and concerns, AI-driven chatbots revolutionize customer care in the travel sector. Businesses can use AI to monitor customer happiness through automated feedback systems and questionnaires, which promotes ongoing enhancements to user experience and service quality.

Revenue Management

By streamlining payment processing, guaranteeing transaction correctness, and producing thorough financial insights, artificial intelligence (AI) revolutionizes revenue management in the travel and tourist industry. Businesses may effectively handle financial reporting, predictions, and bills with AI-powered accounting software, which facilitates improved financial planning and decision-making for long-term success.

Sentiment Analysis

Through real-time social media and online review monitoring, AI-powered sentiment analysis gives travel agencies important insights into the preferences and opinions of their customers. Businesses may better understand client sentiment, spot patterns, and customize services to match changing needs with this data-driven strategy, which eventually increases customer satisfaction and loyalty.

Adaptive Pricing

AI-driven adaptive pricing methods analyse large databases, forecast changes in demand, and instantly modify prices to maximize profits for travel agencies. Businesses can ensure competitiveness and maximize revenue potential by utilizing AI to develop adaptable pricing techniques according to factors including the marginal expense, rival pricing, and demand flexibility.

Language Translation

AI-powered language translation services improve tourists' capacity to explore and interact with local environments by facilitating smooth communication in foreign locations. AI enhances the overall travel experience by enabling tourists to confidently immerse themselves in various cultures and locations through precise translations of menus, signage, and conversations.

2.3.2.5 Real Estate

The following are some ways AI is being used in real estate [25–27]:

Automated Property Valuation

By examining past data, local market patterns, and property attributes, AI systems determine the worth of real estate. By eliminating personal prejudices, this objective approach ensures that buyers, sellers, lenders, and investors receive correct evaluations.

Automated Property Management

By automating processes, reducing errors, and increasing productivity for those in charge of several rental properties, artificial intelligence (AI) is revolutionizing property management. AI allows property managers to focus on strategic aspects by effectively handling activities like maintenance planning, tenant assessment, and lease administration, which leads to faultless operations and increased customer satisfaction.

Optimizing a Real Estate Investment Portfolio

Through machine learning that evaluates massive datasets and forecasts property prices, rental income, and market fluctuations, artificial intelligence (AI) improves the returns on real estate investments. By assessing market movements and improving the equilibrium between risks and benefits using real-time evaluation of information and adaptive modifications, AI-powered risk evaluation algorithms create diversified portfolios.

Automated Lead Identification

The use of AI in real estate improves and expedites the process of finding possible leads. In order to find prospects based on demographics, internet behavior, and property preferences, machine learning algorithms analyze a variety of datasets. AI predicts the likelihood of lead conversion through predictive analytics, which allows agents to allocate resources and concentrate on high-potential leads, leading to improved conversion rates and streamlined procedures.

Predictive Analytics for Market and Investment Research

Through the analysis of historical data and market trends, AI-powered predictive analytics efficiently assess property values, empowering stakeholders to make informed decisions about pricing strategies and investments. Real estate professionals can use AI to generate forecasts that make determining market value easier, allowing them to make well-informed choices about pricing and real estate investments. The real estate sector benefits from enhanced decision-making abilities as well as better market analysis and pricing strategies because AI can predict market trends.

Enhanced Customer Service

Artificial intelligence (AI)-powered chatbots and virtual assistants with Natural Language Processing (NLP) abilities simplify user contact in the real estate industry by facilitating interactive questions, tailored suggestions, and improved user experiences. These advanced algorithmic techniques enable straightforward interaction and effective property searches by understanding and responding to consumer inquiries in normal language. By utilizing AI, real estate websites may help customers identify homes that more adequately and precisely fit their requirements and tastes.

Property Appraisal

Artificial intelligence (AI)-powered automated property appraisal eliminates subjective biases and ensures fair and accurate assessments by analyzing market trends, historical data, and property attributes. Large volumes of data are used by AI systems to produce accurate valuations of properties, assisting lenders, purchasers, vendors, and investors in making informed choices. By improving the accuracy, productivity, and transparency of the assessment procedure, an AI-powered asset analysis benefits the real estate sector.

Investigation

Artificial intelligence (AI) reduces the risk of fraudulent activity, streamlines due diligence labor, and boosts real estate transaction efficiency by analyzing massive datasets, spotting inconsistencies in documents, and improving accuracy in procedures like loan approval. AI-powered solutions examine papers and identify mistakes or discrepancies, guaranteeing adherence to regulations and reducing the possibility of legal problems. Real estate agents can improve workflows, reduce operating costs, and raise the general caliber of deals by automating the due diligence process.

Smart Recommendations

AI-powered property search engines analyze user preferences, previous search history, and property listings using machine learning algorithms to provide tailored recommendations that expedite the house search process and raise customer satisfaction. Based on user preferences, financial constraints, and preferred locations, these services employ artificial intelligence (AI) to provide personalized property recommendations. Through improving user experiences, boosting interaction, and enabling effective property inquiries on real estate platforms, artificial intelligence (AI) transforms property search and suggestion techniques.

Intelligent Data Processing

Through efficient information extraction and organization from a variety of forms, including handwritten or badly scanned files, workflow optimization, and seamless integration into existing systems, artificial intelligence (AI) improves document analysis in the real estate industry. AI-powered tools make it easier to handle and analyze vast amounts of data by precisely extracting data from documents using Optical Character Recognition (OCR) technology. AI improves real estate operations' overall quality, reduces errors, and promotes productivity by automating data processing processes.

Generating Listing Descriptions

By using sophisticated Natural Language Processing (NLP) techniques, AI expedites the creation of real estate listings, creating accurate and thorough descriptions fast, reducing time and guaranteeing uniformity among postings. AI-powered tools can be used by real estate professionals to write interesting and educational listing descriptions that attract potential tenants and purchasers. Real estate platforms may improve search engine visibility, streamline the property listing process, and raise the bar for property listings by using AI to create listings.

Ensuring Adherence and Detecting Corruption

In order to ensure legal compliance, preserve the authenticity of business operations, reduce legal hazards, and promote market transparency, artificial intelligence (AI) solutions like computer vision and machine learning identify and assess illegal actions related to real estate postings. Real estate brokers may detect and stop fraudulent activity with the use of AI-driven solutions that analyze listing data to find irregularities or suspicious trends. By using AI for fraud detection and compliance oversight, real estate platforms increase market credibility and confidence while guarding against any legal problems and guaranteeing that consumer interests are protected.

Enhanced Transactional Procedure

By lowering data input errors, speeding up closing procedures and producing thorough evaluations that enable organizations and brokers to assess and improve efficiency, artificial intelligence (AI) simplifies real estate transactions. By using AI to automate repetitive processes like data entry and document processing, real estate agents may reduce errors and increase transaction efficiency. By using AI for processing transactions, real estate networks may boost efficiency, cut expenses, and improve the general experience for buyers, sellers, and brokers.

Lease Administration and Record Keeping

AI improves efficiency and customer satisfaction in the real estate industry by automating processes like abstraction and summarization, drafting contracts, continually tracking renewals, bargaining with data-driven decisions, and establishing centralized electronic storage. These applications powered by AI, enhance lease management procedures by increasing productivity and accuracy in processes including lease abstraction, record keeping, and renewal handling. In addition to increasing administrative efficiency, real estate professionals can lower compliance risks and boost customer satisfaction by using AI for lease administration and paperwork.

2.3.2.6 Media and Entertainment

The following are some ways AI is being used in media and entertainment [28–30]:

AI in Game Design and Gameplay

By refining mechanisms and enhancing Non-player Characters (NPCs), AI improves game design and produces realistic, difficult levels that improve the player's experience. AI produces procedural material, such as new stages and characters, and builds strong opponents for increased gameplay immersion, guaranteeing a constantly interesting and captivating gaming experience.

Storytelling

AI enhances the production and distribution of content, which helps with storytelling. Authors can produce more engaging stories by using the insights gained from the study of large datasets about character development and story structures. Writers can enhance their stories, elicit certain emotional responses, and forge stronger bonds with readers by using sentiment analysis and emotion identification.

Editing Movies

When it comes to editing full-length films and making powerful movie trailers, artificial intelligence is essential. AI is very effective at identifying highly significant and psychologically charged scenes, which aids editors in making compelling trailers. An example is the science fiction film "Morgan" trailer, which was produced using IBM Watson. AI can also be used to edit entire films. It streamlines the editing process for feature-length productions by using facial recognition to identify main characters and important moments linked to the plot.

Content Recommendation

Recommendation engines driven by AI examine a variety of user data to forecast and offer pertinent content, increasing user happiness and engagement. Machine learning is used by platforms such as Netflix to continuously improve suggestions based on user interactions and A/B testing. By using machine learning to optimize content delivery and user experience, these platforms create customized landing cards based on user attributes. By customizing suggestions based on user preferences, offering users a variety of thumbnails improves content discoverability and engagement. Additionally, movie categorization is improved by machine classification techniques, which also improve platform user experience and search accuracy. AI-driven algorithms improve search results, making it easier for users to locate pertinent material and increasing platform engagement and user satisfaction.

Content Automation

Artificial intelligence is revolutionizing the recreational and journalism sectors by transforming the creation, dissemination, and consumption of content. Beyond merely automating tedious tasks, AI gives creatives the tools they need to produce realistic characters, rich, personalized storylines, and immersive experiences that appeal to a range of audiences. In order to enhance distribution of material, forecast consumer preferences, and increase interaction across multiple platforms, this sort of technology examines enormous volumes of information. AI has the potential to help the industry push the boundaries of innovation, speed up production, and create innovative content that people will find more engaging.

Book Publishing

AI has revolutionized book publishing by automating tedious jobs, cutting expenses, and expediting the publication process. AI improves workflow efficiency from article finalization to reader distribution and empowers publishers to make data-driven forecasts. While enabling tasks like text generation based on preset rules, AI-powered solutions help publishers analyze massive volumes of data to create pertinent and interesting content. When it comes to quickly writing synopses and summarizing books, AI is essential. Through the use of machine learning algorithms, it assists with activities such as designing book layouts and covers. Additionally, based on reader preferences, AI can suggest distribution and marketing channels, improving book promotion tactics.

Personalized Advertising

Streaming platforms were the first to generate revenue through targeted advertising campaigns and subscription arrangements. AI-based advertising has many benefits since it carefully examines consumer behavior using big data analytics and machine learning. AI improves user experiences and helps marketers to efficiently optimize plans by comparing this data with past trends. Prominent media and entertainment firms, like Disney+, use AI solutions to target their advertising and provide more relevant commercials based on the interests of its customers.

Social Media

Social networking sites like Facebook, Instagram, Snapchat, and Pinterest use a range of artificial intelligence (AI) technology, from computer vision to analytics, to provide their customers with more individualized goods and services. By customizing recommendations, ads, and content according to user choices and actions, AI improves the user experience. Additionally, these platforms' AI-driven algorithms assist in identifying and reducing hazardous content, guaranteeing a more secure and interesting user experience.

Journalism

Social networking sites like Facebook, Instagram, Snapchat, and Pinterest use a range of artificial intelligence (AI) technology, from computer vision to analytics, to provide their customers with more individualized goods and services. By customizing recommendations, ads, and content according to user choices and actions, AI improves the user experience. Additionally, these platforms' AI-driven algorithms assist in identifying and reducing hazardous content, guaranteeing a more secure and interesting user experience.

Music Composition

Even though AI technologies are currently mostly focused on entertainment, they are rapidly helping musicians with song generation. These programs have the ability to generate lyrics as well as compose music. Platforms such as Soundraw allow users to compose songs by combining pre-made phrases using artificial intelligence. Similar to this, services such as These Lyrics Do Not Exist use artificial intelligence (AI) to create lyrics depending on predetermined criteria like topic, genre, and mood, making it easier to create original song lyrics. By evaluating user inputs like topic, genre, and mood, these AI technologies assist in creating music and lyrics, offering an advanced instrument for creating tunes and composing.

Podcast

Podcasts have grown in popularity in the technology world because they provide an advanced means of disseminating knowledge. The media and entertainment sector can use AI to produce interactive, tailored, and captivating content that appeals to busy people who favor audio formats. AI speeds up and improves the efficiency of audio editing procedures. A crucial part of artificial intelligence, natural language processing (NLP) analyzes and produces human language, allowing for activities like automatically creating subtitles for viewers with hearing impairments and transcribing audio into text format. Furthermore, AI's inventive skills revolutionize podcasting, improve audience engagement, and change production methods

2.3.2.7 Manufacturing

AI's application in manufacturing [31–33] entails:

Defect Detection

AI revolutionizes manufacturing defect identification by employing cutting-edge technology such as computer vision and machine learning to pinpoint defects with previously unheard-of accuracy. In order to increase accuracy, it continuously learns from manufacturing patterns, automates visual inspections, and analyzes sensor data in real time. AI lowers waste, minimizes rework, and improves overall product quality by identifying flaws early and offering actionable insights, which increases the effectiveness and economy of manufacturing operations.

Connectivity of Assembly Lines

AI-automated assembly lines streamline processes in modern production, eliminating the need for human intervention and ensuring efficient, dependable, and error-free output. Automation significantly boosts efficiency, reduces errors, and enhances overall production because robots can now finish tasks in a preset order.

Predictive Analytics

Through the analysis of sensor data and maintenance logs, AI algorithms forecast equipment faults, allowing for proactive scheduling of repair tasks. By minimizing unscheduled downtime, cutting maintenance expenses, and optimizing production uptime, this predictive strategy improves the overall efficacy and operating efficiency of the equipment.

Real-Time Monitoring and Analysis

AI enables real-time production procedure monitoring while collecting data from various sources. By quickly spotting anomalies and variations, manufacturers may boost output, simplify processes, and take swift corrective action. Data-driven decisions for ongoing operational improvement are made easier by the insightful information that real-time analysis offers.

Quality Control

Visual inspections are automated by AI-powered algorithms that compare photos or videos to predetermined quality standards in order to identify flaws. This automation improves quality control, reduces waste, and ensures continual reliability of goods. Manufacturers have the capability to maintain high standards of quality and reduce product defects.

Process Optimization

Production data is analyzed by AI, especially machine learning, to find inefficiencies and improve manufacturing procedures. By recommending improvements in cycle durations, energy consumption, and material usage, artificial intelligence (AI) raises productivity, lowers costs, and improves overall operational efficiency. For long-term productivity increases, manufacturers can locate bottlenecks, get rid of waste, and put continuous improvement plans into action.

Order Management

Manufacturers can manage complex orders across numerous channels, automate order input, track stocks, and improve inventory planning and order management transparency by implementing AI-based systems. AI guarantees flexible, economical procedures that adjust to changes in the market, demand, customer expectations, and production tactics.

Design and Manufacturing

For a single product, AI-based design software generates several optimum product designs. Engineers are able to develop and test multiple layouts against various production circumstances to get the optimum result, greatly accelerating the design process, by entering criteria such as raw materials, size, weight, manufacturing processes, and cost limitations.

Factory Automation

AI increases efficiency and production by decreasing the need for human operators. In addition to lowering labor costs and improving overall factory performance, AI can create a centralized location for operational information, automate complex tasks, quickly detect anomalies through constant surveillance, and expand output in accordance with need. Artificial intelligence (AI) is transforming the business world by increasing efficiency, precision, and adaptability across a variety of manufacturing techniques, especially in the framework of Industry 4.0. AI technologies, such as machine learning, computer vision, and natural language processing (NLP), improve several aspects of manufacturing processes. AI can evaluate vast volumes of data from sensors, equipment, and production lines to increase output, improve quality, and reduce downtime. By using algorithms to identify patterns in data, AI may anticipate potential issues, suggest improvements, and even independently alter processes in real-time.

Product Development

By analysing data from manufacturing or experimental processes, artificial intelligence (AI) systems speed up product development and assist manufacturers in cutting costs, time, and replication techniques. The development process is streamlined and product innovation efficiency is increased with this data-driven approach.

Price Variance

AI assists manufacturers in selecting the best suppliers and making precise cost estimates for raw materials. Algorithms and dashboards driven by AI monitor supplier dimensions and resource characteristics, forecast typical purchase prices, and provide benchmarks for price comparisons, streamlining procurement management and increasing cost effectiveness.

Control of Warehouses

Innovations in technology have continuously led to advancements in warehouse management, from scanning bar codes to manual stocktaking. With the aid of AI-powered demand forecasting methodologies, warehouses may enhance supply chain management, anticipate shifts in consumer demand, and arrive at intelligent choices regarding stock, transport, and purchasing. AI-related improvements are being incorporated into machines that systematize logistics processes. AI makes it possible to gather data in real time for ongoing logistics planning and warehouse monitoring, which promotes effective stock management and lowers transportation costs by forecasting demand. AI maximizes efficiency and reduces warehouse management expenses by automating processes like item monitoring and sorting, which eventually improves product quality control and boosts sales and profit margins.

2.3.2.8 Automotive

AI applications in the automotive industry [34, 35] include:

Smart Traffic Control

Intelligent traffic management is the use of artificial intelligence (AI) to assess traffic information collected in real time from GPS and surveillance cameras. This data is processed by AI algorithms to enhance road safety, reduce congestion, and optimize traffic flow. Adaptive traffic signal management systems automatically adjust signal schedules in accordance to changing traffic conditions to reduce congestion. By suggesting alternate routes to drivers, dynamic route planning cuts down on travel time. Accident detection technologies with AI capabilities can also identify problems fast, enabling efficient rerouting and prompt responses.

Enhanced Navigation

Beyond conventional GPS, AI-powered navigation provides optimum routes by using real-time data such as traffic and road conditions. By dynamically modifying routes to prevent traffic jams and collisions, these adaptive algorithms give drivers the most efficient routes. In order to accommodate user preferences, cut down on trip times, and improve overall driving experiences, AI-driven navigation systems also include service stations and sites of interest.

Customized Client Service

In the automotive industry, artificial intelligence (AI) produces personalized customer experiences by tailoring conversations and services according to consumer interests. By examining information like previous purchases and driving patterns, AI systems provide tailored suggestions for car options and maintenance plans. Customer engagement, devotion, and satisfaction all increase as a result. AI-powered chatbots also provide prompt assistance, helping customers with purchases or difficulties, ensuring a seamless and personalized experience.

Predictive Vehicle Maintenance

Predictive maintenance of vehicles uses artificial intelligence (AI) to analyze vehicle data in real time, identifying potential issues before they become critical and reducing repair costs and availability. This proactive approach ensures optimal vehicle performance and extends the fleet's lifetime. Because AI-powered software provides actionable insights about vehicle maintenance in real time, boosting efficiency and lowering depreciation, proactive upkeep is displacing preventative maintenance.

Modernization of Manufacturing Processes

Artificial intelligence (AI) helps optimize the automotive manufacturing technique by analyzing production information to identify shortcomings, predict breakdowns of machinery, and improve quality control. Faster production timelines, less waste, and better-quality vehicles result from its ability to automate repetitive processes, improve decision-making, and enable real-time modifications. This results in improved business support functions, a leaner supply chain, and more intelligent project management, all of which improve the process as a whole.

Vehicle Prototyping

By increasing the efficiency of CAD rendering and prefabrication, AI-powered prototyping simplifies the fast prototyping process used in the automotive sector. While ML finds design anomalies and improves simulation processes, it automates repetitive work so designers may concentrate on important details.

CPQ Automationwe

By handling product configuration and price quote generation and handling large amounts of data with ease, AI simplifies CPQ (Configure, Price, Quote) automation. This improves overall operational efficiency by enabling automakers to apply price and discounting rules, handle contracts effectively, and create proposals.

Demand Forecasting

Demand forecasting is powered by AI, which analyzes changes in the business environment and the state of the economy to help businesses modify output and cut down on excess inventory expenses. To provide precise demand forecasts, AI combines with blockchain and IoT technologies to collect extensive data on equipment and shipment status

2.3.2.9 Education

With several applications that have improved the environment, artificial intelligence (AI) in education has completely changed the way we learn. Among these usage scenarios are:

Individualized Education

AI maximizes learning results and promotes engagement by customizing learning paths and content to each student's needs. This strategy guarantees that students experience focused and flexible learning opportunities. By customizing learning experiences to meet the needs of each individual student, boosting engagement, and enhancing overall learning results, artificial intelligence is transforming education. Adaptive systems use AI and ML (machine learning) algorithms to analyse vast amounts of educational data. The information helps evaluate their benefits and drawbacks. AI creates personalized learning paths by fusing the specifics with each person's requirements, preferences, and learning preferences. Through the application of suitable frequency and difficulty depending on the student's level of competency, the AI can provide a customized learning experience that is optimal for helping the student fulfill their educational goals.

Intelligent Tutoring

AI-powered tutoring programs improve students' learning experiences by providing them with individualized advice and feedback. By adjusting to different learning styles, these systems offer focused support and improve comprehension across a range of subjects.

Automated Assessment

In the past, manual grading processes took hours or even days to complete; today, they can be completed in a matter of seconds. Because they are more efficient, students may obtain feedback more rapidly, which enhances their comprehension of their performance. Due to weariness, biases, or different interpretations of the grading guidelines, human examiners may add errors into their rating. In contrast, automated evaluation systems consistently adhere to a predetermined set of guidelines and norms, guaranteeing impartial and equitable assessments for every student. The two primary benefits that AI can provide are efficiency and responsiveness. It takes a long time to grade by hand. The AI system can evaluate a large number of documents quickly. AI in evaluation enables quick responses and mark distribution to students, leading to more efficient learning.

Educational Analytics

AI for educational analytics looks for trends and patterns in student performance data. To increase overall student achievement, educators can use these understandings to inform data-driven initiatives that pinpoint areas of weakness and offer personalized assistance.

Curriculum Enhancement

The subject of education is undergoing major changes as a result of technology breakthroughs that are continuing to affect numerous industries, especially with the development of artificial intelligence (AI). With its ability to produce more individualized, effective, and engaging learning experiences, curriculum design is one of AI's most promising uses. AI is used in curriculum building to enhance and personalize our learning process, making it more thorough, efficient, and individualized. From improving the relevance of course material to increasing the productivity of human teachers, artificial intelligence (AI) is revolutionizing curriculum design and is a crucial component of curriculum creation. By examining educational data to find patterns and gaps and recommending revisions based on current knowledge and changing standards, artificial intelligence (AI) supports curriculum planning. This enables teachers to make data-driven choices, guaranteeing that instructional materials stay current and raise the standard of education as a whole.

Content Creation

AI is essential to the content creation industry since it automates a number of labor-intensive and time-consuming operations. Content like blog entries, social media posts, and articles can be automatically created using large language and image AI models. For professionals and companies that regularly produce material, this might be a useful time-saving tool. Artificial intelligence (AI)-powered programs may apply artistic filters, produce completely new, synthetic media, and even turn raw photographs and videos into attractive graphics. This has a significant effect on sectors like marketing and entertainment, as AI-powered tools for content production can save expenses and enhance content quality, ultimately increasing engagement and generating commercial results.

Interactive Language Learning

AI has an enormous effect on language acquisition because it provides learners with individualized, easily available, and engaging solutions. Artificial intelligence-powered platforms offer a variety of language learning opportunities, from adaptive classes to real-time feedback. With millions of users worldwide, AI-powered language learning services like Duolingo, Babbel, and Memrise are growing in popularity. These platforms use sophisticated algorithms to produce tailored educational experiences that adapt lessons to the skill and development of each individual. AI improves language acquisition by offering immediate guidance on vocabulary, grammar, and pronunciation, making the learning process more engaging and efficient. AI makes language acquisition interesting and customized by mimicking real-world situations and adjusting to each learner's unique learning preferences.

Safe Online Evaluation

By employing sophisticated monitoring and verification methods to stop cheating, AI greatly enhances the fairness and integrity of online tests. This lessens the workload for teachers and guarantees a safe testing atmosphere, encouraging confidence and academic honesty.

Efficient Administrative Management

Administrative duties include everything from managing records to setting up meetings. These tasks are prone to inefficiencies since they frequently call for a great deal of time and attention to detail. By automating repetitive operations and improving decision-making skills, artificial intelligence (AI) offers a smooth method to streamline these tasks. Artificial intelligence (AI) provides technologies that can lessen the workload for human administrators through natural language processing (NLP) and predictive analytics. With its ability to manage scheduling, optimize resource allocation, and streamline student enrollment procedures, artificial intelligence (AI) is revolutionizing administrative assistance in educational institutions. Staff members can concentrate on more important duties when routine questions are handled by chatbots and virtual assistants, which improves operational efficiency.

Task Automation

By automating processes like report management, exam grading, and homework evaluation, artificial intelligence enhances online learning environments. This promotes an atmosphere that is favorable to effective learning and knowledge acquisition while streamlining processes for Edtech companies and increasing productivity.

2.3.2.10 Fashion

AI applications in the fashion industry include:

Trend Forecasting and Buying

AI is essential to the fashion industry since it forecasts trends using data from multiple sources. AI algorithms assist customers in making informed purchases by analyzing consumer behavior and preferences from social media, historical sales data, and fashion blogs. Fashion brands can increase their marketability by ensuring that their collections represent both current and emerging trends.

Merchandising and Analysis

AI-optimized assortment planning and inventory management lead to effective merchandising. AI analyzes enormous databases that include sales, past trends, and customer preferences to identify the best product placement, quantity, and selection. The fashion industry's profitability is increased by this data-driven strategy, which also reduces excess inventory and out-of-stock scenarios.

Technology Design and Creation

AI tools that are included into the design and development technique include virtual prototype creation, pattern optimization for material efficiency, and design recommendations. Designers are able to experiment with fabrics, styles, and colors as a result of the streamlined creative process. The results include enhanced development of goods and successful revisions to design in the fashion sector.

Styling and Visual Merchandising

AI improves visual merchandising by suggesting styles according to consumer tastes and current fashions. AI makes clothing and product combinations suggestions and even allows virtual try-ons, whether in-store or online. This individualized strategy draws clients in and creates an engaging, eye-catching purchasing experience.

Product Recommendations

By examining past browsing and purchase activity, AI improves the fashion e-commerce experience by offering tailored product recommendations. By identifying and accommodating unique tastes and styles, this improves the possibility of a purchase and cultivates client loyalty.

Customer Support

Chatbots and virtual assistants driven by AI offer 24-h customer service by responding to inquiries, providing product information, and assisting with purchases. In the cutthroat online fashion market, these AI technologies increase productivity, decrease response times, and boost consumer happiness by automating repetitive exchanges.

Product Search

AI-powered search engines improve the accuracy and efficiency of consumer queries in online fashion purchases with techniques like visual navigation and speech recognition. These sophisticated features make purchasing smooth and easy by enabling consumers to locate stylish items using pictures, descriptions, or voice queries.

Pricing Optimization

Fashion merchants can use AI to optimize price by examining variables including demand, rival pricing, and past sales data. Retailers may keep a competitive advantage and boost revenue by using this data-driven strategy to help them set competitive prices that strike a balance between profitability and sales volume.

Market Research

AI is capable of efficiently processing and analyzing vast amounts of market research information from various sources, including industry publications, networking sites trends, and consumer feedback. This analysis's analytical information about customer preferences, rival strategies, and industry trends enables fashion firms to make data-driven decisions, identify new possibilities, and swiftly adapt to changing market dynamics. This keeps them competitive and in line with current trends.

2.3.2.11 Information Technology

AI applications in IT [36, 37] include:

IT Support and Helpdesk Automation

An IT helpdesk automation system uses technology and software to automate the support process in any business. Both the company's clients and staff benefit from this since it lowers the possibility of making a mistake and saves a significant amount of time and money. The combination of intelligent systems and service desk automation solutions intended to manage routine support chores and enhance overall customer service efficiency is referred to as artificial intelligence (AI) in IT Help Desk services. Technology help desk teams can automate the creation of tickets, fix common problems, and keep an eye on systems with AI ticketing, freeing up IT staff to work on more difficult problems. Chatbots and virtual assistants with AI capabilities streamline IT support by efficiently handling user inquiries and technical issues, from complex hardware configurations to password resets. The implementation of automation not only increases user satisfaction but also frees up IT staff time to focus on critical projects and offer valuable insights for enhancing IT service delivery processes.

Threat Identification and Cybersecurity

AI constantly tracks internet traffic and user activity to swiftly identify anomalies and potential security risks. A strong cybersecurity posture is facilitated by proactive threat mitigation and automated incident response procedures, which shorten reaction times and protect private information from online attacks.

Industry Intelligence and Data Mining

AI-driven techniques that search through intricate datasets for useful information enable data-driven decision-making. Predictive analytics forecasts trends, whereas prescriptive analytics offers useful techniques for optimization of processes. AI in business intelligence uses natural language processing to make data more accessible and automate report development.

Software Development and Testing

AI is totally changing the software development process by introducing tools and techniques that increase productivity, accuracy, and innovation. By automating code generation and enhancing evaluation and implementation, AI is transforming software design, development, and administration. AI speeds up coding procedures, improves code quality through automated reviews, and automates tedious jobs in software development. By mimicking user behaviors and anticipating possible problems, AI-driven technologies in testing automate the creation, execution, and analysis of test cases, guaranteeing improved software quality.

Because software testing is typically a tough process, automation is necessary. However, AI must be used if software automation is to be incredibly effective and smooth. The use of AI in software testing has completely changed how we do testing. AI has the potential to improve software testing's efficacy, efficiency, and dependability. AI-powered testing solutions can assist in automating tedious and routine processes, allowing human testers to concentrate on more intricate testing situations. Additionally, by detecting and forecasting software flaws, these technologies can improve the precision and comprehensiveness of the testing procedure. In order to optimize the test suite, AI may examine test data and spot trends. To increase test coverage, it may propose eliminating unnecessary tests and adding new ones. AI is also capable of analyzing intricate test logs to more precisely detect flaws and their underlying causes. This helps developers apply more efficient patches by speeding up debugging and offering insightful information about the underlying code problems.

IT Asset Management

A crucial area of finance is asset management, which includes the strategic administration and oversight of different kinds of assets that belong to people, businesses, or institutions. These assets can include a variety of investments, such as equities, bonds, products, real estate, and more. In accordance with the investor's financial goals and risk tolerance, asset management's primary goal is to maximize these assets' performance while lowering risk. In order to make sure that nothing is missing or incorrectly configured, AI-powered solutions automatically search networks and systems for all IT assets. They have the intelligence to record the entire estate. Understanding an organization's assets is one of the core components of IT asset management. AI-powered solutions are capable of scanning a whole network and locating applications and devices, including ones that could have been missed or forgotten. This thorough asset discovery process guarantees that no important asset is overlooked. By automating asset discovery, tracking usage trends, and anticipating maintenance requirements, artificial intelligence (AI) makes IT asset management more effective. It assists in keeping an inventory current, guaranteeing adherence to legal and regulatory obligations. AI-powered asset management improves IT processes, lowers procurement costs, and maximizes resource allocation.

IT Documentation

The computerized method of producing, organizing, and preserving documentation through the use of artificial intelligence technology is known as AI documentation. Consider it the digital counterpart of a neat filing cabinet, but with the added advantages of effectiveness, precision, and speed. By classifying and tagging documents, extracting important insights, and keeping knowledge bases current, artificial intelligence (AI) automates the administration and organization of IT documentation. By consulting documentation, AI-powered chatbots and virtual assistants offer prompt assistance, increasing the effectiveness and speed of IT support and troubleshooting. AI documentation can also improve the way decisions are made. Businesses may quickly make well-informed decisions and get a competitive edge in the ever-changing marketplace by having simple access to vital data. It's critical to select the appropriate AI technology for your documentation requirements. Think at things like scalability, simplicity of use, ease of integration with current systems, and the vendor's degree of technical assistance.

Predictive Maintenance

AI forecasts problems by analyzing past incident data, allowing for preventive steps to stop IT disruptions and enhance important operational KPIs. Organizations can reduce downtime and guarantee seamless business operations by anticipating and addressing possible events.

Capacity Planning

By employing sophisticated forecasting methods, AI examines past consumption patterns to anticipate future resource needs, enabling businesses to proactively grow infrastructure and reduce expenses. By taking a proactive stance, the danger of service interruptions brought on by capacity limitations is reduced and enough capacity is guaranteed to satisfy business demands.

Intelligent Escalation

AI expedites issue resolution and reduces manual intervention by routing events to the appropriate specialists and automating remediation operations. AI guarantees that problems are resolved quickly by optimizing escalation procedures, which lowers downtime and boosts operational effectiveness.

Event Correlation and Noise Reduction

By organizing events into logical categories, AI finds related occurrences and lessens alert fatigue, freeing up IT personnel to concentrate on important issues. By reducing distractions and facilitating quicker reaction times to real problems, this noise reduction increases productivity.

Automated Report Generation

AI ensures accuracy, consistency, and adherence to industry standards by automating the creation of IT reports. By efficiently processing and analysing massive datasets, AI lowers the likelihood of inaccuracies associated with conventional data entry, providing a solid foundation for decision-making processes and compliance with laws and regulations.

Root Cause Analysis

AI-powered solutions look into the underlying causes of IT problems, allowing for early diagnosis and identification, which lowers mean time to resolution (MTTR) and mean time to acknowledgement (MTTA). Organizations can take proactive steps to stop future issues and improve system reliability by identifying the root causes of incidents.

IT Service Management (ITSM)

Service request fulfillment, change management, and issue resolution can all be intelligently automated with AI-driven ITSM platforms. Such systems use intelligent automation and analytical forecasting to boost quality of service delivery, reduce interruptions, and improve the effectiveness of operations

2.3.2.12 Hospitality

AI benefits hospitality businesses [38, 39] in the following ways:

Personalized Recommendations

In order to improve the overall visitor experience, AI algorithms can examine past reservations, browsing patterns, and consumer preferences to offer tailored suggestions for lodging, food, and activities. Recommendation engines driven by AI examine a visitor's past booking history, travel information, and preferences to make recommendations. By analyzing visitor behavior and preferences, AI can suggest spa treatments, room upgrades, and other services that are likely to be popular with them, thereby boosting hotel income. For a more enjoyable and customized experience, the system might propose events according to guest preferences or restaurants that fit in tastes and budget.

Revenue Management

Strong new trends in hospitality technology are driving a flurry of innovation in the sector. These days, hotels use revenue management systems that allow them to customize their pricing plans. The effects of AI on hotel revenue management extend beyond straightforward automation. It involves using sophisticated algorithms and machine learning tools to evaluate enormous volumes of data from many sources, spot trends, and provide predictions more quickly and accurately than is possible for humans. This gives revenue managers the ability to switch from reactive to proactive tactics, foreseeing shifts in the market and visitor behaviour before they happen.

Artificial intelligence (AI) can analyse customer behaviour, previous information, and market developments to enhance pricing strategies, optimize room occupancy rates, and increase revenue for hotels and resorts.

Hoteliers can provide customized pricing that maximizes revenue while improving client happiness by utilizing their guest data and segmentation. These days, every customer wants the best deal on the desired good or service. The mathematical assessment of guest involvement over a range of rates and channels was done by the conventional hotel revenue management systems. AI-powered systems can analyze previously unheard-of amounts of data and produce surprisingly precise projections of demand. This includes historical reservation data as well as external factors like local events, weather patterns, and even social media trends. AI can produce more accurate projections by combining these various data pieces and spotting minute patterns and connections that human analysts might overlook. Additionally, hotels have been able to maximize their revenue by providing guests with more individualized rates and packages thanks to AI in revenue management. For dynamic and profitable pricing, an AI-powered hotel revenue management system offers several advantages.

Guest Sentiment Analysis

One of the most important resources for figuring out what works and what needs improvement is customer feedback. The term "guest sentiment" describes the attitudes, beliefs, and sentiments that visitors have about their stays at a hotel. Numerous platforms, including social media posts, online reviews, direct feedback, and survey results, can be used to communicate this. Hotels can determine areas for growth, assess overall satisfaction levels, and customize their offerings to match visitor expectations through investigating guest opinion. Businesses may increase guest happiness and quickly resolve any issues by using AI algorithms to extract sentiment from customer reviews, social media mentions, and feedback.

Customizing hotel services according to visitor preferences is one of the most effective strategies to leverage guest opinion. Hotels can find recurring themes and visitor preferences by examining sentiment data. Negative comments might be a treasure trove of chances to get better. Hotels show their dedication to visitor happiness by actively responding to and addressing unfavorable reviews. Hotels may demonstrate their commitment to offering great service by quickly resolving client complaints and transforming a bad experience into a pleasant one.

Fraud Detection

By examining transaction patterns, user activity, and historical data, AI can help detect fraudulent behaviors like identity theft or credit card fraud, guaranteeing the security and reliability of online reservations and transactions.

Smart Room Automation

Sophisticated functionalities can now be integrated thanks to recent developments in AI. These developments boost security and energy efficiency in addition to convenience. AI's intelligent and intuitive technology is transforming smart homes. In addition to understanding instructions and responding appropriately, AI considers human preferences and tastes when making decisions. AI recognizes the owner of the house and can recall user speech. By identifying their voices and delivering their desired outcomes, it improves the user's availability. Robots, ambient motion sensors, smart speakers, and thermostats are some of the gadgets that are bringing our living spaces to life and changing the settings based on our preferences. The best thing is that energy conservation benefits us by lowering electricity costs and creating a more ecologically friendly home. Voice assistants like Google Home and Alexa are powered by AI, which allows them to comprehend and analyze human speech. Natural language processing (NLP) is used by these gadgets to decipher instructions and react appropriately. AI makes these interactions smooth and effective, whether it's playing music, sending notifications, or managing other smart gadgets.

Language Translation

Since linguistic obstacles prevent knowledge from being shared globally, language translation plays a crucial role in the scholarly and scientific publishing industry. The obstacle of the language barrier has changed throughout time. In actuality, AI translations are facilitating global connections and communication more easily than ever before. AI translation has numerous corporate uses as well, such as simplifying daily communications with global teams. Real-time inter-language communication is made possible by AI translation platforms, which can process enormous volumes of data in a matter of seconds and provide translations almost instantly. AI-powered solutions can effectively process large volumes of text with little or no human involvement in situations where speed and scalability are critical, such translating user-generated material on social media sites. Beyond linguistic accuracy, incorporating regional and cultural subtleties is one of the biggest obstacles in translating. AI translation systems must comprehend and adjust to the environmental and cultural elements that affect language in addition to translating words if they are to be successful. This is accomplished by using cultural datasets in the training of sophisticated AI models.

Customer Service

AI chatbots offer round-the-clock customer support on several platforms, helping with reservations, inquiries, and information while lowering employee workload and increasing guest satisfaction.

Loyalty Programs

Companies must identify techniques that make their loyalty programs stand out to consumers as they grow more and more common. Predictive AI, also referred to as AI and machine learning, has been utilized for decades to support and enhance loyalty initiatives and programs, although generative AI (genAI) is still relatively new. The efficacy of program benefits and communications can be increased by using AI loyalty programs that are equipped with predictive analytics to proactively engage customers with pertinent offers and experiences in real-time. From client segmentation to reward distribution, AI-driven automation in loyalty programs optimizes workflow and guarantees timely and pertinent communications with clients. Through the analysis of visitor data, AI improves loyalty programs by customizing communications and rewards, boosting engagement, retention, and repeat business.

By determining the likelihood that a specific consumer or segment will accept an offer, such a refer-a-friend, marketers may fine-tune their offer and campaign targeting. Personalized rewards based on consumer preferences and behavior patterns can also be provided with the use of this study. Customized rewards are one of the main ways AI is transforming retail loyalty. It accomplishes this by carefully examining consumer data, such as previous purchases, preferences, and even surfing habits, to build an extensive client profile. By doing this, businesses are able to provide incentives that are pertinent to the customers and strike a highly personal chord with each individual.

A crucial component of increasing shop loyalty is AI-driven chat assistance. It offers clients individualized support, responding to their questions and issues instantly. Additionally, an AI-powered chatbot can provide customers with personalized information on future products, enabling them to put pre-orders for these items ahead of time. By providing effective and customized service, this not only expedites the buying experience but also cultivates loyalty. In conclusion, businesses gain from integrating AI into consumer loyalty programs in a number of ways. Predictive analytics, progressive rewards, fraud detection, tailored incentives and rewards, and gamification components that improve consumer loyalty and engagement are all made possible by AI. Companies that use AI can increase operational effectiveness, save expenses, and use valuable customer data to make well-informed decisions.

Integrated Property Management

Property management has entered a new era with the integration of AI technology, which has completely changed the way properties are run and maintained. Given AI's widespread impact on many facets of our lives, its incorporation into property management systems offers previously unheard-of possibilities for improved decision-making, efficiency, and optimization. An important shift in the way the real estate industry functions has occurred with the combination of artificial intelligence (AI) with property services. Intelligent automation, which may expedite standard procedures like tenant screening, lease renewals, and even complaint handling, is one of the main uses of AI in this industry. Large datasets may be swiftly analyzed by AI systems to spot trends or problems, enabling managers to take action before such concerns worsen. Routine chores like scheduling service requests, handling payments, and sending payment reminders can be handled by AI-powered platforms. In addition to saving time, this automation guarantees a more seamless and effective operation. Additionally, AI can anticipate maintenance problems before they arise, assisting property owners in taking proactive measures to resolve issues and minimize disruption.

One of the most important parts of property management is tenant screening. In the past, property managers were required to manually examine applications, verify references, and assess the fitness of tenants. This procedure frequently results in biases or mistakes and might take a long time. AI is assisting property managers by offering more precise evaluations of tenants. AI systems can evaluate a tenant's dependability by looking at a variety of data, including credit ratings, rental history, and background checks. By doing this, property managers can lower risks and increase tenant satisfaction by choosing tenants who are more likely to take care of the property and pay rent on time. Another crucial aspect of property management is overseeing leases. Managing everything by hand might result in errors and missed deadlines when there are numerous tenants, lease renewals, and rent payments. AI may streamline a number of lease management tasks, such as processing payments, collecting rent, and sending out reminders for lease renewals. AI can also be used by property managers to improve their buildings' security. Real-time surveillance feed monitoring, anomalous activity detection, and warning management or security staff of possible security breaches are all possible with advanced AI systems. In addition to safeguarding the property, this proactive strategy for property protection gives tenants piece of mind.

Hotel Staff Assistance

In certain circumstances, visitors who would rather engage with actual people might be more than happy to engage with AI-enabled technology. Artificial intelligence has made it possible for hotels to respond to customer questions and offer assistance much more quickly and effectively, which lessens the workload for staff and raises customer satisfaction while enhancing and supplementing current procedures. AI makes personalized visitor care possible by integrating the Point of Sale (PoS) and Property Management System (PMS). This enables concierge, cleaning, and front desk employees to reserve, authorize, and manage bookings in real time in addition to keeping an eye on customer preferences and expenditure patterns to provide customized suggestions and enhance the overall guest experience.

AI streamlines intricate data processing and provides insightful information about visitor preferences and behavior to enhance strategic decision-making. Over time, personalization boosts visitor pleasure and spending, resulting in better occupancy rates and return visits. Examples of this include tailored loyalty benefits and mood lighting and temperature settings in the room. The ability of hospitality companies to offer customized guest experiences could be greatly enhanced by AI algorithms. One of the top lodging technology initiatives, according to 68% of hospitality IT experts, is enhancing the physical safety of both customers and employees. Through automated processes that expedite detection and issue alerts on suspicious activity, artificial intelligence (AI) capabilities can increase the efficacy of technologies such as building entry and video surveillance.

Streamlined Lodging Services

By incorporating real-time visitor input into workflows to gauge satisfaction and provide alternatives for room changes, artificial intelligence (AI) simplifies accommodation services. Hotel operators can use it to keep track of amenity maintenance plans and quickly respond to requests and grievances from visitors. Additionally, AI-powered smart mirrors improve visitors' overall stay by giving them easy access to directions and news.

Food and Beverage Service Optimization

Artificial intelligence (AI) is transforming the food and beverage sector by predicting menu item consumer demand, managing stock levels, and customizing dining recommendations depending on customer preferences. In the end, this increases visitor pleasure and profitability in the hospitality sector by streamlining culinary operations, improving service quality, cutting waste, and increasing operational efficiency.

Maintenance and Facilities Management

By anticipating demands, effectively scheduling work, automating processes, and guaranteeing optimal facility conditions, artificial intelligence (AI) improves maintenance and facilities management, reducing interruptions and improving visitor experiences. The hotel's dedication to excellence is strengthened by this proactive approach, which expedites processes, enhances reaction times, and extends asset longevity.

2.4 Conclusions

Most people agree that since machines and robots are already a part of our everyday lives, everyone must come to terms with this new reality. The shift toward automation and data sharing in industrial technologies and processes is known as the Fourth

Industrial Revolution, and it encompasses cloud computing, artificial intelligence, cyber-physical systems (CPS), the Internet of Things (IoT), and cognitive computing. During the Industrial Revolution, civilizations moved from a farming-based system to an industrialized economy, with machines creating commodities in place of humans. This led to increased production and efficiency, lower pricing, more goods, higher incomes, and immigration from rural to metropolitan areas. Industry 4.0 focused on machine connectivity as a result of increased automation and artificial intelligence brought about by the Internet of Things (IoT). On the other hand, Industry 5.0 will place more emphasis on increased human-machine cooperation through cyber-physical systems and technologies. During the Industrial Revolution, massive industries automated manufacture, and an industrial sector replaced economies centered on agriculture and handicrafts. New equipment, energy sources, and labor organization strategies increase the productivity and efficiency of existing industries.

References

1. Philbeck, T., & Davis, N. (2018). The fourth industrial revolution. *Journal of International Affairs, 72*(1), 17–22.
2. Skilton, M., & Hovsepian, F. (2018). *The 4th industrial revolution*. Springer Nature.
3. Ziatdinov, R., Atteraya, M. S., & Nabiyev, R. (2024). The fifth industrial revolution as a transformative step towards society 5.0. *Societies, 14*(2), 19.
4. Lee, M., Yun, J. J., Pyka, A., Won, D., Kodama, F., Schiuma, G., et al. (2018). How to respond to the fourth industrial revolution, or the second information technology revolution? Dynamic new combinations between technology, market, and society through open innovation. *Journal of Open Innovation: Technology, Market, and Complexity, 4*(3), 21.
5. Kurt, R. (2019). Industry 4.0 in terms of industrial relations and its impacts on labour life. *Procedia Computer Science, 158*, 590–601.
6. Akubo, A. A., Odiji, O. L., & Muhammed, M. B. (2025). Fifth industrial revolution and an overview of its impact on human resources. In *Human capital analytics: Exploring the HR spectrum in industry 5.0* (pp. 65–80). Wiley.
7. Malik, S., Muhammad, K., & Waheed, Y. (2024). Artificial intelligence and industrial applications—A revolution in modern industries. *Ain Shams Engineering Journal, 15*(9), 102886.
8. Peres, R. S., Jia, X., Lee, J., Sun, K., Colombo, A. W., & Barata, J. (2020). Industrial artificial intelligence in industry 4.0-systematic review, challenges and outlook. *IEEE Access, 8*, 220121–220139.
9. Kozłowski, J., Sika, R., Górski, F., & Ciszak, O. (2018). Modeling of foundry processes in the era of industry 4.0. In *Design, simulation, manufacturing: The innovation exchange* (pp. 62–71). Springer International Publishing.
10. Dhamija, P., & Bag, S. (2020). Role of artificial intelligence in operations environment: A review and bibliometric analysis. *The TQM Journal, 32*(4), 869–896.
11. Sankar, D. D., & Reddy, S. R. (n.d.). Impact of artificial intelligence in business operations—A comprehensive review. In *Navigating the digital landscape* (pp. 46–56). Bharti.
12. Chen, Y., Biswas, M. I., & Talukder, M. S. (2023). The role of artificial intelligence in effective business operations during COVID-19. *International Journal of Emerging Markets, 18*(12), 6368–6387.
13. Panesar, A. (2019). *Machine learning and AI for healthcare* (Vol. 10). Apress.

14. Jiang, F., Jiang, Y., Zhi, H., Dong, Y., Li, H., Ma, S., et al. (2017). Artificial intelligence in healthcare: Past, present and future. *Stroke and Vascular Neurology, 2*(4), svn-2017-000101.
15. Koski, E., & Murphy, J. (2021). AI in healthcare. In *Nurses and midwives in the digital age* (pp. 295–299). IOS Press.
16. Shaheen, M. Y. (2021). *Applications of artificial intelligence (AI) in healthcare: A review.* ScienceOpen Preprints.
17. Srivastava, A. (2021). The application & impact of artificial intelligence (AI) on e-commerce. *Contemporary Issues in Commerce and Management, 1*(1), 165–175.
18. Ntumba, C., Aguayo, S., & Maina, K. (2023). Revolutionizing retail: A mini review of e-commerce evolution. *Journal of Digital Marketing and Communication, 3*(2), 100–110.
19. Sharma, D. (2021). Impact of AI on e-Commerce. In *Applications of artificial intelligence in business and finance* (pp. 1–28). Apple Academic Press.
20. Srinadi, N. L. P., Hermawan, D., & Jaya, A. A. N. A. (2023). Advancement of banking and financial services employing artificial intelligence and the internet of things. *Journal of Wireless Mobile Networks, Ubiquitous Computing and Dependable Application, 14*(1), 106–117.
21. Gupta, A., Dwivedi, D. N., & Shah, J. (2023). *Artificial intelligence applications in banking and financial services.* Springer Nature.
22. Malali, A. B., & Gopalakrishnan, S. (2020). Application of artificial intelligence and its powered technologies in the Indian banking and financial industry: An overview. *IOSR Journal of Humanities and Social Science, 25*(4), 55–60.
23. Seyfi, S., Kim, M. J., Nazifi, A., Murdy, S., & Vo-Thanh, T. (2025). Understanding tourist barriers and personality influences in embracing generative AI for travel planning and decision-making. *International Journal of Hospitality Management, 126*, 104105.
24. Koo, C., Xiang, Z., Gretzel, U., & Sigala, M. (2021). Artificial intelligence (AI) and robotics in travel, hospitality and leisure. *Electronic Markets, 31*(3), 473–476.
25. Rossini, P. (2000). Using expert systems and artificial intelligence for real estate forecasting. In *Sixth annual pacific-rim real estate society conference, Sydney, Australia* (pp. 24–27).
26. Alsahan, I. M., & AlZaidan, Z. I. (2024). Unleashing the power of artificial intelligence in real estate valuation: Opportunities and challenges ahead. *Journal of Knowledge Learning and Science Technology, 3*(2), 1–10.
27. Seagraves, P. (2024). Real estate insights: Is the AI revolution a real estate boon or bane? *Journal of Property Investment & Finance, 42*(2), 190–199.
28. Nader, K., Toprac, P., Scott, S., & Baker, S. (2024). Public understanding of artificial intelligence through entertainment media. *AI & Society, 39*(2), 713–726.
29. Hallur, G. G., Prabhu, S., & Aslekar, A. (2021). Entertainment in era of AI, big data & IoT. In *Digital entertainment: The next evolution in service sector* (pp. 87–109).
30. Lachman, R., & Joffe, M. (2021). Applications of artificial intelligence in media and entertainment. In *Analyzing future applications of AI, sensors, and robotics in society* (pp. 201–220). IGI Global.
31. Liu, K., Wei, Z., Zhang, C., Shang, Y., Teodorescu, R., & Han, Q. L. (2022). Towards long lifetime battery: AI-based manufacturing and management. *IEEE/CAA Journal of Automatica Sinica, 9*(7), 1139–1165.
32. Plathottam, S. J., Rzonca, A., Lakhnori, R., & Iloeje, C. O. (2023). A review of artificial intelligence applications in manufacturing operations. *Journal of Advanced Manufacturing and Processing, 5*(3), e10159.
33. Kim, S. W., Kong, J. H., Lee, S. W., & Lee, S. (2022). Recent advances of artificial intelligence in manufacturing industrial sectors: A review. *International Journal of Precision Engineering and Manufacturing, 23*(1), 111–129.
34. Soegoto, E. S., Utami, R. D., & Hermawan, Y. A. (2019). Influence of artificial intelligence in automotive industry. *Journal of Physics: Conference Series, 1402*(6), 066081.
35. Madhavaram, C. R., Sunkara, J. R., Kuraku, C., Galla, E. P., & Gollangi, H. K. (2024). The future of automotive manufacturing: Integrating AI, ML, and generative AI for next-Gen automatic cars. *International Multidisciplinary Research Journal Reviews, 1*, 010103.

36. Mohammad, S. M. (2020). Artificial intelligence in information technology. *International Journal of Innovations in Engineering Research and Technology, 7*(6), 168–175.
37. Jakšič, M., & Marinč, M. (2019). Relationship banking and information technology: The role of artificial intelligence and FinTech. *Risk Management, 21*(1), 1–18.
38. Limna, P. (2023). Artificial intelligence (AI) in the hospitality industry: A review article. *International Journal of Computing Sciences Research, 7*, 1306–1317.
39. Law, R., Lin, K. J., Ye, H., & Fong, D. K. C. (2024). Artificial intelligence research in hospitality: A state-of-the-art review and future directions. *International Journal of Contemporary Hospitality Management, 36*(6), 2049–2068.

Chapter 3
The Impact of AI on Work and Workers

3.1 Introduction

The rapid development of artificial intelligence (AI) and automation technology can significantly disrupt the labor market. Artificial intelligence and automation may increase the productivity of some workers, but they can replace the work done by others and are likely to change almost all occupations, at least to some extent. Growing automation comes at a time of growing economic inequality, fuelling fears of technological mass unemployment and new political efforts to address the consequences of technological change [1]. Today, AI is considered the most innovative and promising arena of workplace and workforce management. Forty percent of HR functions in small and large companies worldwide now use AI-enhanced applications. These companies are primarily based in the United States, but European and Asian organizations are also involved. Research by PricewaterhouseCoopers shows that an increasing number of global companies are beginning to understand the value of artificial intelligence to support workforce management. In addition, 32% of HR departments at tech companies and others are reshaping organizations that use AI to optimize "adaptability and learning to best integrate insights from employee feedback and technology." According to a recent IBM report (IBM, 2018), half of the HR leaders surveyed foresee and recognize the possibilities of technology in HR and talent acquisition and development. A Deloitte report shows that 71% of global companies consider human analytics a high priority in their organizations, as it should enable organizations not only to provide good business insights but also to address the so-called "people problem". "Human problems" are also called "human risks". These have several dimensions outlined in the Chartered Institute for Personal Development (CIPD) report, including talent management; healthiness and safety; employee beliefs; multiplicity and equivalence; employee associations; and reputational hazard [2, 3].

S. Majumder, B. Misra, *AI-Empowered Industrial Relations*, Studies in Computational Intelligence 1254, https://doi.org/10.1007/978-3-032-14557-4_3

"People analytics" is an increasingly popular HR practice where big data and digital tools are used to "measure, report and understand employee performance, aspects of workforce planning, talent management, and operations management". Every industry and organization needs staff responsible for everything from recruiting to drafting employment contracts and managing employee-employer relations [4]. AI-enhanced human resources practices can help managers gain seemingly objective wisdom about people even before they are hired, with management having access to information about potential employees that has important implications for tailoring worker protections and preventing occupational, safety and health risks at the individual level. Ideally, people analytics tools can help employers make good hiring decisions. In human analytics, algorithmic decision making could actually be used to support the workforce by matching employee performance feedback and performance pay and labor costs with business strategies and specialized support. Employees must be personally empowered by accessing new forms of information that help them identify areas for improvement, promote personal development and achieve greater engagement.

Figure 3.1 shows that industries consider intelligence, robots, data, technology, skills, workers, tasks, people, labor, etc., when doing their work. Intelligent workplace systems increase workers' reliance on artificial intelligence in the workplace. However, overpromising the possibilities of artificial intelligence in the workplace undermines the trust between employees and intelligent systems. Therefore, trust between employees and AI in the workplace continues to be an important emerging topic. AI applications are rapidly spreading and transforming organizations; improving operations and decision-making; and freeing workers from repetitive, physical, manual, and boring tasks to creative tasks. Applications of artificial intelligence along with robotics and machine learning are becoming important for autonomous

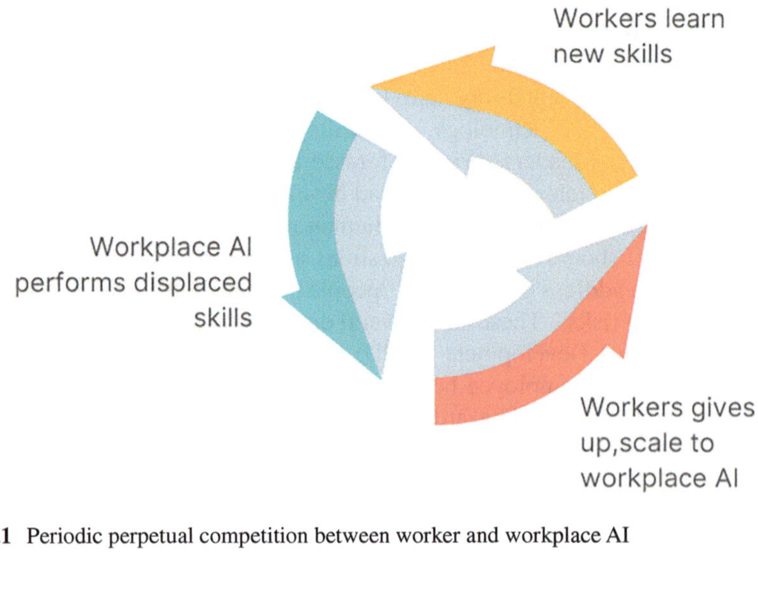

Fig. 3.1 Periodic perpetual competition between worker and workplace AI

vehicles. Chatbots; planning, scheduling, forecasting, and capacity planning; and gaming, marketing, and pricing strategies. While chatbots help employees with things such as online training, customer service, and cognitive therapy, they also benefit from a human touch that extends beyond machine-like interactions.

3.2 Automation and Job Displacement

The rapid progress of technology, especially automation and artificial intelligence, has led to major transformations in numerous industries and economies across the globe. Automation involves the use of technology and machines to complete duties that were formerly executed by individuals. Despite the advantages of increased productivity and efficiency brought by automation, concerns about the possible displacement of human workers have also emerged. Job displacement occurs when automation leads to either elimination or a drastic decrease in the demand for the human workforce. Automation involves the utilization of technology such as robotics, artificial intelligence, and computer systems to complete tasks and operations that people once did. Replacing or adding machines and algorithms to perform repetitive, routine, or complex tasks with little to no human involvement is known as automation. The issue of job loss because of automation is not a new occurrence. Historically, technological advancements have disrupted industries, and workers have been displaced [5].

For example, the Industrial Revolution caused the automation of farming and the implementation of machinery in production, leading to a major shift in the job market. The rapid advancement of computer technology and the digital revolution have sped up automation in recent years, affecting different industries and jobs. The introduction of computerized systems, robotics, and AI has led to major transformations in sectors such as manufacturing, transportation, retail, and services. The effects of job loss and automation on economic development are complex. Although automation can increase productivity and efficiency, thus facilitating economic advancement, it can also result in decreased consumer purchasing power if many workers face job loss or stagnant incomes.

In addition, economic expansion could be impacted by elements such as investment in fresh technologies, adaptability of the workforce, and the capacity to generate new job prospects in growing sectors. Understanding how automation leads to job displacement is important for policymakers and stakeholders to create plans that reduce negative impacts, encourage inclusive growth, and facilitate a smooth transition for both individuals and the overall economy. For years, there has been concern about automation leading to a daily loss of jobs for traditional/manual patterned workers. It substitutes human labor with technology and leads to job loss. Despite the displacement of many workers and the looming threat of more being replaced, digital transformation remains highly impactful. According to projections, automation will result in a loss of 85 million jobs globally by 2025 [6]. A positive portrayal of the impact of artificial intelligence and automation is common. Reflect on the knowledge gained about the water wheel, mills, printing presses, steam engines, and assembly lines. Frequently, the common story is that these were fantastic advancements that lessened the workload for people. However, the technological improvements of today appear to be met with less enthusiasm. This may be due to how close we are to these instances of automation. Our intimacy stops us from focusing solely on advantages and instead compels us to consider the extent to which artificial intelligence affects our lives and means of making a living.

McKinsey & Company estimate that, with different adoption scenarios, automation will replace approximately 400–800 million jobs by 2030, leading up to 375 million individuals needing to transition to different job sectors. In what way could this change not lead to anxiety and worry, especially for vulnerable countries and populations worldwide? Although technical feasibility is crucial, it is not the sole determinant of how quickly or extensively automation will be adopted. Additional considerations involve the expenses of creating and implementing automation technologies for particular workplace tasks, the complexities within the labor market (such as the amount and caliber of available workers and their wages), the advantages of automation aside from replacing human labor, and the approval from regulatory bodies and society [7]. It is easy to identify workers who have lost their jobs due to automation, but the new jobs created indirectly by technology are more difficult to identify, as they are scattered across various industries and locations.

3.2.1 The Role of Automation in Job Loss

The relationship between automation and job loss has been the subject of increased discussion. The worry is that jobs that were previously performed by humans will become unnecessary as automation spreads. Divergent opinions exist regarding how automation contributes to job losses. While some contend that automation will result in a massive loss of jobs, others think it will create new jobs that call for different skill sets. Furthermore, some contend that automation will increase productivity, whereas others believe that it will only result in higher corporate profits. One thing to keep in mind when analysing the impact of automation on job losses is that it can take the place of human labor in certain jobs. For example, many businesses now use automated systems to respond to customer service queries, which reduces the need for human workers to perform these duties. Similarly, automation has recently taken the place of many manufacturing jobs. Automation has the potential to eliminate jobs in some industries while creating new ones in others [8]. For example, there will be new job opportunities in these fields since skilled workers are needed for the development and maintenance of automated systems. Additionally, businesses may be able to grow and add new employees as a result of automation's ability to increase productivity. Profit maximization is a primary driver behind businesses' automation investments. Businesses can lower labor costs and increase productivity by substituting machines for human labor. Although this may result in higher profits for businesses, jobs may not always be created as a result. The skills needed for many jobs will change as automation becomes more common. For example, jobs that formerly required manual labor now depend on data analysis or programming abilities. Workers who may need to retrain to stay relevant in the job market may face challenges as a result of this shift in the skills that are needed. The labor market will surely be impacted by automation. In certain places, it might result in job losses, but in others, it might lead to new career opportunities. It can also result in increased profitability and productivity for businesses. Workers will need to stay aware of how the labor market is changing as automation progresses and acquire new skills as needed.

Automation has long been a talking point, and as technology has developed, it has become increasingly obvious that it will continue to influence how people will work in the future (Fig. 3.2; https://fastercapital.com/topics/automation-and-job-displacement.html). Although there are many potential advantages to automation, such as higher productivity and efficiency, there is also much concern about job displacement. A common concern is that automation displaces human labor,

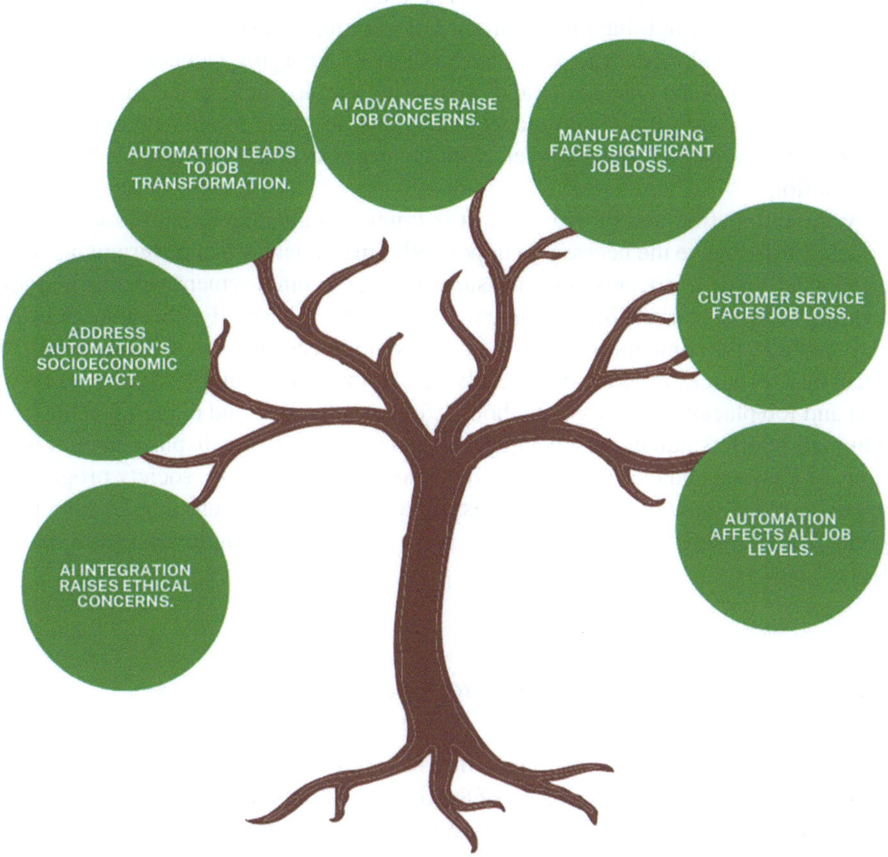

Fig. 3.2 Relation between automation and job loss

deprives people of job opportunities, and escalates economic inequality. The main concerns about automation and job displacement, as well as possible effects on the labor force, the economy, and society at large, will be discussed in this section.

Automation has already had a significant effect on the labor market, and the trend will continue only in the coming years. According to a study by McKinsey and Company, automation could eliminate up to 800 million jobs by 2030. While some jobs are more likely to be affected than others are, almost no industry or profession is immune to the effects of automation. For example, self-driving trucks and delivery drones may soon replace many truck drivers and delivery drivers, whereas automated customer service systems may render human service obsolete. While automation can eliminate many jobs, it also has many potential benefits. Compared with humans, automated systems, such as robots, can handle routine tasks better, freeing time for individuals to concentrate on more stimulating and fulfilling activities. Furthermore, automation has the potential to increase safety in dangerous workplaces and lessen the chances of work-related injuries and fatalities. Automation has the potential to increase productivity and result in greater economic growth, ultimately benefiting the entire society. The job market is constantly changing due to automation, highlighting the importance of training to ensure that workers remain competitive. Employees who are able to adjust to emerging technology and learn new abilities will have an advantage in securing employment in the modern economy. This indicates that governments and businesses need to allocate resources to training programs that equip workers with the necessary skills to thrive in the era of automation.

With automation taking over jobs, it is crucial to guarantee that those who are affected still receive the necessary support [9]. This indicates that governments need to allocate funds to social safety measures such as unemployment benefits and job training to assist workers in switching to different professions. Furthermore, it is the responsibility of companies to invest in their employees and provide them with the necessary resources to thrive in the evolving economy. The complexities of automation and job placement necessitate thoughtful consideration and planning. Although automation offers numerous advantages, it can also lead to the displacement of millions of workers and exacerbate overall economic inequality. As society progresses toward a more automated future, it is essential to allocate resources to training programs, social safety nets, and other tools to prevent employees from being left behind.

3.2.2 The Rise of New Jobs and Skills

Work patterns and functions are changing as a result of technology, and new jobs are created on a regular basis as a result of the digitalization of business operating models. Remoting was considered a luxury 5 years ago, and it was frequently awarded on the basis of performance and trust. Currently, businesses are looking to hire work-from-home (WFH) facilitators to engage, motivate, and take care of employees, who are confident that the WFH setup is here to stay. The need for virtual babysitting is also still growing, as working from home parents finds it challenging to concentrate on their jobs and take care of their children at the same time.

As a result of digital transformation, recruitment teams are beginning to place greater emphasis on new positions, such as technologists, managers of social media and digital marketing, data analysts, managers of process improvement, and managers of transformation.

Innovation gives rise to new job responsibilities and new skill sets, making new jobs more rewarding but also more complex. The workforce's preparation and equipment for these new jobs and skills is currently the main challenge.

Recruiters and hiring managers have the ability to impart knowledge and educate job seekers on transitioning to different careers and the necessary skills. Job seekers can use this information to redirect and adjust their career paths. It is essential for employees and individuals looking for employment to grasp this and its impacts on the future of work and the workforce [10]. Steve Brown, managing director of ChapmanCG, a Will company, said that organizations must keep identifying skills gaps in their employees and assisting them in developing the necessary skills and competencies to succeed. The traditional significance of a college degree is being challenged in the current fast-paced job market, as employers face difficulties in recruiting skilled workers.

In 2022, the manpower group discovered that a record high of 77% of employers faced difficulty in recruiting the skilled workers they needed, marking the highest percentage in the past 17 years. According to a recent LinkedIn analysis (2023), there has been a significant rise in job postings prioritizing skills over traditional academic qualifications, with 19% now doing so compared with 15% just a year ago. According to a report by Deloitte (2022), an impressive 90% of American companies view a skill-oriented approach as crucial to their achievements, which reinforces this pattern. The job market demands the following skills.

3.2.2.1 Digital Skills

One of the most in-demand skills in the future will be proficiency with digital technologies. Nearly half of all professions worldwide will require digital skills to remain employed by the end of 2030. This implies that there will be a strong need for individuals with digital platform expertise and skills [11].

3.2.2.2 Digital Collaboration

In this competitive world, employers want their staff members to be knowledgeable about current market trends. Synchronous digital collaboration tools, such as video conferencing and instant messaging, are attainable to learn.

3.2.2.3 Critical Thinking

One needs to use critical thinking and carefully and purposefully evaluate information to better understand things [12]. A company can thrive with an employer who can develop new ideas and solve problems more effectively.

3.2.2.4 Cognitive Adaptability

With the introduction of digital technologies comes a plethora of opportunities as well as challenges that one will need to manage. Can anyone think through multiple intricate concepts at once and adapt as circumstances change? If so, the person exhibits qualities that recruiters and employers highly value in advanced multitaskers.

3.2.2.5 Social Intelligence

Understanding oneself and others is one of the most important skills for preparing for the future. People who can function in any kind of social setting are highly valued in the workforce. It is also referred to as "street smarts" or "common sense" at times. The capacity to interpret one's own and other people's behavior is known as social intelligence. Social intelligence is a skill that is acquired through interpersonal interaction and learning from mistakes made in social situations. It is a crucial interpersonal ability that promotes success in all facets of life.

3.2.2.6 Sustainable Functioning

Only when corporations make financial investments in restructuring their operations will the world be able to meet their environmental goals and prevent a global catastrophe. Waste generation can be minimized, waste can be recycled whenever possible, waste can be converted into renewable energy sources, and carbon emissions and pollution can be lowered.

3.2.2.7 Data Skills

In practically every industry, data-driven analytics and results are now standard operating procedures. The development of data skills is essential because businesses worldwide generate increasing amounts of data with exceptional diversity and intricacy. Excel in the area that most closely matches your job profile, whether it is data science or data analytics.

3.2.2.8 Leadership skills

Be an effective leader who understands the strengths and weaknesses of the teams to get the most out of others. Fundamental leadership abilities can assist individuals in managing others toward a common goal of business success. The digital revolution is causing industries to change quickly, so tools and technology that are state-of-the-art 1 day might not be the same the next. As computers, people will have to take on novel and challenging tasks, whereas AI will be more than capable of handling routine and everyday tasks [13]. To do this, people need to continuously acquire new abilities and keep up with how the surroundings are changing.

Learning new information and applying it to develop new skills and capabilities will be among the most important abilities as new industries emerge, offering new employment opportunities and possibilities. The World Economic Forum predicts that soft skills such as problem-solving and emotional intelligence will be highly valued in the workplace of the future. Success in specific industries, such as technology and healthcare, has also been linked to critical soft skills such as leadership and flexibility. According to a recent McKinsey analysis, there will be a greater need for highly skilled workers, especially in the healthcare and STEM fields. The need for workers in professions such as office clerks, production workers, and customer service agents decreases concurrently. Work activities that currently take up to 70% of employees' time could be automated with the help of generative AI (gen AI) tools, suggesting that automation will likely become more prevalent. Up to 12 million workers in Europe and the US may need to change jobs as a result of these shifts. Support for upskilling lower-paid employees may be necessary for them to compete in the new market. However, automation and general AI do not provide a complete picture. In general, efficiency is a crucial indicator of success in the workplace of the future. Efficiency is more than just handling urgent crises and using fewer resources to accomplish the same tasks. A noteworthy proportion of participants (40%) ascribe inefficiency to intricate organizational frameworks, whereas a commensurate percentage attributes it to vague job descriptions, matching the most valuable roles to the best talent. According to McKinsey research, up to 30% of crucial positions in many organizations are not filled by the best candidates. Strengthening organizational capacities to outperform rivals. According to the latest McKinsey State of Organizations Survey, only 5% of participants believe that their companies possess the necessary capabilities.

3.3 Rapid Changes in Technology and Hiring

Technological advancements, automation, and an aging workforce are acknowledged as major contributors to skilled labor shortages. Technology is advancing so quickly that there is often a mismatch between what employers want and what employees can do. Artificial intelligence and automation have led to a decline in the demand for certain jobs, whereas the demand for skills in fields such as cybersecurity, software development, and data analysis has increased. An aging workforce and insufficient education and training systems exacerbate the talent shortage.

The shift to skill-based hiring benefits employers and job seekers alike. Companies can now look through a wider pool of talent to find applicants who more closely match their particular needs, which encourages innovation, diversity, and expansion. Using this tactic, job seekers can enhance their existing skills, pick up new skills, and stay competitive in the labor market. It promotes a culture of flexibility and continuous education.

By prioritizing skills over degrees, employers can access a wider pool of talent and find candidates more suited to their specific needs. This approach has many benefits, such as encouraging growth, diversity, and inventiveness from a variety of perspectives and backgrounds. However, there are challenges involved as well, especially in light of the widening talent gap. Technology advancements, aging workforces, and automation are some of the factors contributing to this shortage. Consequently, both employers and job seekers must obtain the requisite skills and expertise.

Many positions no longer only require certain degrees as a prerequisite. Specialized skills obtained through various methods, such as online courses, vocational training, or independent study, are now the primary selection criterion. Through skills-based hiring, job seekers can highlight their interests and talents in a number of ways. Not having a certain degree or certification is no longer a barrier. In a labor market that is always evolving, job seekers can remain competitive by learning new skills and honing their existing skills. Through the promotion of an ongoing learning and self-improvement culture, this approach assists individuals in modernizing and tailoring their skill sets to the needs of the market.

The following is a list of the outlook of the World Economic Forum's 2023 Future of Jobs Report, which emphasizes the importance of a skills-centric approach going forward. Priority should be given to upskilling and reskilling to obtain in-demand skills. The skills that receive the highest scores are: technical literacy; interest and lifelong learning; logical and creative thinking; elasticity, tractability, and agility; enthusiasm and self-awareness; management and social influence; quality regulator; systems thinking; talent management; service positioning and customer facility; resource management and procedures; and artificial intelligence and big data. Compared with the previous three decades, the last 3 years have seen a faster rate of workplace change, and this trend is expected to continue. Owing to a lack of workers, changing employee expectations (particularly among Generation Z), and the rise of disruptive technologies, organizations are now faced with varied job types and skill demands.

John Patterson, the vice president of talent at Macy, Inc., asserts that changes are occurring in the workplace. Skill-based hiring, generative AI, addressing employee grievances, promoting inclusivity, and hybrid work will be influential trends in shaping the future of work. The World Economic Forum's 2023 Future of Jobs Report predicts that 44% of worker skills will face disruption in the next 5 years, with the greatest need being for analytical thinking, creative problem-solving, and technological literacy [14]. The World Economic Forum predicts that 60% of workers will need more training, yet most will not have the necessary resources available. Chief Human Resources Officers (CHROs) and HR leaders are implementing strategies to meet the need for a stronger talent pool. This is achieved by providing employees with enhanced training and development opportunities and emphasizing skills and competencies during the hiring process.

Matthew Daniel, the senior principal for the talent strategy at Guild, advised large corporations on skill development, education, and career mobility, emphasizing the increasing importance of skills. When employers prioritize skills over traditional requirements such as a degree, they can build a diverse and customized talent pool guided by valuable insights that are crucial for keeping up with rapid changes. Daniel suggested that companies thrive by constantly investing in improving their skills. By concentrating on enhancing the skills of employees, aiding them in their career advancement, and fostering flexibility, one can prepare both the workforce and business for any changes that may arise [15].

3.4 Algorithmic Management and Employee Monitoring

Businesses around the world are collecting a growing amount of data about their workers. Often, intrusive surveillance technologies are used to achieve this, leaving workers ignorant of the information being collected about them, why it is being collected, how to access it, or how to object to the practices. Whether the company hires warehouse workers, uses gig workers, or serves as a platform for content creators' videos, the data collected can be used to make automated decisions that could have a large effect on the individuals involved. Algorithm management has become commonplace in some industries, where employment eligibility requires employees to reveal a great deal of personal data. Tracking tools advertise that they can measure output and identify underperforming workers. Algorithms have the authority to determine a person's pay amount, account suspension or termination, and job termination. It is typical for employees to obtain insufficient explanations for the choices they make. Decisions made by an algorithmic "black box" appear to be unchallengeable owing to this lack of transparency. The black box phenomenon primarily affects gig economy workers, content creators, and warehouse workers, but intrusive and opaque surveillance techniques are becoming commonplace in many industries and workplaces.

Since the start of the pandemic, there has been an increase in worker and workplace surveillance due to factors such as the growing blurring of work and home life, the shift to remote work, and the integration of workplace technology into personal devices and spaces. Low-wage workers have taken the lead in the campaign to end workplace surveillance and harms enabled by algorithms, although this is occurring in many industries and at all managerial levels [16]. Worker-led organizations expose the use of algorithmic management to set productivity quotas, set worker benchmarks and pay, and recommend hiring, promoting, demoting, and firing employees. Companies use a range of excuses to support their use of surveillance technology in the workplace, such as the thin pretences that it lessens discrimination, offers metrics that mid-tier management can use to demonstrate compliance, and increases efficiency for labor-intensive jobs such as resume reviews. Nevertheless, the negative consequences of these justifications far exceed them: algorithmic management weakens worker and individual privacy, unfairly divides benefits and risks, and increases the devaluation of labor. It also puts worker-led collective bargaining rights at hazard. Workplace surveillance is essentially a control mechanism, meaning that it has little effect on productivity, efficiency, or safety. This is highlighted by worker-driven initiatives. The ability to use information as a source of power is what unites algorithmic management, worker surveillance, and Big Tech, and this analysis must apply to them all.

This holds for both the power disparity between tech companies and their users and the relationship between employers and employees. Moreover, the rights, liberty, and dignity of workers are compromised in both situations to further the interests of those in control of and with access to information [17]. To rebalance the power between employers and employees, significant restrictions on algorithmic control and surveillance in work environments must be enacted while maintaining employee autonomy and the right to collectively organize.

There is a compelling argument for bright-line laws that outright forbid the use of these devices and, at the very least, create no-go zones around the most invasive forms of surveillance. Such a regime might be advantageous; for example, the use of algorithms in management is increasing. In recent years, worker-led organizing has focused on how algorithmic management erodes worker and individual privacy, risks protected worker-led collective action, worsens working conditions, puts employees' health and safety at risk, and increases the devaluation of work. Policy responses to these demands must respect workers' rights to compensation, privacy, autonomy, and collective bargaining while addressing the pace and scope of this ramp-up.

Organizing tech workers is one of the most effective and direct ways to prevent tech-enabled harm before it occurs [18]. Workers have taken major risks to engage in collective action and reveal harmful technologies and contractual agreements while they are still being developed. In addition to advocating for better working conditions and worker protection and denouncing human rights violations, they have had remarkable success in encouraging employers to renounce contracts with military agencies. Many of the people spearing this effort have been subjected to various forms of retaliation. Because of this, the success of tech policy initiatives across the board depends on the establishment of strong baseline labor laws, including stronger protections for whistleblowers. After all, organized labor is the only real foundation upon which an ethical, responsible, accountable, and just tech sector can be built. Worker-led pushback faces a number of challenges: the industry is making cuts and laying people off while keeping executive compensation levels high. Even before the current economic downturn, many of the first wave of tech worker organizers were fired by tech companies in retaliation for their loudest internal critics. Tech companies, which are already among the most watchful in the world, closely monitor the conduct of their staff members. Amazon even hired Pinkerton agents, private security firms known for breaching labor laws in the late nineteenth and early twentieth centuries, to spy on labor organizers, environmental activists, and warehouse workers. Pinkerton agents denote the operatives hired by the Pinkerton National Detective Agency, established in 1850 by Allan Pinkerton. At first, the agency focused on railway theft incidents, safeguarding trains, and capturing train thieves. As time passed, Pinkerton agents gained a reputation for taking part in numerous criminal investigations, such as apprehending bank robbers, counterfeiters, and forgers. Therefore, policies that promote worker organizing—such as strengthening whistleblower protections, restricting the use of nondisclosure and no-disparagement agreements, and tightening restrictions on employers' use of noncompete clauses—are crucial to reducing the concentration of power in the tech sector [19, 20].

3.4.1 The Algorithmic Management of Work: A Basic Compass

Algorithms are increasingly being used in labor coordination. This could impact industrial relations, job quality, and business models through organizational changes at work. Joint Research Centre Algorithmic Management and Platform Work (JRC AMPWORK) tracks algorithmic management within the EU.

Owing to the use of digital tools, an increasing amount of work is being conducted and monitored. Planning, organizing, commanding, coordinating, and controlling tasks in management can all be performed with algorithms. To understand the consequences of algorithmic management, which spans from work organization to working conditions and job quality, the JRC is conducting new empirical research and aims to provide a strong conceptual basis for this analysis. This area of research builds on previous JRC studies on digital labor platforms and the digitization of the workforce. The JRC defines algorithmic management as the process of using computer-programmed procedures to coordinate labor input within an organization [21]. Artificial intelligence may or may not be used to help with this task, which could involve scheduling and assigning work shifts, drafting and disseminating job-related instructions, assessing worker performance, and determining incentives and sanctions. The management of an organization is the set of duties and procedures that are employed to organize each work process. Algorithm management is the practice of performing one or more of these tasks via algorithms. Algorithm management affects both the businesses that use it and the employees who work there by automating management tasks. These consequences include i) a change in the structure of the workplace, which affects the caliber of the work and the working environment because of factors such as communication, reward, and work pace; ii) altering employment relations and encouraging outsourcing to alter industrial relations; and iii) creating information asymmetry between employers and employees, which lessens their bargaining capacity and their involvement in the production process. Despite the potentially disastrous effects of this technique, there is still a lack of statistical evidence regarding the application of algorithmic management because it is a relatively new and rapidly developing phenomenon. Most of what is known about algorithmic management comes from research on digital labor platforms and platform laborers. JRC research aims to provide significant evidence via the Algorithmic Management and Platform Work survey (AMPWork) study. This joint JRC-ILO study looks at algorithmic management from a global perspective, focusing on industrial relations, job quality, and work organization while examining different countries and industries [22]. The study, which is being conducted in association with the International Labour Organization (ILO), looks at the logistics and healthcare sectors in two non-European countries—South Africa and India—and two European countries—France and Italy. The report claims that algorithmic management is widely employed in conventional industries and offers benefits in terms of increased productivity as well as the simplification and streamlining of work procedures. However, there are significant challenges in the form of concerns about the likelihood of intrusive worker surveillance and the potential decline in job quality.

3.5 The Future of Work: Human-AI Collaboration

Although vital, transparency and data-access measures are insufficient, employers and developers should bear the brunt of responsibility instead of the people who are negatively impacted. Because workplace surveillance is so opaque, it can be especially harmful. It increases the extent of employers' control over employees and their ability to peer into the most private aspects of their lives. As a baseline accountability measure, many proposals for worker data rights regimes focus on transparency and require disclosures regarding the use of algorithmic systems and workplace surveillance to counteract this growing information asymmetry. This covers the parameters, data inputs, deployment techniques, and applications of workplace surveillance systems. These "worker data rights" proposals aim to balance the informational disparities between employers and employees, taking into consideration, in particular, the greater power that employers acquire from the more intrusive data collection made possible by algorithmic systems [9, 23].

Enacting regulations to guarantee that wages are set fairly and that workers can live in the first place is preferable to informing employees that their employer has systematically reduced their pay through algorithmic targeting [24]. Furthermore, there is an incentive for both software vendors and employers to oppose laws requiring them to grant complete access to employee data owing to contractual obligations and claims of trade secrets. The data and the models trained on them, even in cases where all parties are willing to grant workers access, still pose difficult organizational challenges that employers may argue they are unable to resolve. Second, data-access-focused policy frameworks assume the presence of outside actors with the necessary means and aptitude to interpret the data. While many organizations are emerging to address this need, those with the background knowledge and experience required to sift through sometimes enormous volumes of data—workers and their elected representatives, researchers, investigative journalists, and civil society organizations—frequently have relatively less time and resources to devote to such tasks. Furthermore, becoming aware of detrimental business practices is merely the beginning of the process; it does not equate to exercising control or power over them [25]. Therefore, any future policy framework must consider inherent information and power asymmetries. In the end, an approach that uses bright-line rules that limit abusive practices would shift the burden of proof from those who benefit from algorithmic management to those who are most likely to be harmed by the additional work. The way that AI is being incorporated into the workforce is changing how people think about work and productivity. A deeper look reveals a more nuanced story, one of collaboration and augmentation, where AI enables human workers to reach new heights of efficiency, innovation, and creativity. While worries about job displacement and technological disruption are common, this is only one side of the story.

3.5.1 The Role of AI in Enhancing Human Capabilities

Artificial intelligence spans a wide range of technologies, including natural language processing systems and machine learning algorithms. In contrast to common belief, artificial intelligence should be associated not only with job displacement but also with enhancing human capabilities and optimizing workflows. Artificial intelligence will free up human workers to concentrate on higher-value tasks that call for human judgment and creativity by automating repetitive tasks and delivering data-driven insights. AI is fundamentally a tool for maximizing human potential [16]. AI enables workers to perform tasks more precisely and make better decisions by analyzing large amounts of data and finding patterns that are invisible to human cognition. AI-driven diagnostics and predictive analytics, for example, are transforming the way professionals in the healthcare and finance industries manage financial portfolios and diagnose illnesses, respectively.

3.5.2 Fostering a Culture of AI–Human Collaboration

A culture of cooperation and trust between people and machines is essential for the effective adoption of AI in the workplace. To foster employee trust and guarantee that AI systems are used responsibly, transparency, explainability, and ethical AI practices are crucial. To fully realize the potential of human-AI collaboration, organizations should prioritize open communication and support experimentation with AI technologies. It takes more than just implementing new technology to develop an AI-integrated workplace culture. It entails fostering an environment where the team's ability to use AI effectively and trust in the technology's potential is paramount. Organizations can set the stage for AI to significantly contribute to their growth by adopting a mindset that sees the technology as an enhancement tool rather than a replacement [26]. The successful adoption and integration of AI depend on this cultural shift because it fosters synergy between technology and human expertise. It promotes creativity and progressive methods in the contemporary workplace. Establishing an environment that encourages ongoing learning and development is imperative for organizations.

3.5.3 Upskilling and Reskilling for the AI Era

The need for new skills and competencies is growing as AI changes the nature of work. Employers and employees alike need to make ongoing investments in learning and development to adjust to the shifting needs of the digital economy. Online training courses and mentorship programs are two collaborative approaches to upskilling and reskilling that can help close the skills gap and equip workers for success in the AI-powered workplace of the future. Additionally, there are more options than ever to pursue careers in technology. In the era of artificial intelligence, companies must play a critical role in assisting workers in acquiring new competencies. It is not just for the benefit of the staff either. With artificial intelligence, particularly generative AI, or GenAI, changing the nature of work, businesses must upskill their workforce if they hope to stay competitive and survive over the long run. Employers and employees have been alerted to the importance of consumer-grade AI tools such as ChatGPT, which can handle everything from contract reviews to family vacation planning and provide complex topic answers. These tools demonstrate that a variety of job tasks can be completed via technology [27]. This is a prospect that both creates uncertainty about people's jobs and opportunities to use these capabilities productively.

3.5.4 Overcoming Challenges and Mitigating Risks

Although there are many advantages to AI and human collaboration, there are still risks and challenges. Many people have serious concerns about algorithmic biases, job displacement, and ethical ramifications. Proactive steps are needed to address these concerns, such as incorporating fairness, accountability, and transparency into AI-powered decision-making processes and offering channels for continuous communication and feedback.

Businesses need to adapt and change now more than ever because a new era of work marked by AI-human collaboration and innovation is about to dawn. Through the adoption of AI as a mechanism to enhance human capabilities and stimulate creativity, enterprises can set themselves up for prosperity in the digital realm.

When combined, people and machines can transform entire industries, bring about a process revolution, and open new avenues for prosperity and growth [28].

3.6 The Impact of AI on the Labor Market

Recent discussions have focused on the potential effects of artificial intelligence on the labor market and economic growth. Despite the rapid growth of AI research and its potential to increase efficiency and generate employment opportunities, there are concerns among some specialists regarding potential job displacement and growing inequality. According to a Goldman Sachs analysis from earlier this year, generative AI has the potential to increase worldwide productivity and generate fresh employment opportunities, yet it also poses a threat of major upheaval in the job market, endangering approximately 300 million jobs with automation.

Another illustration is the declaration from British Telecom about their plan to cut 55,000 jobs by 2030, with expectations that AI will take over 10,000 of those. Concerns about job loss and predictions of significant productivity gains are being stirred up by the latest technological development, artificial intelligence. Artificial intelligence has advanced significantly in solving problems in situations where it is difficult to create formal rules and where humans have traditionally excelled in decision-making using their previous knowledge or training. Extensive data are becoming increasingly accessible, the cost of computational capacity is decreasing, and the expanding collection of statistical models and algorithms, especially in machine learning, is driving this advancement.

Concerns arise about job displacement for professions once they are considered immune to automation, as AI improves in performing nonroutine tasks. Employment in the legal, medical, and financial fields, which traditionally require advanced education and rely on experience-based decision-making, could increase automation with the introduction of artificial intelligence. Moreover, the implementation of AI could have a negative and disproportionate impact on the socioeconomic categories that have traditionally experienced the highest unemployment rates. The evaluation of racial and gender bias in AI is backed by a growing body of academic research [29]. Recent reports on the gendered effects of AI have indicated that occupational segregation is a persistent source of concern. Intelligent automation is predicted to alter the majority of jobs to some extent, as generative AI grows more proficient at handling nonroutine cognitive tasks. Whether artificial intelligence augments or replaces human talent will have an immediate impact on employment opportunities today.

Recent advances in AI technology, for example, may improve the interpretation of medical scans by radiologists while eliminating the need for administrative staff members, whose primary responsibilities involve entering patient data. The former would probably experience a rise in job losses, whereas the latter would probably see an increase in job productivity, as AI would replace the majority of their activities. Automation is nothing new in and of itself; earlier waves of technological advancement are what led to changes in responsibilities and employment patterns. For example, the automotive industry is using fewer manual assembly lines as a result of the development of robotic arms.

While earlier automation was limited to routine tasks, the ability of generative AI to perform nonroutine cognitive tasks exposes previously isolated professions that were previously thought of as a complement to automation to a replacement. The graph below represents the approximate percentage of US industry jobs that could be automated by generative AI and could be a sign of future changes to the labor market brought about by AI [30]. It is derived from a recent study conducted by Goldman Sachs.

In various fields of work, there is a growing demand for experts in artificial intelligence, with the greatest need being for those in computer and mathematical jobs. There has been a notable rise in job opportunities in architecture, life and social sciences, management, law, and business, with many roles now demanding knowledge of AI. The fact that artificial intelligence is in high demand across a variety of sectors and professions indicates that AI is a technology with broad potential applications (Fig. 3.3).

The administrative and support services industry provides the largest premium for AI skills. In this field, a job listing that asks for AI skills offers a salary almost 18% higher than one that does not. The insurance, finance, and IT industries each offer an 11% premium. Manufacturing provides a 9% premium, whereas professional services are 8% pricier (Fig. 3.4; https://cepr.org/voxeu/columns/demand-ai-skills-labour-market). AI skills are valued differently across different occupational

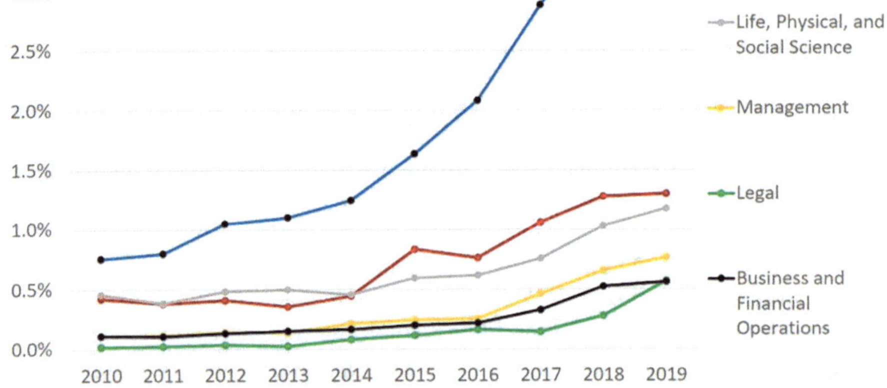

Fig. 3.3 Demand for AI skills across occupations

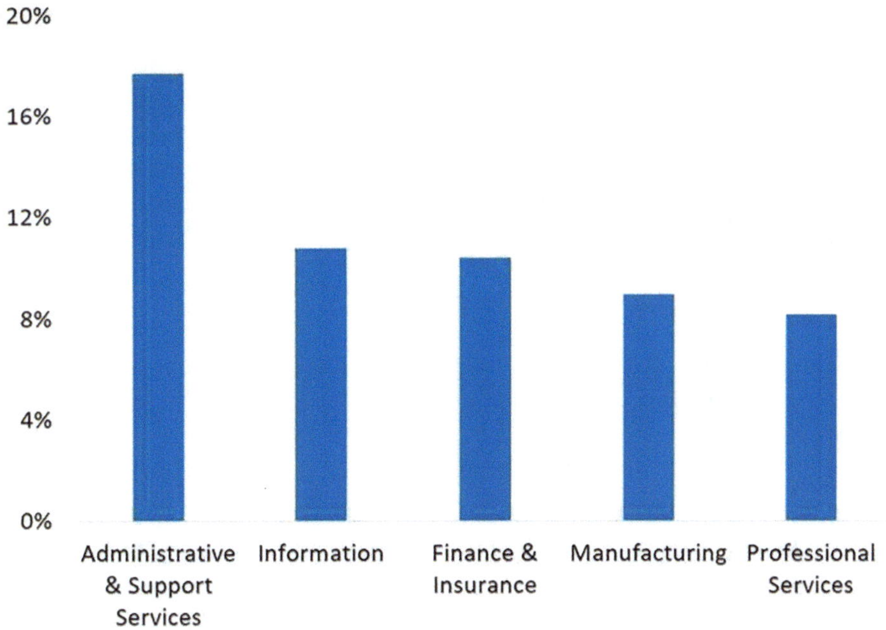

Fig. 3.4 Estimated wage premium for AI skills by industry

groups, according to a similar analysis of wage differences across occupations [17]. Managerial positions offer the greatest salary bump; a job posting related to AI usually pays approximately 11% more than one requiring a comparable set of skills. This amount is much greater than the pay increase of approximately 9% in computer and mathematical jobs that are commonly associated with artificial intelligence [2]. Jobs in business, finance, and life sciences provide a premium of nearly 7.5%, whereas careers in architecture and engineering offer a premium of 5% (Fig. 3.5).

This raises the possibility of an uneven burden of job transition between men and women, to which research has not yet offered a definitive response. Numerous earlier studies have suggested that the manufacturing sector was most vulnerable to automation replacement technologies before the development of generative AI. Men seem to be the most vulnerable to job displacement due to automation because they are more likely to work in these industries. On the other hand, Brussevich discovered that, across all industries and professions, women completed more routine tasks on average than men did [3]. This means that the first group is more likely to lose their jobs to automation. It is now more difficult to predict with precision how gender will affect the labor market in the future because of the use of generative AI. Some recent reports suggest that AI will likely replace white-collar and service workers. Seventy percent of office and administrative jobs in the United States are held by women employees, according to a study on the impact of AI on women's work lives. In the financial services industry, women account for only 25% of senior

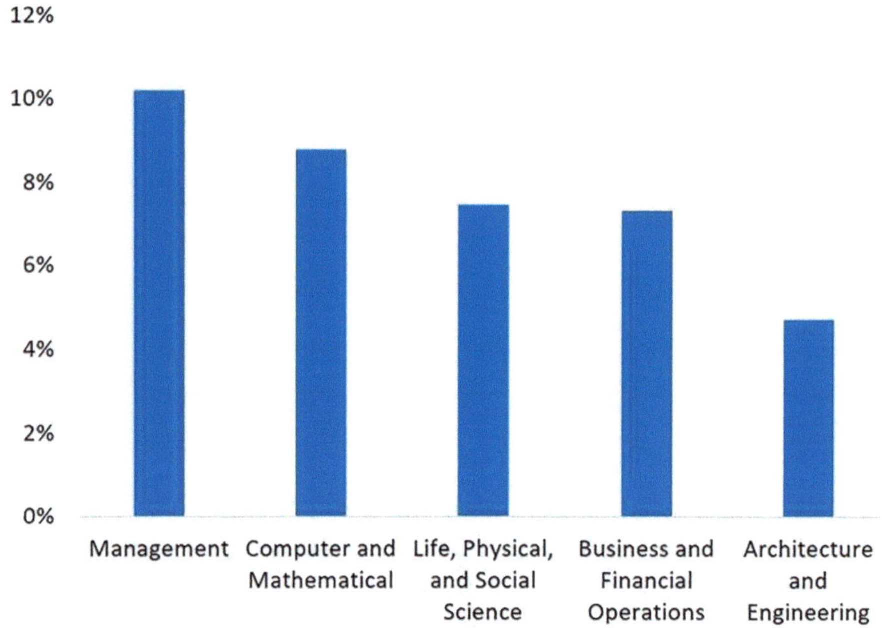

Fig. 3.5 Estimated wage premium for AI skills by occupation

management positions, which are typically assumed to be the least susceptible to artificial intelligence replacement. This information comes from a different study [16].

This implies that the majority of positions in the finance sector that are less prone to being automated by AI are occupied by males. Despite variations in research findings on gender disparities in outcomes, it is evident that AI advancements could exacerbate gender gaps in employment if there are no adequate policies targeting AI integration and employee development [6]. Owing to disparities in educational opportunities and training, AI could create barriers for younger individuals trying to join the workforce by necessitating proficiency in AI-related competencies.

According to the Organization for Economic Cooperation and Development (OECD) report Bridging the Digital Gender Divide (2018), women are less likely than men to have high levels of "digital literacy" in the majority of OECD countries, and this gap grows as women age and find it more difficult to develop new skills while taking on home care and work responsibilities at the same time [5]. Despite having similar interests and skills in their early years, men and women differ in their early careers. This difference is frequently caused by socialization, self-confidence, and conventional gender norms. It can be linked to a different ordering of educational fields. In Europe, women make up only 34% of STEM graduates and 17% of graduates in information and communication technology (ICT), according to the European Commission's (Fig. 3.5) 2021 report. In the labor market, gender disparities in additional AI training and skills lead to unequal competitive advantages, particularly in jobs that stand to gain the most from AI innovation. According to the World Economic Forum's 2018 Global Gender Gap Report, the proportion of female AI professionals worldwide is a mere 22% [23]. If the social and economic barriers that prevent vulnerable groups such as women and adolescents from accessing education and skill development are not addressed, the increased use of AI could ultimately reinforce gender stereotypes and professional differentiation [7, 31].

A labor shortage caused by artificial intelligence and an overabundance of skilled workers could make it simpler for some successful businesses to continue discriminating. Gender-biased relationships can reinforce traditional gender norms and potentially hurt future generations, in addition to preventing women from pursuing certain jobs. Finally, if AI technologies are developed by a team that lacks diversity and is therefore susceptible to unconscious biases and stereotypes or if they are trained on data that are not representative of society, they may be intrinsically biased [8]. AI bias disproportionately impacts groups that have traditionally been left out of data collection and analysis in both scenarios. This may result in bias and discrimination in hiring practices and invasive monitoring practices in the labor market. For instance, gender bias forced Amazon to scrap its AI hiring system, which was implemented in 2018. The algorithm trained itself to penalize resumes containing the word "women" using the input. Several traditional stereotypes, such as the feminization of virtual assistants, have given rise to concerns regarding the fallibility of artificial intelligence. Feminine-voiced virtual personal assistants (VPAs) could contribute to the perception of women as caregivers and support staff.

Task-based theoretical models have received even more attention in research to better identify the various labor market effects of generative AI. Considering variations within a particular profession, job analysis allows for a more accurate identification of the degree to which artificial intelligence has reduced, expanded, or rendered roles obsolete. From theoretical arguments to real-world considerations of how generative AI is transforming society, the conversation surrounding AI has changed. Concerns as well as enthusiasm have been raised by the growing application of AI in many industries. Misinformation, job displacement, income inequality, biases, and societal stability are some of these concerns [32]. To shape AI's future and ensure inclusive and sustainable social and economic progress, cooperation between a variety of stakeholders—including governments, industry, academia, and civil society—is considered essential.

3.7 Case Studies

Germany Programs for Vocational Training Germany have established a well-respected system of vocational training that assists people in gaining the skills required for the workforce, including the ability to adjust to technological improvements. The nation places a strong emphasis on practical, hands-on training that integrates classroom learning with apprenticeships conducted on the job. To guarantee that the skills taught in vocational training programs meet the demands of the industry, these associations work with program designers to construct their programs [33]. This strategy has assisted Germany in maintaining a robust industrial sector and lowering unemployment rates, as people have the skills needed for the changing labor market.

Finland Experiment on Universal Basic Income. In 2017 and 2018, Finland ran a 2-year trial with universal basic income (UBI). A randomly chosen set of jobless people, regardless of whether they were actively looking for work, received a monthly stipend as part of the experiment. The objective was to assess how UBI affects people's social security, employment opportunities, and general well-being. The findings demonstrated that although UBI users reported feeling more secure about their financial situation and overall well-being, there was little change in job outcomes [34]. Nonetheless, the trial revealed significant issues about labor market regulations, societal well-being, and financial security.

Singapore The Skills Future Initiative, a comprehensive national initiative to promote lifelong learning and skill development is Singapore's Skills Future Initiative. The initiative's goal is to give people the information and abilities they need to adjust to the shifting needs of the labor market, especially those brought on by automation. It gives people credit that they can put toward a variety of training courses and programs, including courses for reskilling and upskilling. Encouragement is given for a culture of continual learning, for firms to partake in staff training, and for industry collaboration as a key aspect of the Skills Future Initiative. The program has effectively enhanced the skills of Singapore's workforce and encouraged a mindset of continuous learning [35]. These case studies highlight the importance of implementing preventive actions to address job displacement and enhance the welfare of individuals and communities. Nations can mitigate the adverse impacts of job displacement and equip their workers with the necessary skills for the future economy through investing in vocational training, exploring new approaches such as universal basic income trials, and implementing wide-ranging skills development programs.

3.8 Conclusions

One of the main tasks of artificial intelligence is automation. It eliminates repetitive and time-consuming tasks, allowing employees to focus on more creative and strategic responsibilities. This not only increases productivity but also reduces the risk of errors. By leveraging advances in natural language processing, automated AI systems can perform tasks such as taking notes, reading written content, and making phone calls. In addition, they can manage daily tasks, assess and warn of potential risks, and prepare daily briefings. Artificial intelligence refers to the use of machines and software to perform tasks that traditionally require human intelligence. These machines can range from laptops or cell phones to computer-controlled robots. When one automates intelligently, team members can spend less time on repetitive routine tasks and more time on innovation, creative thinking, problem-solving, and collaboration. Employee productivity is the backbone of any successful business, and AI technology is an important way to achieve this.

References

1. Morandini, S., Fraboni, F., De Angelis, M., Puzzo, G., Giusino, D., & Pietrantoni, L. (2023). The impact of artificial intelligence on workers' skills: Upskilling and reskilling in organisations. *Informing Science, 26*, 39–68.
2. Howard, J. (2019). Artificial intelligence: Implications for the future of work. *American Journal of Industrial Medicine, 62*(11), 917–926.
3. Braganza, A., Chen, W., Canhoto, A., & Sap, S. (2021). Productive employment and decent work: The impact of AI adoption on psychological contracts, job engagement and employee trust. *Journal of Business Research, 131*, 485–494.
4. Majumder, S., & Dey, N. (2022). Knowledge management in various sectors. In *AI-empowered knowledge management* (pp. 37–61). Singapore.
5. Lane, M., & Saint-Martin, A. (2021). *The impact of Artificial Intelligence on the labour market: What do we know so far?* (Working Paper No. 256). OECD Social, Employment, and Migration.
6. Ernst, E., Merola, R., & Samaan, D. (2019). Economics of artificial intelligence: Implications for the future of work. *IZA Journal of Labor Policy, 9*(1), 1–35.
7. Arslan, A., Cooper, C., Khan, Z., Golgeci, I., & Ali, I. (2022). Artificial intelligence and human workers interaction at team level: A conceptual assessment of the challenges and potential HRM strategies. *International Journal of Manpower, 43*(1), 75–88.
8. Farhan, A. (2023). The impact of artificial intelligence on human workers. *Journal of Communication Education, 17*(2), 93–104.
9. Tang, P. M., Koopman, J., Mai, K. M., De Cremer, D., Zhang, J. H., Reynders, P., … Chen, I. (2023). No person is an island: Unpacking the work and after-work consequences of interacting with artificial intelligence. *Journal of Applied Psychology, 108*(11), 1766.
10. Wei, W., & Li, L. (2022). The impact of artificial intelligence on the mental health of manufacturing workers: The mediating role of overtime work and the work environment. *Frontiers in Public Health, 10*, 862407.
11. Tschang, F. T., & Almirall, E. (2021). Artificial intelligence as augmenting automation: Implications for employment. *Academy of Management Perspectives, 35*(4), 642–659.
12. Boustani, N. M. (2022). Artificial intelligence impact on banks clients and employees in an Asian developing country. *Journal of Asia Business Studies, 16*(2), 267–278.
13. Nedzhvetskaya, N., & Tan, J. S. (2024). *The role of workers in AI ethics and governance.* https://doi.org/10.1093/oxfordhb/9780197579329.013.68
14. Todolí-Signes, A. (2021). Making algorithms safe for workers: Occupational risks associated with work managed by artificial intelligence. *Transfer: European Review of Labour and Research, 27*(4), 433–452.
15. Majumder, S., Chowdhury, S., Dey, N., & Santosh, K. C. (2022). Balance your work-life: Personal interactive web-interface. *International Journal of Interactive Multimedia and Artificial Intelligence*. https://doi.org/10.9781/ijimai.2021.08.016
16. Cramarenco, R. E., Burcă-Voicu, M. I., & Dabija, D. C. (2023). The impact of artificial intelligence (AI) on employees' skills and well-being in global labor markets: A systematic review. *Oeconomia Copernicana, 14*(3), 731–767.

17. George, A. S., George, A. H., & Martin, A. G. (2023). ChatGPT and the future of work: A comprehensive analysis of AI's impact on jobs and employment. *Partners Universal International Innovation Journal, 1*(3), 154–186.
18. Dong, X., Tian, Y., He, M., & Wang, T. (2025). When knowledge workers meet AI? The double-edged sword effects of AI adoption on innovative work behavior. *Journal of Knowledge Management, 29*(1), 113–147.
19. Zarifhonarvar, A. (2024). Economics of ChatGPT: A labor market view on the occupational impact of artificial intelligence. *Journal of Electronic Business & Digital Economics, 3*(2), 100–116.
20. Shen, Y., & Zhang, X. (2024). The impact of artificial intelligence on employment: The role of virtual agglomeration. *Humanities and Social Sciences Communications, 11*(1), 122.
21. Shaikh, F., Afshan, G., Anwar, R. S., Abbas, Z., & Chana, K. A. (2023). Analyzing the impact of artificial intelligence on employee productivity: The mediating effect of knowledge sharing and well-being. *Asia Pacific Journal of Human Resources, 61*(4), 794–820.
22. Edelman, B. G., Ngwe, D., & Peng, S. (2023). *Measuring the impact of AI on information worker productivity*. https://doi.org/10.2139/ssrn.4648686
23. Gmyrek, P., Berg, J., & Bescond, D. (2023). *Generative AI and jobs: A global analysis of potential effects on job quantity and quality* (Working Paper No. 96). ILO.
24. Zhao, H., Yuan, B., & Song, Y. (2024). Employees' perception of generative artificial intelligence and the dark side of work outcomes. *Journal of Hospitality and Tourism Management, 61*, 191–199.
25. Bankins, S., Hu, X., & Yuan, Y. (2024). Artificial intelligence, workers, and future of work skills. *Current Opinion in Psychology, 58*, 101828.
26. Majumder, S., & Mondal, A. (2021). Are Chatbots really useful for human resource management? *International Journal of Speech Technology, 24*(4), 969–977.
27. Chowdhury, S., Budhwar, P., Dey, P. K., Joel-Edgar, S., & Abadie, A. (2022). AI-employee collaboration and business performance: Integrating knowledge-based view, socio-technical systems and organisational socialisation framework. *Journal of Business Research, 144*, 31–49.
28. Langer, M., & Landers, R. N. (2021). The future of artificial intelligence at work: A review on effects of decision automation and augmentation on workers targeted by algorithms and third-party observers. *Computers in Human Behavior, 123*, 106878.
29. Hui, X., Reshef, O., & Zhou, L. (2024). The short-term effects of generative artificial intelligence on employment: Evidence from an online labor market. *Organization Science, 35*(6), 1977–1989.
30. Ghosh, S., Majumder, S., & Peng, S. L. (2023). An empirical study on adoption of artificial intelligence in human resource management. In *Artificial intelligence techniques in human resource management* (pp. 29–85). Apple Academic Press.
31. Zirar, A., Ali, S. I., & Islam, N. (2023). Worker and workplace Artificial Intelligence (AI) coexistence: Emerging themes and research agenda. *Technovation, 124*, 102747.
32. Verma, S., & Singh, V. (2022). Impact of artificial intelligence-enabled job characteristics and perceived substitution crisis on innovative work behavior of employees from high-tech firms. *Computers in Human Behavior, 131*, 107215.
33. Tang, P. M., Koopman, J., Mai, K. M., De Cremer, D., Zhang, J. H., Reynders, P., et al. (2023). No person is an island: Unpacking the work and after-work consequences of interacting with artificial intelligence. *Journal of Applied Psychology, 108*(11), 1766.
34. De Stefano, V. (2019). "Negotiating the algorithm": Automation, artificial intelligence, and labor protection. *Comparative Labor Law & Policy Journal, 41*, 15.
35. Webb, M. (2019). *The impact of artificial intelligence on the labor market*. https://doi.org/10.2139/ssrn.3482150

Chapter 4
AI in Collective Bargaining and Dispute Resolution

4.1 Introduction

A successful labour market and industrial relations system must include conflict resolution. Labor conflicts always arise where there are labor relations, and they must be settled quickly, amicably, and fairly for the good of all parties and the overall economy. The foundation established to handle these conflicts is essential to any nation's labor relations framework [1]. Social partners and governments have various tools, from nonformal discussions to formal litigation and possibly even government action to settle specific labour conflicts in the public good. Although there are many options for settling labor disputes, the extrajudicial processes of conciliation, mediation, and arbitration are the only ones that are covered in this study; these are alternatives that do not require going to court or appearing before a labor tribunal [2]. While many different types of conflicts can occur between employees and employers, this study focuses specifically on the mechanisms used to settle disputes in cases of collective disputes, disputes involving the application or interpretation of collective agreements (right disputes) or the process of collective bargaining (interest disputes), which occur between employers and groups of workers most frequently represented by trade unions.

It is worthwhile to review some fundamental ideas and terminology before delving into a discussion of the various collective dispute resolution mechanisms that the newest employee union (EU) Member States have elected to implement. In addition to helping define phrases that are not always used consistently from one country to another, this approach provides a logical foundation for comparing dispute resolution systems, which is necessary. Individual and collective disputes are the two general categories into which work issues fall. Individual conflicts, as the name suggests, concern a single worker, whereas collective disagreements concern groups of workers, typically represented by a trade union. The two subcategories of collective disputes are rights disputes and interest disagreements [3]. When there is

S. Majumder, B. Misra, *AI-Empowered Industrial Relations*, Studies in Computational Intelligence 1254, https://doi.org/10.1007/978-3-032-14557-4_4

disagreement about the application or interpretation of statutory rights or the rights outlined in an existing collective agreement, a rights conflict occurs. On the other hand, an interest dispute relates to situations in which parties cannot agree on the definition of rights and obligations or how those that already exist should be changed. Interest disputes usually occur during collective bargaining when there is no collective agreement or when the collective agreement is being re-negotiated.

Concerning group disagreements, the type of dispute can play a significant role in deciding the appropriate resolution approach, with legal and strategic implications. If there is a valid collective agreement in place during a rights dispute, it may outline the process that the parties involved must adhere to in resolving the dispute. In some countries, laws may mandate specific procedures for resolving collective disputes, such as mandatory arbitration for essential public service disputes involving collective interests. A labour union is a group of employees in a specific trade, sector, or business that aims to advocate for workers during discussions with employers regarding topics such as salary, perks, and work environment. The process of collective bargaining involves labour union representatives negotiating with employers. The procedure leads to a preliminary agreement that needs approval from all members to be completed. Unions in the United States have a lengthy past. Philadelphia shoemakers formed the initial union in 1794 [4]. The Federation of Organized Trades and Labor Unions was established in 1881, and the American Federation of Labor (AFL) was founded 5 years later. Labor unions typically operate with a democratic framework, conducting elections to select officials who make decisions in the best interest of the members. Workers contribute money to the labour union. In exchange, the labour union serves as a representative for the workers. To establish a union, a group of local employees acquires a charter from a national labour organization. The majority of labor unions in the U.S. are managed by two major organizations—the Change to Win Federation (CtW) and the American Federation of Labor and Congress of Industrial Organizations (AFL-CIO). The AFL-CIO was established in 1955 following the combination of the two organizations. CtW broke away from the AFL-CIO in 2005. Most unions have similar structures and operate in comparable manners. In the United States, an employer must engage in negotiations with a union sincerely, but they are not obligated to accept every condition. Negotiations occur between the union's bargaining unit, which consists of members responsible for ensuring fair compensation and representation, and the employer through various rounds. A Collective Bargaining Agreement (CBA) is eventually reached and signed by both parties. The Collective Bargaining Agreement details salary levels and covers additional employment provisions such as holidays, sick leave, perks, work hours, and job conditions [5]. Once the CBA is signed, the employer must obtain a union representative's permission to make any changes, but CBAs have an expiration date, leading to negotiations and a new agreement between the labour union and management.

4.1.1 *Steps of Collective Bargaining*

When both parties state their positions and make their demands, negotiations can start. These beginning demands, like other negotiations, only layout the groundwork. Usually, both parties anticipate some degree of compromise and recognize that the ultimate agreement will lie halfway between these two extremes. If all proceeds according to the plan, union members may vote on a preliminary agreement. The procedure is finished, and a contract that regulates the employment relations for a predetermined amount of time is signed if they accept it. Negotiators from both sides will need to return to the negotiation table if workers reject the agreement. It is legally obligatory for both sides to engage in good faith negotiations during the collective bargaining process. This implies that they both need to actively engage in talk and convey their desire to establish a foundation for a settlement.

The steps of collective bargaining (Fig. 4.1) are as follows: (i) **Preparation**—both parties must prepare. People with both organizational expertise and the ability to negotiate effectively should make up the negotiation team. An essential component of this planning phase is comprehending working conditions and employee unhappiness. An important aspect of this stage is establishing goals for the negotiations and, if applicable, going over the previous contract. To be more prepared for settlement, the administration must also plan and anticipate union demands. One issue is management rights, which provide an organization with total autonomy in areas of hiring, moving personnel to various positions, and other management-related activities, **(ii) Negotiation**—the parties decide on a timetable for talks as well as ground rules, such as how often to meet and what matters should be discussed first. For example, both parties may decide that the most difficult issue to resolve—compensation—will be settled last or first, (iii) **Formation:** Both sides present their initial proposals face to face. These meetings can begin 60–90 days before the current contract expires. It will likely include sample opening sentences and options for handling potential situations. The key to a successful proposal is to come to the table with "let us do it". There is a discussion at the beginning, after

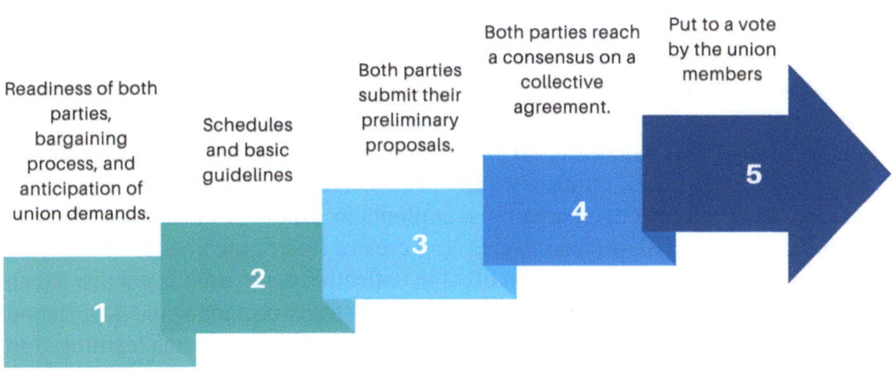

Fig. 4.1 Steps of collective bargaining

which each party usually returns to decide which requests they can and cannot fulfil. A second meeting is typically scheduled at this stage to carry out the conversation. Many conditions-related topics are covered, such as pay, benefits, working conditions, working hours, vacations, sick leave, pension schemes, and other services. Simple issues are typically discussed first since they are more amenable to compromise [6]. Private discussions are held at all times, (iv) **Presentation:** reaching a consensus on a collective agreement always requires several meetings. Hundreds of sessions are frequently needed to establish an agreement in this lengthy procedure. Both sides make counterproposals and propose compromises until an agreement is reached. Negotiators with experience are aware that sometimes they have to give or compromise. The union may bring an improper allegation against the employer if there is reason to believe that an improper practice that was not bargained in good faith took place. Some employers switch to win–win negotiations instead of using hostile tactics. This paradigm takes a win-win strategy rather than a "us and them" or "win and lose" stance. Together, the union and the employer collaborate to resolve disputes. This means that instead of taking a less compelling stance, both sides discuss the matter at hand while seated at the same table as equals [7]. Employers and certain unions are dubious about this strategy. This requires that both parties be trained to resolve conflicts, change their minds about each other, and establish a relationship between employers and employees, **(v) Settlement**—union members must ratify and cast their votes on any collective deal reached by two negotiating parties. The procedure proceeds if the member declines. The entire staff is obligated to approve the contract, and at times, administrators must evaluate it first. The existing contract will be replaced (or, in the event of a new union, begin with the initial contract) if top management accepts the contract and the majority of employees vote in support of it. The management and union bargainers resume talks if both parties reject the contract. After the contract is signed by both sides, the administration begins.

4.2 AI Facilitates More Efficient Negotiations

In ever-evolving industrial relations, the integration of artificial intelligence (AI) into collective bargaining is a significant paradigm shift. As unions and employers grapple with increasingly complex economic realities, technological advances and changing workforce dynamics, AI is emerging as a powerful tool for improving bargaining effectiveness, efficiency and fairness. This study explores the multifaceted role of AI in collective bargaining, explores its potential to change traditional practices, provides data-driven insights, and creates fairer outcomes for both workers and organizations. The inclusion of AI in collective bargaining is not just a technical innovation; it represents a fundamental transformation of how labour negotiations are conducted in the twenty-first century. Using machine learning algorithms, natural language processing and predictive analytics, AI can solve long-standing problems in the negotiation process, such as information asymmetry, protracted negotiations and the difficulty of quantifying complex compromises [8]. This study explores various applications of AI in collective bargaining, from data analysis and strategy development to real-time negotiation support and contract monitoring. Through a series of case studies, this book explores real-world applications of AI in labour negotiations and highlights both successes and challenges. In addition, the metrics used to evaluate the effectiveness of AI in this context are examined, and the ethical aspects of its use are discussed. As this complex landscape is navigated, AI is not a panacea for all collective bargaining. Rather, it is a powerful tool that, when used thoughtfully and ethically, can improve human decision-making, foster collaborative negotiation, and potentially lead to more sustainable contracts that benefit both employees and employers. As the forefront of this technological revolution in workplace relations is approached, it is imperative that thoughtful dialogue is engaged in by all stakeholders—unions, employers, policymakers, and technologists—to ensure that AI is acted upon as a force for positive change in the workplace. In the rapidly evolving landscape of the twenty-first century, AI has emerged as a revolutionary force in various social and economic sectors. Its potential to revolutionize employment and labour relations is particularly important because it presents both unprecedented opportunities and complex challenges. This essay explores the multifaceted role of AI in shaping the future of work, labour negotiations, and the broader dynamics of industrial relations. AI, broadly defined as the development of computer systems capable of performing tasks that normally require human intelligence, has made significant advances in recent years. From machine learning algorithms capable of processing massive amounts of data to natural language processing systems capable of understanding and generating human-like text, AI technologies are becoming increasingly complex and pervasive. As these technologies continue to evolve, their impact on the workplace and labour relations will become increasingly profound. Integrating AI into work and employment is a double-edged sword. On the other hand, it provides an opportunity to improve efficiency, decision-making, and productivity. AI-powered systems can analyse complex datasets to identify patterns and trends, automate routine tasks, and provide valuable information to employers and employees [9]. On the other hand, the rise of AI has raised concerns about job mobility, privacy, and the potential deepening of inequality in the workplace. In addition, the ethical aspects related to the use of AI in the workplace are discussed, and an overview of the further development of AI in shaping the dynamic between employers and employees is given. Importantly, the integration of AI in work and employment is not only a technological but also a socioeconomic problem. It intersects with wider debates about the future of work, workers' rights and the changing social contract between employers and workers. By looking at these intersections, a closer look at how AI can be used to create fairer, more efficient, and harmonious workplaces in the digital age can be taken. Collective bargaining is the technique by which employees, via their unions, bargain with their employers to decide on terms such as wages, perks, conditions of employment, hours, vacation time, regulations regarding workplace health and safety, how to manage work and family obligations, and more. One strategy for resolving issues at work is collective bargaining.

4.3 Understanding AI in the Context of Labor and Industrial Relations

Before specific applications of AI in business and professional life are explored, a thorough understanding of AI and its importance in the field is important. AI encompasses a wide range of technologies and approaches, including but not limited to machine learning, which are algorithms that can learn from data and make predictions or decisions on the basis of that data. NLP: The ability of computers to understand, interpret and produce human language. **Computer vision:** systems that can interpret and understand the visual information of the world. **Robotics:** the design and operation of robots that perform physical tasks. **Expert** systems: AI programs that mimic human expert decision making. In work–life relationships, AI can be applied to various aspects of workforce management, negotiation, dispute resolution and decision-making. Its potential applications range from automating administrative tasks to providing advanced analytics for strategic decision-making. The importance of AI in work–life relationships stem from its ability to process and analyse large amounts of data, identify patterns and trends and make predictions or recommendations on the basis of this analysis. This feature can be particularly valuable in the following areas:

(i) Workforce Planning and Optimization: Organisations can increase operational efficiency and personnel alignment with business goals by implementing workforce planning and optimization initiatives. These methods entail assessing the number of employees now on staff, projecting the number of workers needed in the future, putting policies in place to improve performance, expediting scheduling, and fostering organisational success.

(ii) Performance Management and Evaluation: The process of performance management is continuous and aims to match the ambitions and objectives of employees with the strategic priorities of the organization. It entails routine contact between managers and staff members to evaluate duties, standards, and outputs. Organizations can attain overall success, maximize staff productivity, and support professional development when they use effective performance management systems. Providing employees with tools, feedback, and recognition that they need to grow both personally and professionally is the goal of performance management.

(iii) Payroll and Benefit Analysis: The process of determining and allocating employee compensation, including wages, salaries, and other payments, is known as payroll. It entails keeping track of deductions for things such as taxes, social security, and health insurance costs. The process of weighing the advantages and disadvantages of employee benefits, such as paid time off, health insurance, and retirement programs, is known as benefit analysis. Employers can use this study to find the most beneficial and affordable benefits to provide to their staff.

(iv) Labor Market Analysis and Forecasting: Examining patterns and trends in the labor market, such as the rise in temporary, part-time, and low-paying positions, is known as labor market analysis. The analysis of labour supply and demand at the firm and worker levels is performed via microeconomic theory. Policy makers should find formal labour market projections generated by means of an economy-wide model that appeals to a number of factors.

(v) Collective bargaining and negotiation: Collective bargaining is a method by which employers and employees, or their representatives, negotiate terms and conditions of service. It entails making written agreements, exchanging ideas, resolving conflicts, and exchanging suggestions.

(vi) Compliance and Risk Management: In the context of corporate operations, compliance and risk management are two different but connected ideas. Ensuring that an organization complies with applicable laws, regulations, and internal procedures. It entails determining, assessing, and monitoring compliance risks to prevent fines, monetary losses, and other serious consequences.

(vii) Employee engagement and satisfaction: In the field of human resources, employee satisfaction and engagement are two different but connected ideas. The degree of excitement, devotion, and passion a worker has for their work and the company is referred to as employee engagement. It all comes down to an employee's drive and emotional commitment to the company's success. On the other hand, personal satisfaction is concerned primarily with the fulfilment and contentment that a person experiences in their employment, including aspects such as pay, work–life balance, and working conditions.

As AI advances, its role as a shaper of labour and industrial relations is likely to expand, potentially redefining traditional paradigms of labour and industrial relations. There are various potential applications of AI in labor and industrial relations. The applications of AI in labour and industrial relations are diverse and far-reaching. The following are some key areas where AI is making significant inroads (Fig. 4.2).

4.3.1 Recruitment and Talent Acquisition

AI-enabled systems can simplify the hiring process by automating resume screening, performing initial candidate assessments and even predicting candidate success on the basis of historical data. These tools can help reduce bias in hiring decisions and improve the efficiency of talent acquisition processes [10].

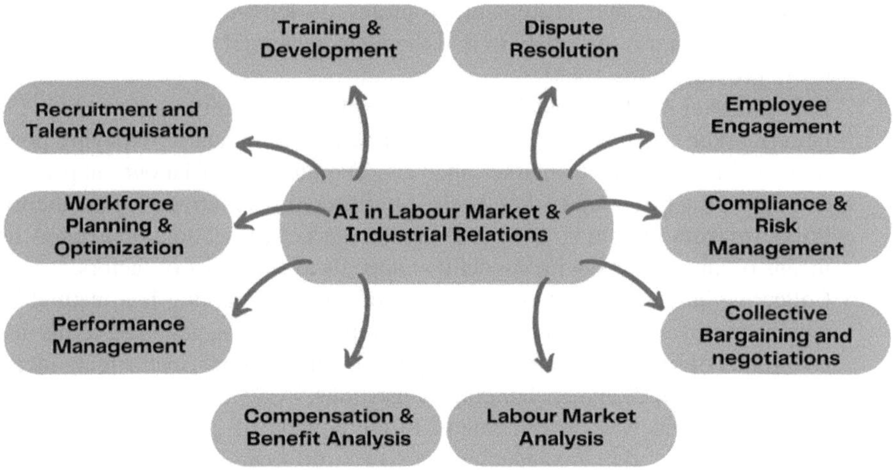

Fig. 4.2 Potential applications of AI in labor and industrial relations

4.3.2 Workforce Planning and Optimization

AI algorithms can analyse workforce data to optimize staffing levels, predict turnover and identify skills. This can help organizations make more informed decisions about hiring, training and resource allocation.

4.3.3 Performance Management

AI can provide more objective and data-driven performance reviews by analysing various metrics and identifying patterns in employee performance. This can lead to fairer assessments and more targeted development plans.

4.3.4 Compensation and Benefits Analysis

AI systems can analyse market data, internal salary structures and individual performance metrics to recommend fair and competitive compensation packages. This can help organizations maintain fair pay and optimize their compensation strategy [11].

4.3.5 Labor Market Analysis

AI-powered tools can analyse labour market trends, predict future skill requirements and provide insight into salary dynamics. This information can be valuable to both employers and unions in negotiations and strategic planning.

4.3.6 Collective Bargaining and Negotiations

AI can help in collective bargaining by analysing historical data, simulating different scenarios and providing negotiation support. This can lead to a more informed and potentially fairer outcome in employment negotiations.

4.3.7 Compliance and Risk Management

AI systems can monitor workplace operations, identify potential compliance issues and report risks related to labour laws and regulations [9]. This can help organizations proactively address potential issues and maintain good working relationships.

4.3.8 Employee Engagement and Satisfaction

AI-based methods can be used to measure employee morale, identify factors affecting job satisfaction, and provide insights to improve workplace culture and engagement. AI is able to analyse employee activity-based data to determine a person's preferences, capabilities, and shortcomings as well as forecast future performance. Additionally, real-time data are essential to the personalized interaction approach.

4.3.9 Dispute Resolution

AI can help resolve workplace disputes by providing objective analyses of situations, recommending solutions on the basis of historical data and even facilitating online dispute resolution processes [12]. Making well-informed decisions is aided by AI algorithms that examine prior AR data to forecast the possibility of dispute settlement outcomes. With the aid of predictive analytics, it evaluates risk indicators and suggests the best courses of action to improve the precision and efficacy of dispute resolution efforts.

4.3.10 Training and Development

AI can customize employee learning experiences, recommend appropriate training programs and track skill development over time. This can lead to more effective and targeted employee development initiatives. When these applications are examined in more detail, it becomes clear that the potential to transform almost every work-life relationship is held by AI. However, both the benefits and challenges associated with these applications are considered, which are explored in the following sections.

4.4 Benefits of AI in Labor and Industrial Relations

The incorporation of AI into labour and industrial relations has many potential advantages for companies and workers alike. Among the principal benefits are as follows: (i) **Enhanced** efficiency and productivity-routine tasks can be automated by AI, freeing up human labor for more intricate, innovative, and strategic endeavors. This has the potential to greatly increase an organization's overall productivity and efficiency, (ii) **Data-driven decision-making-**AI's capacity to handle and evaluate enormous volumes of data can offer management and labor union decision-makers insightful information. Making better informed and impartial decisions in domains such as policymaking, remuneration, and workforce planning is essential, (iii) **Improved fairness and** reduced bias-AI systems, when developed and used appropriately, can aid in minimizing human bias in a variety of processes, such as hiring, performance reviews, and pay decisions. This may help promote more fair work practices, (iv) **Personalized employee experience:** AI can make it possible to take more individualized approaches to employee engagement, training, and development [11, 13]. AI can assist in customizing experiences to each employee's distinct needs and goals by evaluating individual preferences and performance data, (v) **Enhanced compliance and risk management-**AI-powered monitoring and analysis can assist businesses in adhering to labour laws and regulations, lowering the possibility of expensive infractions and court cases, (vi) **Improved** workplace safety—to improve overall workplace safety, AI systems can monitor working conditions, anticipate possible safety hazards, and notify management to take preventive action, (vii) **Enhanced communication and collaboration**-AI-powered solutions can breakdown organizational silos and promote a more connected workforce by facilitating improved communication and collaboration. Even though these advantages are substantial, it is crucial to remember that achieving them requires careful AI system design, execution, and continuous management.

4.5 Challenges and Ethical Considerations

Although AI has much to do in the field of labour and industrial relations, there are many obstacles to overcome and ethical issues to consider when implementing it. Among the crucial concerns are the following: Concerns about AI's potential to automate jobs and displace workers are among the most urgent concerns. AI has the potential to significantly disrupt traditional employment patterns, which could exacerbate social tensions and income inequality even though it might also open up new job opportunities. AI is frequently used in workforce management, which involves gathering and examining a large amount of employee data. This increases data security, privacy, and the possibility of personal information being misused. While AI has the potential to lessen human bias, poorly built or trained AI systems have the potential to reinforce or even magnify preexisting biases in areas such as hiring, performance reviews, and pay decisions [14]. Many AI systems function as "black boxes," making it challenging to comprehend and justify their decision-making processes. This is especially true of systems built on intricate machine learning algorithms. Trust and accountability issues may result from this lack of transparency. The growing prevalence of AI in the workplace has the potential to exacerbate existing disparities by expanding the skills gap between workers who understand AI and those who do not. Employees who must interact with or be managed by AI systems on a regular basis may experience issues with job satisfaction and quality of work, as these systems proliferate in the workplace. In the workplace, AI systems may be asked to make morally challenging decisions or to support their decision-makers. Ensuring that these systems are in line with ethical standards and human values is a major challenge. Legal and regulatory challenges: As AI technology develops quickly, legal and regulatory frameworks may not keep up, leading to uncertainty about matters such as worker rights, liability, and compliance. Ethical decision-making: In the workplace, AI systems may be asked to make morally challenging decisions or to support their decision-makers. Ensuring that these systems are in line with ethical standards and human values is a major challenge. It is anticipated that AI will permeate more deeply into workforce management functions such as hiring, training, performance reviews, and strategic planning [15, 16]. Increased data-driven decision-making and more individualized employee experiences are anticipated outcomes of this integration. AI is predicted to replace repetitive and routine tasks in the workplace, meaning that jobs will change and require more skills to work alongside AI. Skills such as creativity, emotional intelligence, critical thinking, and complex problem-solving may fall under this category. There will likely be an increased focus on developing ethical frameworks and governance structures for AI in the workplace. This may involve the creation of new roles such as AI ethics officers and the establishment of AI ethics committees within organizations. Instead of being intended for replacement, future AI systems are likely to be created with human-AI collaboration in mind. This cooperative strategy might help allay worries about employment displacement and improve AI's general efficacy in the workplace. AI-powered solutions that provide customized learning experiences on the basis of individual needs, preferences, and career goals are likely to play a larger role in individualized employee training and development. It is anticipated that developments in AI and machine learning will increase the accuracy and application of predictive analytics in areas such as labour market trends, employee turnover, and workforce planning. With the ability to provide scenario modelling and data-driven insights to support negotiations between labor unions and employers, AI tools may find their way into collective bargaining processes. The emergence of new laws and legal frameworks to address issues such as algorithmic bias, privacy concerns related to AI, and the effect of AI on employment rights should be anticipated as AI becomes more prevalent in the workplace. The integration and consequences of AI in labour and industrial relations are anticipated to differ considerably among nations and areas, depending on variables such as technological frameworks, legal frameworks, and cultural perspectives on AI.

4.6 Continued Debate on the Societal Impact of AI

AI in the workplace has wider societal ramifications and will likely continue to be the focus of policy talks and debates. These ramifications include how AI affects social security systems, income distribution, and the nature of work itself. It will be essential for all parties involved—employers, workers, labour unions, legislators, and AI developers—to maintain constant communication and cooperation as these trends develop. This will make it easier to ensure that the advancement and application of AI in labour and industrial relations are in line with ethical standards, societal values, and the objective of establishing just, fruitful, and satisfying work environments. The incorporation of AI into labour and industrial relations is signified as a paradigm shift in how employment, work, and the relationship between employers and workers are viewed. As this essay has shown, AI has enormous potential to increase productivity, facilitate better decision-making, and produce more engaging and customized work environments. AI has the potential to revolutionize almost every facet of labour relations, ranging from expediting the hiring process to enhancing workforce planning and enabling more successful collective bargaining [17]. However, several difficulties are associated with the use of AI in this field. It is important to carefully consider issues such as algorithmic bias, job displacement, privacy concerns, and the potential to exacerbate existing inequalities.

AI is a major paradigm shift in the constantly changing field of labour relations concerning collective bargaining processes [18]. AI has become a potent instrument for improving the efficacy, efficiency, and fairness of negotiations, as unions and employers address more complicated economic realities, technology breakthroughs, and shifting workforce dynamics. The potential of AI to revolutionize conventional practices, offer data-driven insights, and produce more equitable results for workers and organizations is examined in this study, which delves into the complex role of AI in collective bargaining.

The introduction of AI into collective bargaining is a real revolution in labour negotiations for the twenty-first century, not just a technical advancement. AI uses natural language processing, machine learning algorithms, and predictive analytics.

This research explores the different ways in which AI is used in collective bargaining, ranging from data analysis and strategy development to real-time negotiation support and agreement monitoring. Practical applications of AI in labour negotiations will be explored via several case studies, highlighting both achievements and difficulties. The ethical issues that arise when using AI will also be discussed, along with the metrics used to assess its efficacy in this situation. It is essential to recognize that AI is not a magic bullet for every problem with collective bargaining, as this difficult terrain is negotiated. Instead, it is viewed as a potent instrument that, when applied wisely and morally, can enhance human decision-making, encourage more cooperative bargaining, and possibly result in more long-lasting agreements that are advantageous to both employers and employees [19]. At this critical juncture in industrial relations history, employers, unions, legislators, and technologists must have meaningful conversations to guarantee that AI becomes a driver of positive change in the workplace.

4.7 Case Studies

Let us look at a few case studies that illustrate the potential advantages and difficulties of AI in labour and industrial relations to gain a better understanding of its practical applications:

4.7.1 Case Study 1: AI-Powered HR Platform of IBM

Watson Career Coach is an AI-powered HR platform created by IBM that uses machine learning to provide employees with individualized career advice. The system evaluates a worker's qualifications, experience, and aspirations for her career before recommending possible career routes within the business. It also suggests jobs and training courses that are pertinent. The benefits are, i.e., (i) individualized professional growth for staff members, (ii) increased mobility and retention of talent within the company, and (iii) data-driven perspectives for organizing the workforce. The challenges are as follows: (i) employee privacy and data security need to be preserved; (ii) ensuring that the AI system's recommendations are impartial and that AI-driven advice is balanced with human judgment when making career decisions [20].

4.7.2 Case Study 2: AI Recruiting Tool of Amazon

To automate the resume screening process, Amazon created a recruiting tool in 2014 that was powered by AI. However, the business found that the system was biased against female applicants—especially those applying for technical positions. This was a result of the AI training on hiring records from the past, which revealed gender biases from the tech industry's past. In this case, the benefits are (i) the possibility of improved efficiency in the rescreening process and (ii) the ability to swiftly handle a high volume of applications. Challenges include (i) bias in algorithms that replicate and magnify past discrimination, (ii) transparency issues with the AI decision-making procedure, and (iii) negative impacts on diversity and inclusion efforts [21].

4.7.3 Case Study 3: AI-Driven Recruitment Process of Unilevers

Unilever has introduced an AI-powered hiring procedure for entry-level jobs. Throughout the process, candidates receive real-time feedback, submit video interviews that are analysed by AI for language and facial expressions, and play games based on neuroscience to gauge their aptitude. The benefits are (i) shorter hiring times and lower hiring costs, (ii) a more varied pool of candidates, and (iii) better applicant experience through prompt feedback.

The challenges are as follows: (i) addressing privacy and data use concerns in video analysis, (ii) guaranteeing the validity and fairness of AI-based assessments, and (iii) balancing AI evaluations with human judgment in hiring decisions [22].

4.7.4 Case Study 4: AI-Powered Workforce Planning of Siemens

For workforce planning, Siemens has created an AI system called Future Sight. The system uses data from both internal and external sources to forecast future skill needs, identify possible skill gaps, and suggest workforce development tactics [23]. The benefits are (i) a proactive strategy for meeting upcoming skill requirements, (ii) the use of data to inform workforce planning decisions, and (iii) better workforce capability alignment with business strategies. Challenges include (i) ensuring the dependability and accuracy of AI forecasts, (ii) addressing possible worries about job insecurity among staff members, and (iii) weighing AI recommendations against human strategic planning knowledge.

4.7.5 *Case Study 5: Union AI Guidelines of the UNI Global*

Guidelines for the moral application of AI in the workplace have been created by the international federation of trade unions, UNI Global Union. These guidelines cover topics such as accountability, transparency, and how AI affects jobs and working conditions.

The benefits are (i) the proactive involvement of labour unions in forming AI policies, (ii) a focus on defending employees' rights in the AI era, and (iii) a framework for discussing AI implementation between employers and employees. Challenges include (i) ensuring that guidelines are widely adopted and followed, (ii) adapting to quickly changing AI technologies, and (iii) finding a balance between worker safety and innovation.

These case studies highlight the intricate interplay between the advantages and difficulties of using AI for labour and industrial relations. They emphasize how crucial it is for the effective application of AI in the workplace to consider ethical issues, meticulous planning, and constant communication among all parties involved [24].

4.8 Future Prospects

There are a number of exciting new developments in store for collective bargaining as AI technologies continue to advance and our knowledge of their uses grows. Future AI systems may be able to manage some aspects of negotiations independently, perhaps with the assistance of predetermined guidelines and goals set by human negotiators. These AI agents could handle routine matters, freeing human negotiators to focus on more complex issues. The speed and intricacy of scenario modelling and predictive analytics in collective bargaining could be significantly increased by the integration of quantum computing and AI. This might make it possible to analyse in real time a vast number of variables and possible results. Emotional progress Affective computing and AI may enable systems to recognize and react to negotiators' emotional states. This could be useful in reducing conflict and determining when to reach a compromise [25]. Blockchain technology and AI may be combined to create intelligent smart contracts that automatically carry out agreements based on predetermined criteria, improving transparency and lowering conflict. AI systems may facilitate a move toward more ongoing negotiation procedures in which the terms of contracts are dynamically modified in response to data analysis of labor demands, business performance, and economic conditions that occur in real-time. Cutting-edge VR technologies have the potential to produce immersive, AI-powered negotiation environments that facilitate remote, highly productive, and engaging bargaining sessions. It may become customary to create AI ethics boards composed of a variety of stakeholders to supervise the creation and application of AI in collective bargaining procedures. While these possibilities are exciting, they also highlight the need for careful implementation and continued ethical thought to guarantee that AI fairly serves the interests of employers and employees. With the potential to improve efficiency, fairness, and negotiation outcomes, the incorporation of AI into collective bargaining represents a significant evolution in labour relations. The case studies and analysis in this chapter serve as examples of how AI tools can offer insightful information, facilitate data-driven decision-making, and assist in locating original solutions to challenging labor-related problems. However, there are additional difficulties and moral issues with using AI in this situation that need to be properly considered [26]. Data privacy, algorithmic bias, openness, and equal access to technology are issues that require constant attention and cooperative problem-solving from all parties involved. A framework for evaluating AI effects and directing future advancements in collective bargaining is provided by the metrics suggested for its assessment. It will be essential to periodically review and improve these metrics as these technologies develop further to ensure that they fully account for the spectrum of AI impacts on labour negotiations and results. There is a plethora of exciting future possibilities for AI in collective bargaining. These technologies, which range from sophisticated AI negotiation agents to the integration of emotional AI and quantum computing, have the power to completely change the field of labour relations. However, to fully realize this potential, a careful and sensible strategy that upholds the core ideas of collective bargaining is needed while leveraging the power of AI to generate more reasonable and supportable labour settlements [27].

In summary, using AI for collective bargaining is a revolutionary process that affects fundamental elements of the working–employer relationship rather than merely being a technological advance. To guarantee that AI is a tool for empowerment and justice in the workplace, cooperation among all stakeholders—unions, employers, technologists, and legislators—is essential as this new territory is navigated. By doing so, AI can be used to build a future for labour relations that are more effective, fair, and sensitive to the demands of businesses and employees in our quickly evolving global economy.

4.9 The Role of Unions in an AI-Powered Workplace

Workers can utilize collective bargaining as a potent instrument to ensure that AI and algorithmic technology improve their jobs rather than worsen their working conditions. Indeed, workers have secured only a number of contracts that give them authority over how AI will affect their jobs. With the advent of AI and machine learning technologies, nonroutine jobs such as producing code and human-sounding prose and scheduling are being automated in novel ways, which is expected to increase productivity for some employees. It makes sense, however, that many people are anxious that they will not be able to take advantage of AI technology [28]. According to research from the Economic Policy Institute, even while worker productivity has increased over the previous few decades, the gains have gone "everywhere but the pay checks of the bottom 80% of workers". Legislators need to reinforce the freedom to form a union and participate in collective bargaining to supplement these rights, as demonstrated by the instances established by unions. Lawmakers should consider taking more legislative action in addition to utilizing current worker protections to guarantee that workers benefit from the application of AI in their place of employment. The application of the current law can shield employees from some of the possible risks associated with hiring and using AI in the workplace.

In a 2022 letter on electronic hiring and algorithmic management, Jennifer Abruzzo, the chief counsel for the National Labour Relations Board (NLRB), argued that many of the AI innovations employed by companies are already prohibited under legal standards. She also pushed the committee to approve a framework that would shield employees from monitoring and algorithmic management that interferes with regulated activities. The Equal Employment Opportunity Commission issued technical assistance in 2021 on compliance with the Americans with Disabilities Act and algorithmic methods for making choices in hiring and employment as part of a larger initiative on algorithmic equality. Lawmakers can also consider how current legislation already controls the application of AI across the Biden administration. Congress and administration policymakers need to address workers' needs first when they respond to the use and development of AI. They should do this by enacting laws that support workers' ability to form unions, guarantee that AI enhances rather than replaces workers, prepares the workforce for the adoption of AI, and assists in addressing the needs of displaced workers. Legislators in Congress are pushing for laws that would shield workers from some of the risks posed by AI, such as the Stop Spying Bosses Act and the No Robot Bosses Act. Algorithmic management platforms have been implemented for duties ranging from hiring and training to planning and appraisal reviews, as well as expanding the automation of tasks, with tasks previously handled by humans being managed by AI—no matter how unintelligent—as organizations become increasingly dependent on technology.

These technologies are frequently marketed as removing human subjectivity from decision-making and enhancing productivity and efficiency. However, algorithms far too frequently reproduce and amplify bias and inequality, escalate calls for increased worker productivity, and utilize employee data in harmful and covert ways. Today's workforce is largely unaware of the data being collected about them or how they are used to evaluate their performance because automated, proprietary systems from a third party make these decisions and do not reveal their inner workings. This can result in unclear hiring and firing decisions. Owing to an algorithmic performance evaluation system that emphasizes student test results over all other factors, more than 200 teachers in Washington were fired in 2011 for doing poorly, sometimes even though they had received excellent personal ratings. This methodology, however, was defective since it failed to account for factors such as poverty or learning difficulties that are outside the control of teachers. Certain automated management systems use discriminatory practices against workers or job candidates that would be against the law if performed by humans. Examples of these systems include blood vessel systems that reject applicants who are statistically more likely to be pregnant or sick or AI evaluation systems that associate worker productivity with personal attributes such as gender, race, or weight. It is nearly difficult to establish prejudice if workers do not have exposure to the algorithms that companies utilize. Most applications of AI in the workplace increase the power of employers. AI's ability to disempower workers through surveillance, algorithmic management, downsizing and reassignment has been widely seen as a technology that employers use more than workers do on the job [29]. However, AI is a technology designed to disrupt the link between human decisions and analytical processes. The notion that AI technologies developed in relation to customer service are fundamentally incompatible with the project of creating a workforce is being examined. The potential for these technologies to be rethought and reworked as tools of solidarity and activism is also being considered.

For unions considering the use of AI for empowerment, three key points emerged:

4.9.1 Redesigning Technology to Match Values

Noncommercial versions of IBM Watson were developed for commercial usage, with the expectation that organizations would use it to "flow the flow" and minimize it. as much interpersonal communication as possible in-service transactions. However, according to the organizational model, unions have different relationships with their members. By leveraging technology to initiate and deepen interactions with members rather than cutting them short, they seek to let members exercise collective power in the workplace. The Utility Workers Union (UWU) extensively reconfigured the chat so that the application supported this philosophy. Instead of the original "information delivery" approach, it changed the programming of the chat. Members continued to obtain relevant information, but it was presented with a perspective that acknowledged the inherent relationship between power dynamics in the workplace and the implementation of work rules. This strategy established the foundation for upcoming companies.

4.9.2 Workers Involved in the Process of Design

Much preparatory effort is needed to develop a chatbot's "brain" so that it can respond to queries in an empowering way. Initially, the union approached this task as a single job, but it was subsequently determined that it would be more beneficial to split the work into two categories: "administrators," who were union representatives tasked with gathering chatbot data, and "experts," who served as workplace delegates and provided answers to queries [30]. Employees on both ends of the dialogue felt empowered by this division of labour from the back office, and new leaders who felt at ease participating in advocacy in a digital environment emerged.

4.9.3 AI Assists Unions in Workplace Mapping

The talk functioned as more than simply a means of exchanging questions and answers; it also gave the organizers insight into the main concerns that workers had and who was posing them in the workplace. Having this type of map made it easier for organizers to become ready for site visits. They were also highly helpful in fields such as home care, where employees did not share a physical workspace, enabling the union to organize and bring up issues that might have been hard to comprehend otherwise. "It revolutionizes the ability to have online conversations through the program and through the web portal," a UWU representative stated. It is the capacity to seamlessly find issues, activists, and future leaders through online enquiries. All things considered, it appears that AI unions may be advantageous, but only if they are prepared to intentionally reinterpret it in terms of organisational philosophy and regard it as an extra instrument for organizing people as opposed to an expense or labor-saving technique. The main objective of the publication "The New Role of Trade Unions in the Age of Artificial Intelligence" is to provide a comprehensive, in-depth analysis of the evolution of the role and importance of trade unions in the context of the development of AI. This study aims to bridge the gap between the study of technology and working life, offering a fresh perspective on how AI shapes the workplace and how it affects unions [31]. It aims to provide unions with actionable recommendations to navigate the changes driven by AI. Advancing Worker-Centric AI: This book aims to promote a worker-centric approach to AI. It advocates the active involvement of trade unions in the governance of AI ensures that AI serves the interests of workers and promotes fair and just workplaces. By achieving these goals, the New Role of Unions in the Age of AI hopes to make a significant contribution to the literature on AI and work. It aims to set the agenda for future research in this critical area and shape the debate on trade unions in the age of AI [32].

4.10 AI-Assisted Dispute Resolution Mechanism

AI is becoming a more potent weapon at the dynamic nexus of law and technology, with the potential to completely change several facets of judicial practice. In the domain of dispute resolution, AI has a particularly significant impact. AI is becoming a more potent weapon at the dynamic nexus of law and technology, with the potential to completely change several facets of legal practice. In the domain of dispute resolution, AI has a particularly significant impact. Traditionally, dispute resolution processes such as mediation and arbitration have relied heavily on human judgment and communication. However, with AI, these practices change significantly. The ability of AI to process massive amounts of data and learn from patterns offers new opportunities to resolve disputes more effectively and efficiently. From automating routine tasks to predicting outcomes and even acting as mediators or arbitrators, AI shapes the dispute resolution environment [33]. In this section, the role of AI in dispute resolution is explored, and how mediation and arbitration practices are changed by AI is examined. The potential benefits and challenges of AI in this context are explored, emerging ethical and legal aspects are discussed, and the future of dispute resolution in the age of AI is considered. As this new frontier is navigated, valuable insights are aimed at helping clients understand and leverage the potential of AI in dispute resolution.

4.10.1 Understanding AI and Its Capabilities

Artificial intelligence (AI) is a general phrase that describes the use of machines, particularly computer systems, to simulate processes related to human intelligence. Learning, reasoning, problem-solving, perception, and language comprehension are some of these mechanisms. AI is not a single concept; rather, it is a collection of tools and techniques that let computers mimic human thought processes and behavior. Machine learning, which uses algorithms that automatically become better with practice, is a crucial application of artificial intelligence. Without the need for specialized programming, machine learning algorithms employ statistical approaches to learn from data and spot patterns to provide judgments. This ability to learn from data makes machine learning particularly effective in data-intensive fields such as law. Natural language processing, or NLP, is another type of artificial intelligence that combines computer communication with human language [34]. The field of natural language processing (NLP) makes it possible for computers to comprehend, interpret, and generate human language. This eliminates the need for coding when communicating with users. NLP can analyse legal texts, extract relevant information and even create legal documents. The capabilities of AI are vastly and constantly expanding. In the context of legal processes, AI can automate routine tasks, analyse large amounts of data to gain insight, predict outcomes on the basis of historical data, and facilitate decision-making [35]. AI can, for example, automate the review of documents, predict the outcome of legal disputes, assist in legal investigations, and even act as a mediator or arbitrator in dispute resolution. However, the capabilities of AI extend beyond these current applications. As technology continues to advance, legal processes are poised to be transformed by AI in ways that can only be imagined. In the following sections, how AI is used in dispute resolution is explored, with a particular focus on its role in mediation and conciliation.

4.10.2 The Current State of Dispute Resolution

Dispute resolution is an integral part of the legal system and provides mechanisms for parties to resolve disputes without going to court. The two most common dispute resolution methods are mediation and arbitration. A third party who is impartial, known as a mediator, assists conflicting parties in coming to a mutually agreeable resolution through the mediation procedure [36]. The mediator facilitates communication, promotes understanding and helps the parties find and clarify possible solutions. Through the flexible and private mediation process, participants can decide how their issues will be resolved. In contrast, arbitration is an official procedure wherein a neutral third person, known as the arbitrator, hears arguments from both sides and considers the relevant evidence before rendering a decision in a dispute. Arbitration may be binding or nonbinding depending on the agreement of the parties. It is often quicker and less formal than a court process but still provides a final resolution to the dispute. Despite the advantages of these traditional methods of dispute resolution, they also have challenges and limitations. Both mediation and arbitration can be time-consuming and expensive, especially in complex disputes. They require the involvement of experienced mediators or arbitrators, who may only occasionally be readily available. In addition, the effectiveness of these methods often depends on the willingness and ability of the parties to negotiate in good faith, which is only sometimes guaranteed. Additionally, while mediation and arbitration can be more efficient than litigation, they still involve a significant amount of manual labor [37]. This includes reviewing documents, conducting research, scheduling meetings, and drafting contracts or resolutions. These tasks can be labor intensive and time consuming, increasing the cost and duration of the dispute resolution process. Faced with these challenges, there is a growing interest in using technology to improve the effectiveness and efficiency of dispute resolution. This is where AI comes into play. In the following sections, how AI is used to transform mediation and arbitration practices is explored, with new ways to resolve industrial disputes being provided.

4.10.3 AI-Assisted Communication and Negotiation

AI can facilitate communication and negotiation in mediation in several ways. For example, natural language processing (NLP) can analyse interactions between parties and identify patterns, emotions, and critical issues. This can help mediators understand the dynamics of disputes and develop more effective resolution strategies. AI can also be helpful in negotiations. For example, AI algorithms can model negotiation scenarios, predict outcomes, and recommend optimal negotiation strategies. By doing so, the parties may be able to decide more wisely and come to advantageous accords. Self-executing contracts with terms encoded directly into the code are known as smart contracts, and they are driven by blockchain technology. They eliminate the need for mediators and conflict settlement by automatically upholding the contract's obligations. In mediation, smart contracts can be used to implement and monitor the terms of the mediation agreement, which ensures compliance and reduces the risk of future disputes.

4.11 AI in Arbitration and Predictive Analytics

As in brokerage, AI is starting to transform the brokerage landscape. From predictive analytics to AI arbitrators, the use of AI in mediation is expanding the boundaries of dispute resolution. One of the most important applications of AI in mediation is predictive analytics. AI algorithms can analyse past brokerage cases to identify patterns and trends, predict outcomes and provide strategic insights [38]. Predictive analytics can be used, for example, to estimate the probability of success in arbitration, estimate a potential award and even predict the behaviour of arbitrators based on their past decisions. AI can also automate and improve the document review and evidence analysis process in arbitration. AI technology can swiftly and precisely analyse extensive document quantities, detect pertinent details, and pinpoint inconsistencies or irregularities. This can reduce time, lower expenses, and enhance the quality of evidence showcased in arbitration. The idea of AI arbitrators is the most advanced use of AI in arbitration. AI systems are capable of overseeing arbitration processes, examining evidence, and rendering judgments. Although mostly theoretical and sparking ethical and legal debates, this signifies a potential change in arbitration methods [39]. AI usage in arbitration provides various advantages. It has the potential to improve the efficiency and cost-effectiveness of arbitration, offer fresh perspectives and tactics, and could result in more reliable and anticipated results.

Predictive analytics applies certain data manipulation techniques to preexisting datasets to find novel trends and patterns (Fig. 4.3). Future results and trends are then predicted via these patterns and trends. The performance and trends for the future can be forecasted via predictive analysis. Generally, six steps are involved in the process of predictive analysis.

(i) Problem Definition: Describing the problem that needs to be solved before delving into the data is necessary. It is crucial to set the objective in a larger framework. Therefore, defining the goals, deliverables, scope, and necessary data is the first stage.

(ii) Data collection: Data gathering is performed during the collecting phase. Data from many sources are prepared for analysis through predictive analytics. To train a predictive model, one needs correct and pertinent data. Make sure that the information is correct and pertinent to the issue at hand. For more comprehensive findings, several forms of historical and present data from a range of sources, such as call centre records, transactional systems, and sensors, are incorporated.

(iii) Data Analysis: Existing datasets and their potential applications in enhancing predictions and achieving goals should be ascertained by a data analyst. Prior to entering the data into the predictive analytics model, identifying any issues by understanding the methods and motivations behind the data collection can be helpful.

(iv) Statistical analysis: After the data have been gathered, they must be sorted to identify the most pertinent information. One cleans the data and performs a

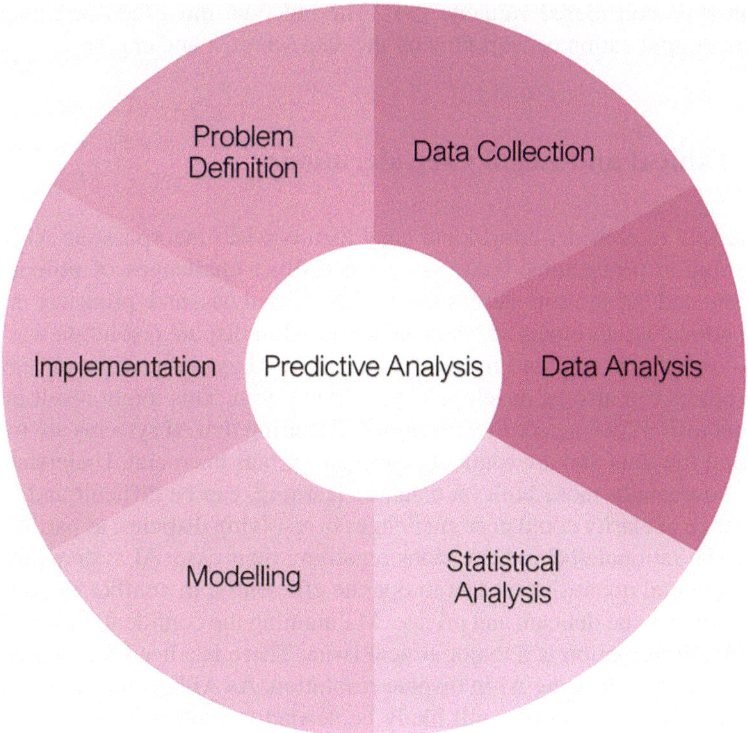

Fig. 4.3 Process of predictive analytics

quality check at this phase. There are several reasons why quality control and data purification are crucial. Data relevance is also checked while cleaning. In the event that any of your data are erroneous, corrupted, or duplicated, ensure that the data are formatted correctly. Using proper statistical tools, statistical analysis involves the quantitative testing and validation of assumptions [40–43].

(v) Modelling: In this step, it should be evident which of the many impact factors that have been identified and examined is best fitted by a prediction model. The predictive model is developed, tested, and validated during the model construction stage. Dividing the data into a training set and a testing set is necessary to train the model. When assessing the model's performance, the testing set is utilized to gauge how well the machine learning algorithm performs. As this can result in poor performance on fresh data, ensuring that the model is balanced with respect to the training set is imperative. One can employ regularization, early halting strategies, and cross-validation to prevent overfitting.

(vi) Implementation: The predictive model is deployed and used on fresh data once model testing and validation are finished. Reports and findings are obtained, and then the information is used to automate decision-making. Only when novel predictive analytics insight significantly alters the course of the process can it be considered valuable [44]. The outcome must then be linked to the proper application or workflow by the data scientist and engineer.

4.12 Ethical and Legal Considerations

It is essential to consider ethical and legal factors when incorporating AI into conflict resolution procedures. Addressing the distinct challenges of utilizing AI in mediation and arbitration necessitates careful analysis and proactive handling. Several ethical issues emerged when the use of AI in dispute resolution was considered. Knowledge is acquired from information by AI systems; if the information is biased, biases can also be developed by the AI system. This might result in inequitable conclusions during conflict resolution. Ensuring that AI systems are trained on varied and fair data and are routinely checked for bias is crucial. Understanding AI systems, especially those built on machine learning, can be difficult and complex. The absence of clarity could pose challenges in resolving disputes, as parties deserve to know the rationale behind decisions regarding their case. AI systems frequently need substantial quantities of data to operate efficiently. In conflict resolution, this information may be delicate and private. Maintaining the confidentiality and protection of this information is a major ethical issue. There is a need for clearer regulatory frameworks for using AI in dispute resolution. As AI becomes more prevalent in this field, new regulations will likely be needed to govern its use. Determining liability in the event of mistakes or harm caused by an AI system can be complicated. The question of whether the creator of the AI system, the user, or the AI system itself is responsible is raised. These liability issues must be addressed as AI becomes part of dispute resolution processes. The legal standing of decisions made by an AI system functioning as a mediator or arbitrator is questioned [45]. The implementation of these decisions like those made by human mediators or arbitrators is also considered. These legal questions are crucial and must be addressed. Navigating the integration of AI into dispute resolution requires addressing ethical and legal considerations. In this way, it can be guaranteed that the application of AI in conflict resolution is not only efficient but also open and considerate of the rights of every party involved.

4.13 The Future of AI in Dispute Resolution

In the future, the role of AI in resolving disputes is ready to grow and change. There are some forecasts regarding how AI could continue to change dispute resolution and the role of legal professionals in this developing environment. With the continued advancement of AI technology, predictive analytics will become more advanced. AI systems have the ability to analyse increasingly intricate data and produce more precise predictions. This might result in better decision-making during conflict resolution. AI systems offer guidance and suggestions grounded in a thorough examination of previous instances, legal doctrines, and pertinent information. Fully automated dispute resolution systems may become more prevalent in the future. These systems can handle the complete dispute resolution process, from start to finish, without the need for any human intervention. This could improve the effectiveness and availability of resolving conflicts, particularly for minor disputes that could be too costly for traditional methods. AI will continue to play a role in helping with mediation and arbitration. AI technology can assist mediators and arbitrators by automating routine tasks, providing data-driven insights, and facilitating communication and negotiation. As these tools continue to develop, they will become increasingly important in resolving disputes. In this changing environment, the responsibilities of legal professionals will also shift. Legal professionals are expected to cooperate with AI instead of being replaced by it, using its ability to improve their work [46]. Legal professionals need to acquire fresh skills and knowledge, such as understanding AI technology and its effects on law and ethics. Legal professionals will have a significant effect on the development of AI in settling disputes. They must confront ethical and legal obstacles, support the just and clear application of AI, and assist in creating regulatory structures.

4.14 Conclusions

In this chapter, it was discovered that the dispute resolution industry is ready for transformation by AI. AI provides various tools and techniques that can improve communication and negotiation in mediation and automate document review and evidence analysis in arbitration, leading to more efficient, accessible, and effective dispute resolution. Nevertheless, the incorporation of AI in resolving disputes poses substantial ethical and legal hurdles. Concerns regarding bias, transparency, privacy, and liability must be thoroughly considered to guarantee fairness, transparency, and respect for the rights of all parties in utilizing AI for dispute resolution. In the future, AI is expected to have more significant involvement in conflict resolution. With the progress of AI technology, there will be increased opportunities for resolving conflicts via tools such as predictive analytics and fully automated dispute resolution systems. In this changing environment, legal professionals must be willing to adjust and develop. They must acquire fresh expertise and information, confront the ethical and legal dilemmas that surface, and have a significant impact on moulding the future of AI in dispute resolution. AI has great potential to transform dispute resolution. As this uncharted territory is ventured into, the way disputes are resolved can be redefined, ensuring that they are efficient, accessible, and fair. By accepting AI and its potential, a future for resolving disputes that is both technologically advanced and based on justice and the rule of law can be created.

References

1. Vaughan-Whitehead, D., & Vazquez-Alvarez, R. (2019). Convergence in the EU: What role for industrial relations? In *Towards convergence in Europe* (pp. 1–34). Edward Elgar Publishing.
2. Addison, J. T., & Teixeira, P. (2019). Strikes, employee workplace representation, unionism, and industrial relations quality in European establishments. *Journal of Economic Behavior & Organization, 159*, 109–133.
3. Kurt, R. (2019). Industry 4.0 in terms of industrial relations and its impacts on labour life. *Procedia Computer Science, 158*, 590–601.
4. Ackers, P. (2020). Industrial relations and the limits of the state: Can a left Labour government resurrect comprehensive sectoral collective bargaining and restore trade union power? *The Political Quarterly, 91*(1), 173–181.
5. Cooke, F. L., Xu, J., & Bian, H. (2019). The prospect of decent work, decent industrial relations and decent social relations in China: Towards a multilevel and multidisciplinary approach. *The International Journal of Human Resource Management, 30*(1), 122–155.
6. Stuart, M. (2019). The industrial relations of training and development. In *The Wiley handbook of vocational education and training* (pp. 165–185). Wiley.
7. Gardawski, J., & Towalski, R. (2019). Labor market and industrial relations. In *Diversity of patchwork capitalism in Central and Eastern Europe* (Vol. 84). Routledge.
8. Lin, M. Z. N., Tanaka, M., Minni, V., Nguyen, H., Thet, K. S., & Macchiavello, R. (2019). *Industrial relations and workplace communication in Myanmar garment sector*. International Growth Centre.
9. Kaine, S., & Boersma, M. (2018). Women, work and industrial relations in Australia in 2017. *Journal of Industrial Relations, 60*(3), 317–336.
10. Özkiziltan, D. (2019). Authoritarian neoliberalism in AKP's Turkey: An industrial relations perspective. *Industrial Relations Journal, 50*(3), 218–239.
11. Kochan, T. A. (2019). Industrial relations and human resource policy in Korea: Options for continued reform. In *Korea's political economy* (pp. 663–697). Routledge.
12. Lee, T. L., & Tapia, M. (2021). Confronting race and other social identity erasures: The case for critical industrial relations theory. *ILR Review, 74*(3), 637–662.
13. Zhang, C., & Lu, Y. (2021). Study on artificial intelligence: The state of the art and future prospects. *Journal of Industrial Information Integration, 23*, 100224.
14. Huang, M. H., & Rust, R. T. (2018). Artificial intelligence in service. *Journal of Service Research, 21*(2), 155–172.
15. Ertel, W. (2018). *Introduction to artificial intelligence*. Springer.
16. Brynjolfsson, E., Rock, D., & Syverson, C. (2019). Artificial intelligence and the modern productivity paradox. *The Economics of Artificial Intelligence: An Agenda, 23*, 23–57.
17. Jarrahi, M. H. (2018). Artificial intelligence and the future of work: Human-AI symbiosis in organizational decision making. *Business Horizons, 61*(4), 577–586.
18. Dwivedi, Y. K., Hughes, L., Ismagilova, E., Aarts, G., Coombs, C., Crick, T., … Williams, M. D. (2021). Artificial Intelligence (AI): Multidisciplinary perspectives on emerging challenges, opportunities, and agenda for research, practice and policy. *International Journal of Information Management, 57*, 101994.
19. Syam, N., & Sharma, A. (2018). Waiting for a sales renaissance in the fourth industrial revolution: Machine learning and artificial intelligence in sales research and practice. *Industrial Marketing Management, 69*, 135–146.
20. Cockburn, I. M., Henderson, R., & Stern, S. (2018). *The impact of artificial intelligence on innovation* (Vol. 24449). National Bureau of Economic Research.
21. Kennedy, N. (2018). *The industrialization of intelligence: Mind and machine in the modern age*. Routledge.
22. Bughin, J., Hazan, E., Sree Ramaswamy, P., Dc, W., & Chu, M. (2017). *Artificial intelligence the next digital frontier*. McKinsey Global Institute.

23. Campbell, R. W. (2023). Artificial intelligence in the courtroom: The delivery of justice in the age of machine learning. *Revista Forumul Judecatorilor, 15*. https://doi.org/10.2139/ssrn.4425791
24. Glikson, E., & Woolley, A. W. (2020). Human trust in artificial intelligence: Review of empirical research. *Academy of Management Annals, 14*(2), 627–660.
25. Budhwar, P., Malik, A., De Silva, M. T., & Thevisuthan, P. (2022). Artificial intelligence–challenges and opportunities for international HRM: A review and research agenda. *The International Journal of Human Resource Management, 33*(6), 1065–1097.
26. Chaudhry, M. A., & Kazim, E. (2022). Artificial Intelligence in Education (AIEd): A high-level academic and industry note 2021. *AI and Ethics, 2*(1), 157–165.
27. Chowdhury, S., Dey, P., Joel-Edgar, S., Bhattacharya, S., Rodriguez-Espindola, O., Abadie, A., & Truong, L. (2023). Unlocking the value of artificial intelligence in human resource management through AI capability framework. *Human Resource Management Review, 33*(1), 100899.
28. Benbya, H., Davenport, T. H., & Pachidi, S. (2020). Artificial intelligence in organizations: Current state and future opportunities. *MIS Quarterly Executive, 19*(4), 9–21.
29. Raisch, S., & Krakowski, S. (2021). Artificial intelligence and management: The automation–augmentation paradox. *Academy of Management Review, 46*(1), 192–210.
30. Popa-Roman, G., & Faghian, C. (2024). How artificial intelligence (AI) can influence the institutions of collective bargaining and the initiation of collective labour disputes and strikes, as amended by Law No. 367/2022 (as Amended by OUG No. 42/2023). *Revue Européenne Du Droit Social, 65*, 52.
31. Majumder, S., Chowdhury, S., Dey, N., & Santosh, K. C. (2022). Balance your work-life: Personal interactive web-interface. *International Journal of Interactive Multimedia and Artificial Intelligence*. https://doi.org/10.9781/ijimai.2021.08.016
32. Molina, O., Butollo, F., Makó, C., Godino, A., Holtgrewe, U., Illsoe, A., et al. (2023). It takes two to code: A comparative analysis of collective bargaining and artificial intelligence. *Transfer: European Review of Labour and Research, 29*(1), 87–104.
33. De Stefano, V., & Taes, S. (2023). Algorithmic management and collective bargaining. *Transfer: European Review of Labour and Research, 29*(1), 21–36.
34. Ghosh, S., Majumder, S., & Peng, S. L. (2023). An empirical study on adoption of artificial intelligence in human resource management. In *Artificial intelligence techniques in human resource management* (pp. 29–85). Apple Academic Press.
35. Majumder, S., & Dey, N. (2022). Artificial intelligence and knowledge management. In *AI-empowered knowledge management* (pp. 85–100). Springer Singapore.
36. Zeleznikow, J. (2021). Using artificial intelligence to provide intelligent dispute resolution support. *Group Decision and Negotiation, 30*(4), 789–812.
37. Voss, E., & Bertossa, D. (2022). Collective bargaining and digitalization: A global survey of union use of collective bargaining to increase worker control over digitalization. *New England Journal of Public Policy, 34*(1), 10.
38. Cichobłaziński, L., Soares Filho, S., & Ribeiro, L. T. F. (n.d.). *The GPT chat is capable of mediating to prevent strikes? Interview with artificial intelligence*.
39. Maiti, S., & Choi, J. H. (2021). Investigation and implementation of conflict management strategies to minimize conflicts in the construction industry. *International Journal of Construction Management, 21*(4), 337–352.
40. Hodge, S. D., Jr. (2024). Is the use of artificial intelligence in alternative dispute resolution a viable option or wishful thinking? *Pepperdine Dispute Resolution Law Journal, 24*, 91.
41. Labor, A. (2021). Collective bargaining and unions in today's workplace. In *Contemporary nursing E-Book: Issues, trends, & management* (p. 260). Elsevier.
42. Doellgast, V., & Wagner, I. (2022). Collective regulation and the future of work in the digital economy: Insights from comparative employment relations. *Journal of Industrial Relations, 64*(3), 438–460.
43. Majumder, S., & Dey, N. (2022). Knowledge management system. In *AI-empowered knowledge management* (pp. 63–84). Springer Singapore.

44. Liu, M., Zhang, H., & Sui, Y. (2024). Workplace artificial intelligence regulation in China: Between efficiency and social stability. *ILR Review, 77*(5), 813–824.
45. Todolí-Signes, A. (2019). Algorithms, artificial intelligence and automated decisions concerning workers and the risks of discrimination: The necessary collective governance of data protection. *Transfer: European Review of Labour and Research, 25*(4), 465–481.
46. Goyal, U., & Goyal, A. (2023). The evolution and effectiveness of Online Dispute Resolution (ODR) platforms: A comprehensive analysis of ADR in the digital age. Part 2. *Indian Journal of Integrated Research in Law, 3*, 1.

Chapter 5
Legal and Ethical Considerations in AI-Driven IR

5.1 Introduction

Artificial Intelligence (AI) has applications in labour and industrial relations for workforce management, negotiations, dispute resolution, and policymaking. It can be used for everything from delivering advanced analytics for strategic decision-making to automating administrative duties. AI is pertinent to labor and industrial relations because of its capacity to gather and analyze vast volumes of data, identify patterns and trends, and produce predictions or recommendations based on this research. Workforce planning and optimization, performance management and evaluation, compensation and benefits analysis, labour market analysis and forecasting, collective bargaining and negotiations, compliance and risk management, employee engagement and satisfaction, and other related fields can all benefit from this capacity. AI is expected to play a bigger part in labour and industrial relations as it develops, thereby upending preconceived notions about what it means to work and be employed. AI has a wide range of applications in labour and industrial relations. Here are a few major domains where AI is becoming increasingly prevalent [1]. By automating resume screening, interviewing candidates, and even projecting candidate success based on past performance, AI-powered solutions can expedite the hiring process. These technologies can enhance the effectiveness of talent acquisition procedures and lessen prejudice in recruiting decisions. AI systems are capable of analysing worker data to forecast employee attrition, find skill gaps, and optimize employment numbers. This can assist companies in allocating resources, hiring personnel, and providing training with better information. By evaluating numerous variables and seeing trends in employee performance, AI can offer more unbiased and data-driven performance reviews. Fairer evaluations and more focused development strategies may result from this. The systematic field of industrial artificial intelligence (AI) is centred on creating, evaluating, and implementing

S. Majumder, B. Misra, *AI-Empowered Industrial Relations*, Studies in Computational Intelligence 1254, https://doi.org/10.1007/978-3-032-14557-4_5

different machine learning algorithms for industrial applications that have long-term performance.

Modern platforms for sensing, connectivity, and big data analytics when paired with an organised Industrial AI approach will make it possible to integrate computer models and physical systems. In the setting of the Industry 4.0 movement, industrial artificial intelligence (AI) involves the combined application of technologies like the Internet of Things, Cyber-Physical Systems, and Big Data Analytics, where embedded computing devices, smart objects, and the physical environment work together to achieve goals [2]. Numerous sectors including automotive, aerospace, healthcare, semiconductors, energy, transportation, mining, construction, and industrial automation could benefit from utilizing industrial artificial intelligence (AI) to enhance productivity, efficiency, and uptime through analyzing operating conditions' hidden connections. When it comes to predictive maintenance, industrial artificial intelligence (AI) can identify early system alterations, estimate the system's remaining usable life, and further optimize maintenance chores to minimize downtime.

5.2 The Importance of Ethical Development and Use of AI

Ethical AI ensures that the rapid progress of technology upholds human dignity and fundamental social values. This model represents a dynamic and adaptable approach to the proper utilization of technologies such as AI, rather than a rigid set of rules. To ensure the responsible development and implementation of artificial intelligence technology, a range of stakeholders, including engineers and government officials, use a set of principles known as AI ethics. This entails using AI in a way that is sustainable, safe, reliable, and compassionate. People frequently receive personalized recommendations from artificial intelligence, based on things like past searches, purchases, and other online activity [3]. AI significantly affects business through transportation scheduling, inventory control, and product optimization, among other things. Stakeholders, from engineers to government officials, use the set of guiding principles known as AI ethics to ensure that AI technology is produced and used properly.

Bias can be avoided, user privacy and data can be protected, and environmental dangers can be decreased with a strong AI code of ethics. Corporate codes of ethics and government-led regulatory frameworks are the two main ways that AI ethics can be implemented. By addressing ethical AI concerns on a national and international level and creating the foundation for ethical AI in organizations, both approaches support the regulation of AI technology. Beyond academic research and organizations, a wider public is now involved in the discussion of AI ethics. Large tech companies such as Google, IBM, and Meta have put together teams to address ethical concerns arising from gathering vast amounts of data. Simultaneously, academic research has been used by government and intergovernmental organizations to inform the development of regulations and ethics policies. AI ethics have been the subject of a lot of discussion lately. The argument put up for this topic is that humans need to figure out how prevent AI from becoming rogue and putting people in danger. Some of the most recent AI-based systems on the market, such as face recognition software, are already being used by hospitals and law enforcement agencies. However, it's still unclear how these technologies will impact humans in the long run at this point [4]. Alongside technology improvements, social obligations must also advance. It is our duty to think about how these technologies might impact human lives. One must make sure that the choices they make in their profession, whether it be research or development, are morally correct in order to protect humans and machines in the future. Beyond a doubt, AI is changing everything around us. AI is making it possible for machines to analyse data much like people do for the first time. Additionally, ML is evolving at an astounding rate. This might be frightening if we don't know how to control it. But AI will also result in many beneficial advancements. AI has made it possible for humans to drive, diagnose illnesses, and even identify criminals. As a result, AI is a highly contentious subject. People have been debating the future of artificial intelligence (AI) and how it will impact our lives for decades. Some people worry that people won't be able to control AI once it takes over and becomes sentient. Some people think that in order to increase productivity and efficiency, artificial intelligence should be incorporated into more facets of society. People need to understand that artificial intelligence will eventually be used, but there are numerous varieties of AI and different effects they can have on society. Since there isn't a single right solution, people should think about the AI ethics concepts before making their own choice. The ability of a computer or robot to carry out tasks that a human would normally complete is known as artificial intelligence (AI). Creating machines with thought, generalization, meaning-finding, and experience-based learning is referred to by this term frequently [5]. From basic mathematical problem-solving to intricate simulations of human thought processes, the term covers a broad spectrum of endeavors. Artificial Intelligence is already having a big impact on our daily lives, even though it sounds like something from The Matrix.

5.3 The Ethical Considerations of Artificial Intelligence

Significant ethical concerns regarding artificial intelligence's use, ownership, responsibility, and long-term repercussions on mankind have been raised by the technology's quick development. As engineers, ethicists, and policymakers look to the future of AI, current discussions about control, power dynamics, and the possibility that AI will surpass human capabilities highlight the need to address these ethical issues now. As a result of the White House's recent $140 million funding commitment and additional policy recommendations, significant efforts are being made to identify and resolve these challenges in order to fully realize the huge promise of artificial intelligence.

5.3.1 Bias and Discrimination

Large volumes of socially biased data are used to train AI systems. As a result, these prejudices may get embedded in AI systems, which could then amplify and reinforce unjust or discriminatory outcomes in important domains like criminal justice, hiring, financing, and resource allocation. For instance, if a business employs AI to evaluate resumes and screen job candidates, the AI system is probably taught using past information about the business's successful hiring practices. However, the AI system might identify and reinforce biased factors in the past data, including racial or gender biases, and discriminate against candidates who don't fit the company's recruiting practices. Many U. S. Agencies recently published alerts detailing their strategies for addressing bias in AI models and holding businesses accountable for allowing discrimination to continue on their platforms.

5.3.2 Transparency and Accountability

AI systems often operate as "black boxes," offering minimal transparency into their internal mechanisms and decision-making procedures. Transparency is crucial in important areas like autonomous vehicles and health care for understanding decision-making processes and accountability. It is vital to clarify accountability to take appropriate corrective action if AI systems make errors or cause harm. Scientists are working to enhance interpretable AI, which helps in defining the model's equity, precision, and possible prejudice, to address the opaque obstacles.

5.3.3 Possession and Ingenuity

When a painter completes a picture, it becomes their property. However, it becomes less obvious when a human artist just types a text prompt into an AI system that was built by another individual or group to produce a piece of digital art. Because regulators are unable to keep up with the rapid growth of AI, this emergent issue—who owns the AI-generated art, who can commercialize it, and who is at danger of infringement—is always evolving. As human creators employ other people's AI systems to create digital art, legislators must continue to clarify ownership rights and provide guidelines to prevent possible violations.

5.3.4 Deception and Social Exploitation

Incorrect data, deception, and disinformation are commonplace in politics, competitive industry, and many other fields. Algorithms using artificial intelligence have the capacity to spread misleading information, influence public opinion, and widen social differences. Election tampering and political stability are seriously threatened by technological advancements like deepfakes, which can create audio-visual content that looks real but is actually fake. To address this issue, attention and efficient countermeasures are required.

5.3.5 Privacy, Security, and Surveillance

The accessibility of vast amounts of personal data frequently determines how effective AI is. As AI is used more often, questions about data collection, storage, and use surface. China, for instance, is allegedly discriminating against and repressing particular ethnic groups as a result of its widespread surveillance network, which is supported by technologies like facial recognition software. In the realm of artificial intelligence, safeguarding individuals' privacy and human rights is of utmost importance, necessitating robust safeguards against data breaches, unauthorized access to personal information, and protection from extensive surveillance.

5.3.6 Job Displacement

AI-powered automation has the ability to replace human jobs, causing economic disparity to grow and resulting in widespread joblessness. Others argue that while AI will replace knowledge workers like robots are replacing manual labor, it also has the potential to generate more jobs than it eliminates. It is essential to implement proactive measures such as retraining programs and fair transition policies for affected workers, in addition to providing comprehensive social and economic support systems, in order to minimize the impact of job displacement.

5.3.7 Autonomous Weapons

The ethical implications of AI-driven autonomous weapons development are being brought into question. International treaties and rules regarding the use of these weapons are essential because of worries about responsibility, abuse, and the erosion of human oversight on life-or-death choices. To prevent catastrophic consequences, it becomes essential to guarantee responsible deployment. To address the ethical issues brought up by AI, cooperation between engineers, lawmakers, ethicists, and the general public is required. Responsible AI deployment requires putting in place strict regulations, guaranteeing transparency in AI systems, encouraging inclusivity and diversity in development, and promoting constant dialogue [6]. AI's amazing potential can be used you while adhering to moral standards to create a future where socially conscious AI is the standard by proactively addressing these issues.

5.3.8 Human-Centered Design

The best interests of people must be taken into consideration while designing AI systems. It entails taking into account how AI might affect people and societies. When creating and implementing AI systems, developers must put principles like autonomy, well-being, and dignity first. In order to take into account various viewpoints and choices, they should also include stakeholders in the development procedure.

5.3.9 Protection of Humans

AI systems must not injure humans. This might entail making sure autonomous cars follow safety procedures, preventing mistakes in medical diagnoses, and reducing bias in systems that make decisions. Protecting human lives, dignity, and well-being requires rigorous design, testing, surveillance, and safeguards.

5.3.10 Accountability for the Environment

Another worry is how AI will affect the environment. Natural resources may be strained by processes that use a lot of energy and materials. Sustainable methods, such as minimizing needless computing demands and optimizing for energy efficiency, must be given top priority in ethical AI.

5.3.11 Use Terms of AI

There are primarily three terms associated with AI (see Fig. 5.1) which is discussed as follows:

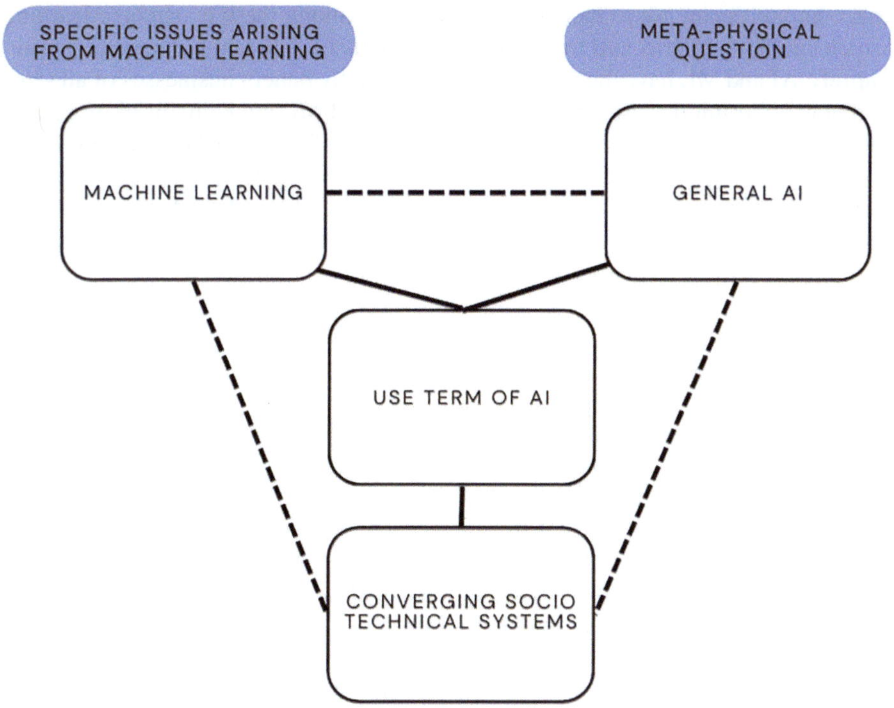

Fig. 5.1 Use terms of AI

5.3.11.1 Machine Learning

Artificial intelligence, which encompasses the idea of a machine that can mimic intelligence in humans, is distinct from machine learning. Machine learning aims to teach a machine how to perform a certain activity and get precise outcomes by identifying correlations. The goal of machine learning, a subfield of artificial intelligence (AI), is to create statistical models and algorithms that can acquire knowledge from information and get better without being explicitly programmed. It tackles various challenges, including ethical concerns, biases, and technical limitations 1 2 3. In this regard, artificial intelligence relates to the overall capacity of computers to imitate human thought processes and perform operations in real-life situations, while machine learning refers to the techniques and procedures that enable systems to identify patterns, make choices, and improve themselves by means of experience and information. Organizations are increasingly utilizing AI and ML technologies to deal with and analyze massive volumes of data, enhance choice-making, provide insights and suggestions in real time, and generate accurate forecasts and predictions. Deep learning is an even more advanced method of machine learning. Deep learning models use large neural networks, which logically process data like a human brain, to find complex patterns and make predictions without requiring human assistance. All things considered, machine learning offers numerous benefits that companies can use to increase productivity. Among these is machine learning, which can find patterns and trends in vast amounts of data that humans might miss entirely. AI and ML have the potential to significantly benefit businesses of all sizes, and new opportunities are always emerging. AI and ML are being used by companies across many industries in various ways to transform their business processes. By incorporating AI and ML capabilities into their strategies and systems, organizations may enhance customer and employee experiences, boost productivity and efficiency, make better data-driven decisions via statistical analysis, and reconsider their approach to use existing data and available resources.

5.3.11.2 General AI

AI is a branch of computer science that makes it possible for software to operate at a level comparable to that of humans when solving new and challenging jobs. An AGI system, on the other hand, can handle issues in a variety of fields without the need for human assistance. AGI may self-teach and tackle problems for which it was never trained, rather than being restricted to a particular scope. Therefore, AGI is a theoretical depiction of a fully functional artificial intelligence that uses generalized human cognitive capacities to handle challenging tasks. AGI enables machines to mimic human thought and behavior in order to resolve any complicated issue. Since these machines are built with extensive knowledge and cognitive computing skills, they perform identically to humans. Strong artificial intelligence (AI) is referred to as AGI. The application of artificial intelligence to particular tasks or issues is known as weak or narrow AI, which is in contrast to strong AI.

The hypothesis of mind-level AI is essentially concerned with teaching machines to comprehend the basic elements of consciousness and acquire human behavior. AGI can plan, acquire cognitive skills, make decisions, manage ambiguous situations, incorporate past knowledge into decision-making, and increase accuracy thanks to its solid AI base. Artificial General Intelligence (AGI) enables machines to carry out inventive, imaginative, and creative activities. Here are five real-world instances of AGI capabilities:

I. Inventiveness: Theoretically, an AGI system could read, understand, and enhance human-generated code perception of the senses. If artificial intelligence (AI) systems comprehend the enormous volumes of human-written code, find new techniques that can be enhanced, and then rewrite the code they have found, they can become smarter on their own. Even though AI-based devices can now sketch and compose music, more development of AI is required to show human-level creativity for self-optimization.
II. Color recognition: It is a subjective form of perception that AGI would be very good at. Additionally, it would be able to recognize three dimensions and depth in still photos.
III. Fine motor abilities: Because of the fine motor skills, humans can effortlessly recover any thing from their pockets. Reinforcement learning was recently used

to teach a robotic hand how to solve a Rubik's cube. Even though the demonstration is noteworthy, it highlights the challenges of training robot fingers to manipulate insignificant objects like keys with a single hand.

IV. Understanding natural language (NLU): Human language is very context-dependent in its meaning. NLU would be made possible by the intuition that AGI systems would possess.

V. Getting around: The current Global Positioning System (GPS) is capable of locating a specific place. When completely developed, AGI would surpass current technologies in its ability to project movement through physical surroundings.

VI. The capacity for empathy: Although deep learning models have not yet shown the genuine creativity that humans possess, they do allude to the potential of AGI. Neural network architecture is still unable to reproduce the emotional reasoning necessary for creativity. For instance, NLP models provide text output based on the linguistic datasets and patterns they are trained on, whereas humans react to a conversation based on their emotional perceptions.

Examples of Artificial General Intelligence

I. ROSS intelligence. Another name for ROSS is the AI attorney, which is a legal expert system. In less than 3 s, it can mine data from over one billion text documents, analyze the data, and offer accurate answers to challenging queries.

II. Watson by IBM: When Watson defeated two of the most well-known Jeopardy winners in 2011, it caused a stir. It is now possible to go through data, extract insights, predict user needs, and more with the Watson toolkit.

III. AlphaGo: Another illustration of restricted intelligence that excels at a certain kind of problem solving is AlphaGo. A computer program called AlphaGo is capable of playing the board game Go. Go is an intricate game that is hard for people to learn. In a five-game encounter in 2016, AlphaGo defeated world champion Lee Sedol.

IV. AlphaFold 3: AlphaFold 3, created by Google DeepMind, is capable of predicting the structures of DNA and RNA, two of life's fundamental building components, in addition to protein structures. This speeds up drug research by enabling the creation of models with different molecular configurations.

V. Model of language The generative Pre-trained Transformer: OpenAI's GPT-3 and GPT-4 are release versions of a computer that can produce human language automatically. General human intelligence can be reliably simulated by the technology. While the AI output is frequently faulty, there are instances where the wording is identical to human output.

VI. Music AIs: Dadabots is an AI algorithm that can produce a stream of its own approximate music if it is fed a collection of existing music. Artificial intelligence (AI) music generators are starting to compete with human musicians by creating songs that create a lot of internet buzz. For instance, Suno can create all the components of a song by itself by adding voices and instrumentals to AI-generated lyrics.

Research on Artificial General Intelligence Is Being Driven by the Following Technologies

I. Generative AI

"Generative artificial intelligence" (generative AI) is a subset of deep learning that enables an AI system to utilize learned data to produce unique, realistic content. In reaction to human requests, generative AI models are trained on huge data sets to generate text, music, or pictures that naturally imitate handmade material. Generative models can imitate human inventiveness and creativity by learning from vast datasets, opening the door for increasingly complex types of artificial intelligence. Generative AI has applications in a wide range of domains, such as virtual storytelling, creative design, and content creation. Organizations can utilize generative AI algorithms, such as LLMs from AI21 Labs, Anthropic, Cohere, and Meta, to tackle challenging problems.

II. Computer vision

Computer vision technologies have made it possible for systems to retrieve, assess, and comprehend spatial information from visual data. Autonomous vehicles utilize computer vision models to assess real-time video feeds and securely navigate around obstacles. Deep learning methods have already made it possible for computer vision systems to streamline complex image processing tasks including object detection, classification, and surveillance. Computer vision systems can navigate complex scenes, help with object handling, and improve human-computer interaction by extracting features, identifying objects, and comprehending spatial relationships. Computer vision is essential to developing AGI capabilities, from augmented reality to driverless cars. For example, developers use Amazon Rekognition to simplify image analysis for a range of computer vision applications.

III. Robotics

Realizing embodied intelligence, in which machines engage with the physical world and manipulate items in real time, depends heavily on robotics. It is crucial for teaching AGI systems the physical manipulation and sensory perception abilities they require. Robotic systems can demonstrate adaptive and context-aware behaviors that are comparable to human intelligence by combining sensorimotor feedback, dexterous manipulation, and autonomous navigation. Research in robotics has the potential to advance artificial general intelligence (AGI) by allowing robots to see, respond, and learn in dynamic situations. For example, a robotic arm with AGI capabilities could see, pick up, and peel oranges much like a human. Before assembling robotic systems, engineering teams researching AGI use AWS RoboMaker to visually design them.

IV. NLP

A subfield of artificial intelligence called natural language processing (NLP) enables computer programs to comprehend and produce human language. Machines can now comprehend, interpret, and produce human language more accurately and fluently thanks to NLP technologies. NLP systems may communicate with users in a natural and intuitive way by utilizing techniques like machine translation, sentiment analysis, and question-answering. This helps to close the gap between people and robots. NLP systems use machine learning and computational linguistics technology to transform language data into simple representations called tokens and understand their contextual links. The forefront of AGI research is being driven by sophisticated NLP models, such as transformer architectures and large language models. For example, companies can use Amazon Lex, an NLP engine, to develop conversational AI chatbots.

5.3.11.3 Converging Socio-Technical Systems

A socio-technical system (STS) is a framework that takes into account the intricate interactions between a system's technical and social components with the goal of optimizing both for successful and efficient results. It acknowledges that human and technological systems are interrelated and interconnected, and that both must be taken into account when designing and implementing systems. This concept highlights the integration of AI into societal and technological frameworks, where both machine learning and general AI play a role in shaping industries, governance, and societal norms. It reflects the transformative impact of AI on various aspects of human life. Among the socio-technical systems are:

I. Hardware: The traditional definition of technology is hardware, which includes mainframes, workstations, peripheral devices, and connecting devices. A socio-technical system cannot exist without any hardware component.
II. People can be either individuals or teams, and they must consider their independence and responsibilities. Employees in an organization create and utilize software and hardware, adhere to legal and regulatory requirements, and share and manage data.
III. Software: Software is nothing more than executable code. Software includes things like operating systems, tools, and application programs. Software is a crucial part of the socio-technical system. Social conventions and practices, such maximizing these parameters, storing data in these types, seeking these data, etc., are often included into software design.
IV. Law and regulations: There may be laws pertaining to privacy protection, rules governing the testing of chips for military applications, etc. Organizational and governmental laws and regulations must be complied with. If those who violate them are apprehended, they face particular social penalties.
V. Data: What data is gathered, who should have access to it, and what formats should they be stored in are all part of the socio-technical systems design.

Sociotechnical System Layers

The STS stack is composed of several layers. Even though these layers are separate systems in and of themselves, they work together as the STS and have an affect on and influence other layers and systems outside of it.

I. The layer of equipment: It includes a collection of hardware devices, some of which could be phones, laptops, computers, etc. Some form of embedded system is present in the majority of the devices.
II. The layer of the operating system: systems that integrate various software programs with hardware. For the system's higher software layers, this layer offers a collection of shared resources. Because it enables communication between software and hardware, this layer serves as a bridge to the latter.
III. The communications and data management layer: The layer that connects the operating system and the application to enable proper use and management of information is known as the communications and data management layer. This layer expands the capabilities of the operating system and offers an interface that enables interaction with more sophisticated features, like system database access and remote system access. Because it sits between the operating system and the application, this is commonly referred to as middleware.
IV. Application Layer: The software that clients or end users view and utilize is known as the application layer. It is frequently the STS layer that is most apparent and offers the user interface. More specialized functionality is offered by this layer to satisfy certain organizational needs. This layer may contain a wide variety of application programs.
V. Business layer: The business activity-supported procedures that specify internal technology utilization and business operations make up the business process layer. This layer is made up of a number of procedures that support company operations and involve both human and computer systems. Software system usage is defined and implemented.
VI. The layer of organization: At this level, high-level strategic processes, corporate rules, regulations, and policies are established and must be adhered to when utilizing the system.
VII. Social layer: The social layer includes end users and customers as well as the external culture, legal framework, and regulatory environment. The laws, rules, and culture that control how the system functions are established.

5.4 Ethical Issues in Generative AI

Generative AI ethics encompasses the ethical, societal, and legal considerations surrounding the implementation of AI systems that are capable of generating content. Authenticity and Truthfulness focus on the blending of real and AI-generated content, like deep fakes, that may mislead or deceive. These are the main components of Generative AI Ethics. Historically, uniqueness of items created by humans has been associated with authenticity. The ability of It is difficult to confirm the authenticity of new products when AI is used to produce artwork and articles. Deepfakes, which are realistic-sounding but entirely fake audio, images, or videos, present a serious threat to generative AI. These works seriously jeopardize the truth, especially when it comes to politics, the media, and public opinion. They also make it impossible to tell fact from fiction. It gets harder to determine authenticity when Generative AI creates content on its own without human input [7]. After training on large datasets, generative AI models may create content that plagiarizes existing works. These situations make one wonder about originality and the possibility of inadvertent plagiarism. With the increasing use of generative AI, there is a rising demand for technologies that can verify content and differentiate between AI-generated and human-created outputs. At this point in AI development, machines do not have authenticity in emotions because true experiences and feelings are lacking. With the growing influence of AI systems across various aspects of society, the significance of bias and fairness in the ethics of generative AI is on the rise. Bias and fairness are crucial to make sure the data used in training generative AI is impartial, preventing the possibility of discriminatory or unjust results. Biased algorithms can amplify societal biases, leading to unfair results and worsening systemic inequalities. Bias occurs when a generative AI model mirrors societal, cultural, or data-specific prejudices. The reason could be biased training data, as well as the architecture and design of the model. Biased AI models can lead to decisions and ideas being misrepresented. Fairness ensures that AI systems operate consistently for all user groups. Achieving fairness in AI systems can boost trust from the public, promote inclusivity and diversity, and ensure fairness and equality in critical decisions. Clarity and openness in generative AI are crucial concepts, especially with the widespread adoption of AI models across various fields. Clarifying and making understandable the decision-making of generative AI is crucial for ensuring transparency and explainability, especially when its results can have important real-world impacts [8]. It is because generative AI can produce a wide range of intricate outputs, it is crucial for users to comprehend how and why the AI is generating particular outcomes. The term "transparency" describes the degree of openness regarding the architecture, training data, and procedures of the AI model. The capability of the model to provide understandable interpretations for its outcomes is known as explainability. Explanations that are too straightforward could mislead users. Explanations should be tailored to the target audience and properly represent the model's decision-making process. Accountability and Responsibility outline who is accountable if a generative AI produces damaging or false information.

It is imperative to define clear guidelines and mechanisms due to the potential consequences of AI-driven outputs. Being accountable means taking responsibility and accountability for the results produced by an AI system. There has to be a way to figure out who or what is responsible if an AI system malfunctions or harms people. The duty to make sure AI acts morally and correctly is related to responsibility. The AI system must be designed, developed, deployed, and monitored as part of one's responsibilities. There are moral and legal ramifications to accountability and responsibility. When AI goes wrong, liability establishes who is responsible for paying for it—the AI itself, the developer, the business, or the user. It is morally our duty to make sure AI doesn't reinforce negative attitudes or behaviors. The idea of intellectual property aims to handle issues related to the ownership of AI-generated content and the creators' rights in the content creation process [9]. Human creativity's intrinsic value and appreciation could suffer if machines create art, music, or literature. If AI produces a work that is commercially successful, it should be clear to whom will profit monetarily. Authenticity and originality are two more aspects of intellectual property.

Inadvertent plagiarism may duplicate already-published copyrighted material, raising moral questions about inadvertent intellectual property violations. The socioeconomic ramifications, such as probable job losses or the decline in value of human-generated content, are covered by the terms "economic" and "social" impact. The economic implications are connected to job growth and replacement as generative AI has the ability to both create new jobs in the tech field and replace existing ones in information production and repetitive tasks.

By simplifying procedures and encouraging creativity in fields like data analysis, design, and content production, generative AI can boost company productivity and innovation. Customized media platforms and AI-driven creation solutions are just two instances of how these products and services could lead to entirely new business models. The social impact may have an impact on education by decreasing the importance of human interaction in the classroom while also allowing AI tutors or content generators to personalize learning. The creation of deepfakes and fake news using generative AI presents serious obstacles to the trust and distribution of information. Privacy and security protect people's privacy, particularly in the context of AI-generated content that may misuse or impersonate people. Since these models are becoming more prevalent in a variety of applications, AI ethics are especially important [10]. To ensure that AI operates safely for users and respects their rights, these issues need to be addressed. With security worries focusing on hostile attacks, tampering, reliance, and manipulation, privacy concerns deal with data exposure, monitoring, profiling, and dehumanization. Especially when developing AI models, it is crucial to obtain explicit consent before utilizing user data. The decrease in chances for practice is associated with the decline of human abilities as generative AI is able to produce content, designs, and outputs that previously depended on human work. They might eventually exhaust their chances to hone their skills, leading to a decline in skill level. Relying too much on generative AI can lead to developing a dependency on automation [11]. The loss of intuitive decision-making due to an overreliance on AI may overshadow the value of human intuition and accumulated knowledge in various fields where they have traditionally been essential.

Creativity could be lost if generative AI begins dominating the creative field, alongside human emotions and firsthand experiences. Loss of traditional skills, including those with cultural or historical importance, may happen alongside a decline in experiential learning if Generative AI starts making decisions. This is due to the fact that Generative AI has the potential to make certain manual or traditional abilities irrelevant.

5.5 A Conceptual Framework for Solving Ethical Issues in Generative AI

Users should be able to address ethical concerns related to generative AI using the proposed conceptual framework. Before deploying the Generative AI system, it is important to consider Contextual Clarity and Purpose, ensuring that the exact goal is established. This involves understanding the potential environments and applications while ensuring they conform to agreed upon societal standards. To achieve transparency and accountability, it is crucial to keep thorough records of the AI design, training data, and decision-making logic.

It is necessary to create responsibility protocols in order to clearly define roles at every stage, from development to deployment. Informed consent is a component of data rights and privacy that guarantees the use of sensitive or personal data only with express consent. Robust mechanisms for data anonymization should be implemented to reduce the possibility of personal identification. To verify the credibility of AI-created content, authenticity protocols must include verification systems, specifically in important areas such as academic research and news. It is important to consider watermarking as a method to monitor the inclusion of identifiable signatures in AI-generated content, ensuring transparency about its origin. Evaluation of potential dangers and vulnerabilities within generative AI systems is essential for ensuring security and resilience. AI models must receive regular updates in order to defend against emerging threats. While feedback loops are essential for refining models by incorporating feedback on unintentional biases or discriminative outputs, fairness audits must also address bias mitigation to detect and reduce biases in training data and model outputs.

Economic and Social Considerations should be responsible for developing plans for seamless labor market transitions as well as for analyzing possible job displacements in order to assess the impact on employment. Ethical concerns ought to take potential business models into account. The public should be informed about the ethical ramifications and applications of generative AI through awareness campaigns as part of public engagement and collaboration. Planning feedback is necessary in order to gather and take into account public opinions regarding the use of generative AI. Continuous Evolution should make sure that new problems, difficulties, and solutions are integrated into the framework through regular reviews. The provided visual representation in Fig. 5.2 may depict the proposed theoretical framework. Awareness includes two aspects: (a) Recognizing Ethical Concerns, which aids in recognizing the instances and locations where ethical dilemmas related to generative AI may surface; and (b) Understanding the Capabilities and Constraints of Generative AI. The evaluation includes three components: (a) User Analysis, which determines the individuals and ways in which Generative AI outcomes are influenced, (b) Analysis of risk evaluates potential dangers, such as misuse or misinterpretation of created content by users. Benefit Assessment examines the potential benefits of AI capabilities, such as improved decision-making and innovation. Decision-making involves two main components: (a) creating definite

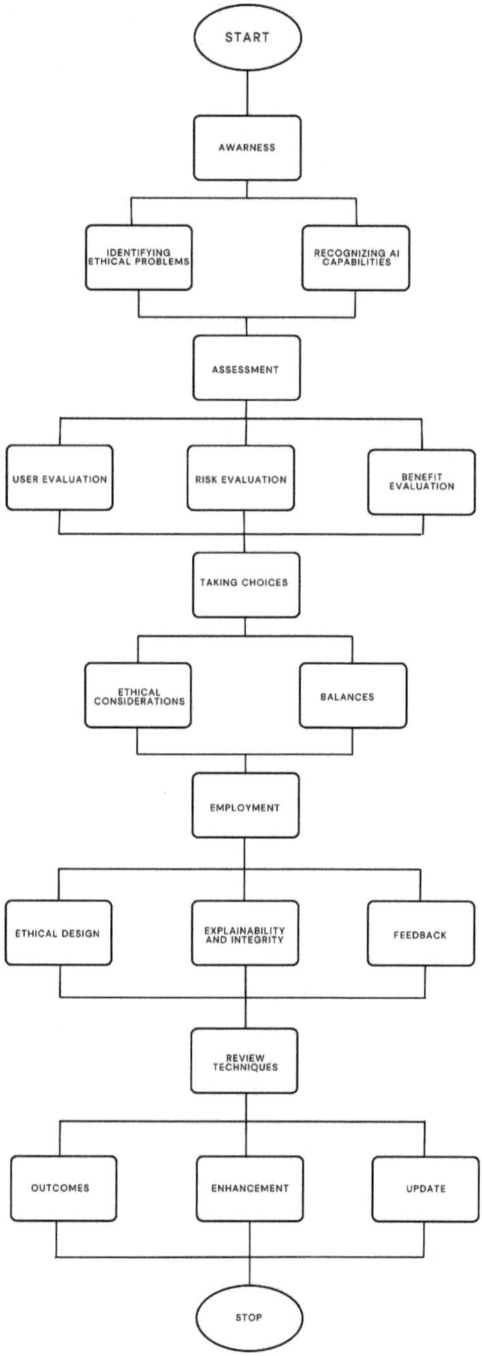

Fig. 5.2 Block Diagram of the conceptual framework for solving ethical issues in generative artificial intelligence

rules rooted in commonly accepted moral standards, like privacy, openness, and equality; and (b) finding a middle ground by weighing the pros and cons while taking into consideration the varied needs and issues of users. Execution involves three components: (a) The field of Design Ethics ensures that generative AI systems are created and operate in an ethical manner. (b) Transparent explanations of the AI's decision-making process and functioning will be available for users and other stakeholders. (c) Feedback mechanisms will allow users and stakeholders to provide input on the AI's outcomes and address any ethical concerns that may come up. The review process is composed of three parts as outlined below: (a) Unforeseen ethical issues will be monitored over time to identify any emerging concerns; (b) The AI system will be adapted according to feedback to change societal norms and observed results. To ensure the framework remains relevant and valuable, updates will consider the latest industry discoveries and advancements.

5.6 Shaping the Future of Work Through Collaboration of AI

Emerging technologies are rapidly transforming the work environment. It is the duty and opportunity of Global Shapers to shape the Future of Work. An attempt was made to comprehend the needs and viewpoints of youth regarding the Future of Work through the cross-hub collaboration Shaping the Future of Work. The workplace is changing, but employees are growing less engaged with their jobs despite leaders' efforts to change it since the pandemic.

5.6.1 The Future of Work Is Collaborative & Community-Centric–The Need

People need teamwork to be fundamental to their working lives because they enjoy it so much. This means that a major cause of worker disengagement is probably the preference for structure over collaboration. Collaboration needs to be a primary organizational value and function as a regular working practice in order to increase employee engagement, loyalty, and satisfaction. Leaders can generate real impact and realize employees' potential by utilizing collaborative working methods. Restoring employee power is essential for organizations to make a meaningful difference. People can make meaningful contributions to the organization and grow into leaders when they believe that their opinions and ideas are valued. According to Rachel Happe, the founder of Engaged Organizations and The Community Roundtable, "you have more ears on the ground being responsive if everyone is looking out for the needs of the organization and feels like they are empowered to do something.". The magic that occurs when people meaningfully unite around a common goal to learn and collaborate is called "Collaborative Impact," and it will be the driving force behind organizations' future success. Better ideas and more room for innovation will result from asking all staff members to contribute their knowledge, experiences, and viewpoints. Nevertheless, a lot of companies have a CEO disease, which makes it difficult for executives to receive candid feedback from their workforce [12]. Though they might not agree with the responses, leaders must be prepared and eager to bring up challenging subjects and pose questions. Real development frequently occurs during these difficult talks. If there is trust and psychological safety (i.e., a sense that one won't be shamed or punished for sharing one's thoughts), people will feel more at ease sharing. You'll also stop people from offering their candid opinions in private conversations that take place in the hallway by establishing these welcoming and secure areas for discourse.

5.6.2 The Vital Role of AI in Shaping Modern Workplaces

The modern workplace requires the incorporation of AI technology since it boosts productivity, fosters innovation, and modifies management practices. In addition to staying current with technology, adapting to AI at work means creating a culture that embraces change, encourages lifelong learning, and maximises the advantages of the collaborative partnership between humans and machines. The modern workplace is an ecosystem where technology and human creativity coexist to produce a dynamic atmosphere that promotes innovation and long-term success. In other words, the company's capacity to adapt to AI in the job will determine the success of future. Just as significant as the established advantages, which include cost savings and higher productivity, are the enormous effects on employee experience and engagement [13].

By using AI to simplify processes, organisations may create a more harmonious and fulfilling work environment. This paves the path for a more promising and sustainable future in which technology augments, not replaces, human potential. In the workplace of the future, productive human-AI cooperation will take precedence over AI taking the place of people. Increased cognitive variety may result from this combination, which combines human creativity and emotional intelligence with artificial intelligence's computing strength and data-processing skills [14]. For example, AI may help create more efficient work procedures, but its development and application still need human oversight and ethical direction.

To fully realise the potential of human-AI cooperation, businesses must support training and development programs that provide employees with the skills they need to work effectively with AI. This encompasses soft skills like AI and data analysis as well as hard talents like moral judgement, adaptability, and problem-solving techniques. Future office design will be greatly and broadly impacted by artificial intelligence. By democratising knowledge and increasing productivity and creativity in the workplace, artificial intelligence (AI) has the potential to fundamentally alter the way people work, learn, and interact.

In order to fully exploit this potential, it is important to carefully consider the ethical, societal, and human factors that impact the integration of AI in the workplace. The goal is to utilize AI in order to establish a work environment that is more dynamic, inclusive, and fulfilling, where human contributions are valued and enhanced, in addition to increasing economic efficiency during this era of revolution. This achievable future of the workplace is enhanced by artificial intelligence [15]. By being proactive in addressing issues and working together with AI, businesses can tap into incredible opportunities for growth and creativity. Despite being complex, the journey to implementing AI in the workplace presents a promising future for both businesses and employees when approached with thoughtful planning and ethical deliberation.

5.6.3 *Enhancing Productivity with AI Tools*

The constant innovation in AI technology has made it possible to access a variety of tools that are targeted to specific fields, fulfilling specific needs (see Table 5.5.1). People may now do both personal and professional duties more rapidly thanks to the development of AI tools. Productivity tools aren't new, of course, but they've gotten even more potent since artificial intelligence was included. Software programs that employ artificial intelligence to help us do activities faster and with less effort are known as AI productivity aids. They can be anything from algorithms that can anticipate the next line of code that might need to write to smart assistants that arrange emails.

In specific sectors such as human resources, marketing, law, and finance, artificial intelligence (AI) can significantly aid in streamlining processes and enhancing productivity. The objective of artificial intelligence is to improve human skills and efficiency, not to entirely substitute them. For this purpose, the list below presents a few of the best AI tools in order to enhance efficiency in different fields.

I. **Human Resources**

   (a) **Juicebox (YC S22)**: The recruiting sector has not innovated in the last 10 years. AI has made it possible to disrupt it with software that has the ability to think and act. Juicebox is a hiring platform driven by AI. To find, evaluate, and hire the greatest personnel, it creates agentic processes. This software for visualizing data has the ability to automatically gather details from various spreadsheets, such as employee information, performance

Table 5.1 Various AI tools in various application domains

Human resource	Marketing	Legal	Finance
Juicebox	Canva	ClickUp	bill
Workable	Copy.ai	Lax Machina	Blue dot
Turing	surfer	amto.ai	docyt

appraisals, and survey results, to create reports. By utilizing natural language processing, Juicebox is able to evaluate employee dedication, productivity, and contentment.

(b) **Workable**: Every business will aim to use AI to improve performance and efficiency across all departments and functions, both now and particularly in the years to come. The widespread use of AI is causing a rapid change in behavior that will drastically alter the recruiting and human resources environment. Workable Assistant offers assistance at every stage of hiring and human resources process and can be easily incorporated into Workable. It automates every stage of the recruitment process to find the most suitable candidate. It supervises the meeting, evaluation, and also the termination process. It allows clients to evaluate candidates for a specific position without any biases.

(c) **Turing**: In order to protect people and property in a world that is becoming more complicated, Turing AI has developed an all-in-one platform that uses AI to deliver flexible, simple, and robust cloud video security solutions. Through artificial intelligence (AI) assistance, over two million developers worldwide can be located, evaluated, connected, and supervised, streamlining remote recruitment for employers and developers alike.

II. **Marketing**

(a) **Copy.ai**: An artificial intelligence writing tool called Copy.ai creates a variety of material, such as blog headlines, emails, social media posts, web copy, and more, using machine learning. To assist customers with the copywriting process, Copy AI is based on OpenAI's GPT-3 large language model (LLM). Customers could utilize Copy.ai without restrictions for 7 days during its initial free trial period. Copy.ai has been able to launch a freemium service with a use cap as compute prices have decreased. Using innate pattern recognition enables users to access templates, grammar transformations, and innovative suggestions.

(b) **Canva** Pro: Canva is a comprehensive visual communication tool that enables anyone to design. Beautiful presentations, infographics, films, t-shirts, websites, social media postings, and more may be easily made using this method. Anyone with an idea to share, be it an executive, entrepreneur, or student, can use Canva. Canva is an online graphic design tool that is free to use. Create presentations, posters, movies, logos, social media postings, and more with it. It produces and customizes videos, infographics, posters, lesson plans, and more. This is A comprehensive design platform that allows users to create images using templates and pre-made design elements. It is useful for creating blurbs, social media posts, introductions, and a wide variety of visual designs.

(c) **Surfer**: Regarding Search Engine Optimization (SEO), this tool is advantageous for improving content strategy and increasing traffic and visibility on a website. It provides an assessment of keyword usage, content length, and headers.

III. **Legal**

(a) **Lex Machina**: Lex Machina legal analytics offer precise, useful data that forecasts the actions of judges, lawyers, and parties in US courts by fusing machine learning with the expertise of legal professionals. In order to provide reliable and thorough data, Lex Machina collects raw data from cases, including downloading millions of court papers. In order to provide the superior Legal Analytics that lawyers depend on, the data is first taken straight from court dockets, then it is assembled, cleansed, and improved using a special blend of artificial intelligence and in-house legal professionals. It is then updated every 24 h.

(b) **ClickUp**: The three separate but complementary tools that make up ClickUp are AI Writer for Work, AI Knowledge Manage, and AI Project Manage. When combined, they significantly speed up repetitive chores, allow to devote limited time to creativity and leadership. amto.ai is a multifunctional productivity tool that enables users to centralize their tasks, produce reports and data on inputted information, monitor billable hours, schedules, and appointments, and perform additional functions. Generative AI is utilized to create the documents and also offers suggestions for language, tone, and missing clauses.

IV. **Finance**

(a) **BILL**: BILL uses artificial intelligence (AI) to convert invoices into digital bills that can be paid with a single click. Additionally, people can avoid manually entering (and re-entering) the data because two-way active sync with the majority of top account software maintains books current. It is a cloud-based tool that automates AR/AP processes. It increases productivity by streamlining the billing and invoicing process. It allows companies to regulate expenses and budgets across different areas.

(b) **Docyt**: This is an accounting platform that helps a person to manage and automate back-office chores. It provides reports and statistics that help improve the financial control of the business. It is useful for tracking expenses, budget, and cash flow. Docyt retrieves information from a financial institution and revenue system. To provide with useful insights into earnings, Docyt then arranges that data into a number of daily reports. Find out how Docyt can provide complete insight into a person's daily earnings. Docyt AI stands out in the financial sector by tackling the main issue facing the sector: delivering real-time accounting data, including live P&L statements. Docyt AI improves the effectiveness of financial teams, boosts profitability, saves time, and offers a real-time perspective of an organization's financial health by fusing AI efficiency with human expertise. Small business owners may recoup hundreds of hours of lost productivity annually and avoid thousands of dollars in penalties, late fees, and accounting headaches with Docyt's AI-based document-driven platform.

(c) **Blue dot**: a useful AI ally to comply with taxes promptly. It employs natural language processing to exploit external data and improve the expense management workflow.

Research indicates that incorporating generative AI results in notable productivity enhancements, with individuals achieving up to a 66% increase in performance in different business scenarios. Customer service effectiveness has shown tangible advantages, including a 14% rise in problems solved per hour, as well as enhanced customer satisfaction and employee loyalty. This shift in productivity tools marks a major change in the work methods, offering ongoing enhancements in efficiency and effectiveness in different industries and roles.

5.7 Conclusions

AI is changing the way of job responsibilities. Automated technology is taking over routine tasks, enabling human workers to concentrate on tasks requiring creativity, critical thinking, and emotional intelligence. Data analysis and insights powered by AI improve decision-making processes, resulting in more well-informed strategies. Although AI can automate certain tasks, it also opens up chances for further developing and updating skills. In order to stay current, people can learn new abilities that enhance AI technology, like understanding data, programming AI, and mastering machine learning. Businesses have the option to spend money on training initiatives in order to prepare their employees with the essential abilities to effectively work alongside AI systems.

AI's capacity to rapidly process and analyze large quantities of data results in increased efficiency and productivity. Chatbots, virtual assistants, and AI-enabled tools make communication and tasks more efficient, enabling employees to concentrate on important duties. Predictive analytics assist organizations in making proactive decisions by optimizing resource allocation and performance. Ethical considerations are becoming more important as AI is being increasingly incorporated into the workplace. It is essential to guarantee fairness, transparency, and accountability in AI decision-making procedures. An AI implementation that is focused on humans ensures that technology enhances human abilities, rather than taking over them, encouraging teamwork and creativity. People who adopt a growth mindset and actively search for chances to acquire new skills will be more prepared to handle changing job demands. Continuously learning and being open to change are extremely valuable qualities to possess. Generative AI presents groundbreaking potential in various fields. Nevertheless, the advanced features also bring about distinctive moral issues. The suggested conceptual framework outlines a method for addressing identified ethical concerns in Generative AI. These guidelines should be followed when developing and deploying Generative AI models to ensure responsible use that maximizes benefits and minimizes potential risks.

References

1. Tzimas, T. (2021). *Legal and ethical challenges of artificial intelligence from an international law perspective* (Vol. 46). Springer Nature.
2. Erskine, T. (2024). AI and the future of IR: Disentangling flesh-and-blood, institutional, and synthetic moral agency in world politics. *Review of International Studies, 50*(3), 534–559.
3. Kalusivalingam, A. K. (2018). Ethical considerations in AI: Historical perspectives and contemporary challenges. *Journal of Innovative Technologies, 1*(1), 1–8.
4. Abràmoff, M. D., Tobey, D., & Char, D. S. (2020). Lessons learned about autonomous AI: finding a safe, efficacious, and ethical path through the development process. *American Journal of Ophthalmology, 214*, 134–142.
5. Kieslich, K., Keller, B., & Starke, C. (2021). AI-ethics by design. Evaluating public perception on the importance of ethical design principles of AI. *arXiv preprint arXiv:2106.00326.*
6. Haner, J., & Garcia, D. (2019). The artificial intelligence arms race: Trends and world leaders in autonomous weapons development. *Global Policy, 10*(3), 331–337.
7. Zohny, H., McMillan, J., & King, M. (2023). Ethics of generative AI. *Journal of Medical Ethics, 49*(2), 79–80.
8. Kirova, V. D., Ku, C. S., Laracy, J. R., & Marlowe, T. J. (2023). The ethics of artificial intelligence in the era of generative AI. *Journal of Systemics, Cybernetics and Informatics, 21*(4), 42–50.
9. Uddagiri, C., & Isunuri, B. V. (2024). Ethical and privacy challenges of generative AI. In *Generative AI: Current trends and applications* (pp. 219–244). Singapore.
10. Zlateva, P., Steshina, L., Petukhov, I., & Velev, D. (2024). A conceptual framework for solving ethical issues in generative artificial intelligence. In *Electronics, communications and networks* (pp. 110–119). IOS Press.
11. Huang, Y., Arora, C., Houng, W. C., Kanij, T., Madulgalla, A., & Grundy, J. (2025). Ethical concerns of generative AI and mitigation strategies: A systematic mapping study. *arXiv preprint arXiv:2502.00015.*
12. Thomas, G. A., Botha, R. A., & Greunen, D. V. (2018). A virtual-community-centric architecture to support coordination in a large scale distributed environment: A case study of the South African Public Sector. *IFIP Advances in Information and Communication Technology, 334*, 62–75.
13. Edirisinghe, C., & Cheok, A. D. (2024). AI-human collaboration: Redefining roles in the modern workplace. *PaKSoM, 2004*, 37.
14. Ashri, R. (2019). *The AI-powered workplace: How artificial intelligence, data, and messaging platforms are defining the future of work.* Apress.
15. Mirbabaie, M., Brünker, F., Möllmann, N. R., & Stieglitz, S. (2022). The rise of artificial intelligence–understanding the AI identity threat at the workplace. *Electronic Markets, 32*, 73–99.

Chapter 6
Future Trends and Opportunities in AI Driven Industrial Relations

6.1 Introduction

In the realm of labor and industrial relations, AI can be utilized for different aspects of managing employees, bargaining, solving conflicts, and creating policies. It's possible uses vary from making administrative tasks automatic to offering advanced analytics for making strategic decisions. AI technology is growing in significance within human resources and relations with employees. AI-based tools provide considerable benefits to HR professionals, enabling them to save time, boost productivity, and make well-informed decisions. AI allows HR professionals to concentrate on the welfare and contentment of their employees, guaranteeing their safety and promoting reconciliation when needed by offering fast and convenient access to pertinent information [1]. AI simplifies tasks, freeing up HR professionals to focus on building meaningful relationships. The use of technology in HR and employee relations is essential, with AI playing a key role in improving efficiency and effectiveness in the workplace. Artificial Intelligence (AI) is transforming HR and Employee Relations by bringing in sophisticated solutions that boost efficiency, precision, and employee contentment. AI helps emergency room professionals focus on strategic and people-centered aspects of their jobs by automating tasks, analysing large datasets, and offering actionable insights. AI integration in ER not just streamlines workflows but also greatly enhances engagement and compliance across organizations, improving decision-making and customizing employee experiences. AI-powered analysis is revolutionizing the ER department's insight into workforce information. These tools analyze patterns in employee conduct, productivity, and commitment, allowing HR professionals to make more knowledgeable choices. AI has the ability to examine patterns that could indicate problems like high turnover rates or inefficiencies within departments, leading to taking proactive actions. AI plays a crucial role in enhancing accessibility for employee relations, providing various resources in different languages and formats to cater to a diverse

S. Majumder, B. Misra, *AI-Empowered Industrial Relations*, Studies in Computational Intelligence 1254, https://doi.org/10.1007/978-3-032-14557-4_6

workforce. AI-driven virtual assistants and chatbots can offer instant replies to employee questions at all hours, creating a more comprehensive method of employee communication. This increased accessibility enhances employee experience by simplifying the process for staff to obtain required information and assistance, regardless of location or time limitations [2]. Adopting AI in HR and employee relations offers numerous advantages that greatly improve the efficiency and timeliness of these critical roles. This is the impact of AI: Enhancing Efficiency and Productivity by automating tasks, allowing HR and ER professionals to focus on strategic duties. This change not just increases effectiveness but also improves the standard of work, enabling teams to concentrate on aspects that need human perspective and skill. Boosted scalability: With workplace problems growing intricate and teams working with constrained resources, AI intervenes to streamline processes. This enables the company to manage a larger workload efficiently without sacrificing quality or responsiveness [3]. Improved decision-making through analysis of large data sets is made possible with AI technology. This technology offers in-depth analyses of trends and patterns, enabling the team to make informed decisions and implement ongoing improvements overall. Reduction in costs: AI reduces costs related to managing employee relations by automating routine tasks. AI frees HR and ER professionals from monotonous tasks, reducing time wasted and potential legal costs, thus providing a cost-efficient option for businesses. By managing these ordinary tasks, AI frees up the team to focus on more meaningful and rewarding work, leading to greater job satisfaction and productivity. By incorporating AI into HR and employee relations plans [4], companies are not only staying current with technology but also establishing a benchmark for operational excellence and strategic foresight within the company.

6.2 Exploring Emerging Trends and Advancements in AI for Industrial Relations

AI is expected to become more deeply integrated into various aspects of workforce management, from recruitment and training to performance evaluation and strategic planning. This integration will likely lead to more data-driven decision-making and personalized employee experiences.

6.2.1 The Future of AI in Employee Relations Departments

Every employee in HR affirms that "our staff is our most valuable resource!" and this belief remains constant going forward. If the businesses are to succeed, they must provide support, training, development, promotion, and recognition to the employees. Each employee requires both a sympathetic ear and a supportive hand. This will remain the same.

Regrettably, issues with harassment and discrimination are unlikely to disappear. There will always be a requirement for a courteous employee relations professional to listen to an individual's story and then conduct a thorough investigation. Technology can assist businesses in this endeavor. The chatbots are able to receive a report, but they lack the ability to make decisions. They are unable to console a crying and distressed employee after the incident. They are unable to determine if this individual should be given leeway on production requirements due to the recent death of their mother. Human workers will continue to require human resources support in their daily work routines [5]. There is no doubt that AI is among the highest priorities. We're investigating, communicating with the customers, involving the community, seeking advice from experts, and acting quickly. Nonetheless, businesses are engaging in it with a sense of responsibility.

6.2.2 *Combining AI and Employee Relations at HR Acuity*

Business take pride in the trust they have built with the employee relations community. One way companies have achieved this is by showing that HR Acuity's [6–9] technology is built on dependable best practices. The incorporation of artificial intelligence (AI) into industrial relations is transforming the work environment, labor interactions, and organizational configurations. Below are a few important developments and trends:

6.2.2.1 AI-Driven Automation and Labor Dynamics

The use of artificial intelligence technology to do repetitive tasks, data processing, and decision-making that typically require human intelligence is known as AI-powered automation. There are numerous solutions that streamline processes, encourage flexibility, enhance collaboration, and make remote work easier. AI technologies are being more and more used to automate regular tasks, boosting labor productivity and enabling employees to concentrate on intricate and high-value activities. This change enhances productivity and enhances employee competencies, ultimately enhancing the overall work value. Nevertheless, this movement prompts worries about job loss and the necessity for retraining, as some positions may no longer be needed because of automation. Due to the characteristics of the workforce, many job jobs involve some repetitive duties. Employees are overworked and unable to concentrate on more difficult duties as a result. This isn't going to help increase efficiency. Automation driven by AI boosts productivity by automating monotonous tasks and allowing employees to focus on higher-value work.

6.2.2.2 Enhanced Monitoring and Performance Management

Performance management is a crucial process that uses goal-setting, assessment, feedback, and improvement techniques to match team and individual efforts with overarching corporate objectives. Performance management also enables firms to promptly detect and resolve performance gaps or difficulties. Organizations may improve performance and guarantee the best results by proactively taking remedial action, offering the required support, and implementing focused interventions through continuous performance monitoring and assessment. AI algorithms are being incorporated into tools for monitoring employee behavior and performance. Using algorithmic management may improve performance evaluations accuracy, yet it poses ethical concerns about privacy and worker autonomy. Industrial relations must find a way to optimize productivity without compromising employees' rights and well-being. An AI-enhanced performance management platform makes it simple to track each person's achievement as well as the performance of the entire organization and each department. AI monitors performance indicators and can notify if employees are not on pace for achieving the target metrics when they modify their objective accomplishment. The chore of managing performance reviews is far less intimidating with AI. You can balance formal and informal reviews by using AI to help you establish a consistent cadence or cycle for your review process. It can effortlessly distribute reviews throughout a formal review cycle and even remind managers and individual staff to do reviews on time. For a variety of reasons, such as inadequate time, money, or training, managers may find it difficult to provide feedback. In handling performance, artificial intelligence (AI) removes the discomfort and hesitation that come with giving direct, encouraging, and action-oriented assessment.

6.2.2.3 Creation of New Employment Opportunities

Despite fears of job loss, AI is also creating new markets and employment opportunities across various sectors, including transportation, healthcare, and education. For businesses developing a long-term plan centered on generative AI, the technology has the potential to do more than just automate tasks—it can also create jobs for people. The demand for skilled workers who can manage and work alongside AI technologies is increasing, suggesting a shift in the types of jobs available in the future.

For instance, machine learning engineers, data scientists, and specialized researchers are needed for the design and development of AI systems. Professionals of this kind are in more demand and are paid highly. Additionally, experts in cybersecurity and AI ethics must support the implementation of AI. Ethics professionals have the chance to make sure that AI systems' decisions are in line with moral and social norms as awareness of the ethical implications of AI grows. At the same time, cybersecurity experts are needed to safeguard systems against outside threats due to the security dangers connected with AI. AI has the potential to improve medical diagnostics, speed up drug research, and facilitate telemedicine in the healthcare industry. Professional profiles like "health data analysts," who decipher and examine data gathered by AI systems to offer more accurate and individualized diagnoses, are made possible by this. Additionally, in order to operate and maintain the machines and robots that are replacing manual labor, manufacturing workers must learn new skills. Data analysts, AI programmers, and machine learning specialists are among the new professional opportunities being created by the integration of AI into high-tech production methods. Entrepreneurs can now investigate new company prospects thanks to the democratization of AI technologies. Emerging startups are promoting economic growth and employment creation in industries including AI consultancy, tailoring AI solutions for specialized markets, and AI-driven inventions. For example, small business owners can provide distinctive goods and services to customers all over the world through AI-powered e-commerce platforms. People must adjust as AI continues to change the employment environment and labor market in order to remain competitive and relevant in their jobs. Focusing on mastering highly sought-after skills like programming, machine learning, and data analytics is one strategy to adjust. People should also keep up with the most recent advancements in AI and how they affect their respective sectors. This may entail networking with colleagues and professionals, attending conferences, and reading trade journals. People may prosper in a world where artificial intelligence is revolutionizing the way we work by accepting change and never stopping learning new things.

6.2.2.4 Transforming Workplace Environments

AI adoption is expected to improve the quality of workplace environments by increasing collaboration spaces and enhancing overall employee experience. This transformation is crucial for fostering a more engaged and productive workforce, which is a key focus for industrial relations professionals.

6.2.2.5 Legal and Contractual Adjustments

As businesses adopt AI technologies, there is a growing need to modify contracts to address emerging risks associated with AI, such as data usage and algorithmic decision-making This necessitates a proactive approach in industrial relations to ensure that labor agreements reflect the realities of an AI-driven workplace.

6.2.2.6 Focus on Employee Self-Service Tools

New AI trends involve creating self-service tools that enable workers to access information easily and simplify processes. This change enhances not just productivity but also fosters a climate of openness and independence in companies.

6.2.2.7 Documentation for Policies

By automating the development, revision, and dissemination of HR policies, artificial intelligence significantly enhances policy management. By guaranteeing that policies are up to date and consistent, this automation lessens the administrative load on HR departments and improves adherence to legal requirements [9]. AI may also tailor how these policies are communicated to different employee groups, making sure that everyone is aware of their rights and obligations under the company's regulations.

6.2.2.8 Balance Between Work and Life

Workers desire a balance between their personal and professional lives. Increases in workload put them under pressure with the manual system, even when they are not working. Employee productivity may suffer as a result. Where workers' workloads are lessened by automation driven by AI, giving them greater flexibility and a better work-life balance. By automating different tasks, this technology can manage the burden.

AI advancements are greatly impacting industrial relations by changing labor dynamics, improving productivity, and generating fresh job prospects. As these patterns progress, stakeholders in industrial relations must adjust and tackle the challenges and opportunities brought about by AI technologies. The incorporation of Artificial Intelligence (AI) into industrial relations is poised to bring about major changes in the workplace. As AI technologies become more prevalent in organizations, a number of trends are beginning to emerge that will impact the future of work, employee involvement, and how organizations function.

6.2.3 Enhanced Communication and Collaboration

AI-powered tools are facilitating seamless communication and collaboration among teams, especially in remote and hybrid work environments. These tools [10] not only streamline productivity tracking but also enhance the overall employee experience by making it easier for teams to connect and collaborate effectively, regardless of their physical location. This trend is likely to continue, fostering a more inclusive and connected workplace culture.

Virtual teams are growing commonplace as the globe grows more digitally connected. Successful teamwork and communication are essential when members are spread across time zones, nations, and continents. This is where artificial intelligence (AI) enters the picture; it is transforming the way we collaborate by improving communication and teamwork in remote teams. Virtual teams can cooperate more successfully and efficiently by utilizing AI-powered tools and platforms to get around time zone and geographical barriers. Language hurdles, cultural disparities, and technological constraints are some of the particular difficulties faced by virtual teams. Misunderstandings, poor communication, and a lack of trust among team members can result from these difficulties. These obstacles can be overcome, though, if the appropriate methods and resources are used.

6.2.4 Improved Accessibility and Inclusivity

Information is strength in the modern age. Because the internet is so widely available, we have access to a wealth of information and concepts. But not everyone has easy access to this data. Accessing websites, articles, and multimedia content is difficult for people with impairments for a variety of reasons. Artificial Intelligence (AI) has become a potent instrument in recent years for increasing the accessibility and inclusivity of online material. By providing information in multiple languages and formats, AI helps accommodate diverse workforces and ensures that all employees have equal access to important resources and support. This focus on inclusivity is expected to grow, as organizations recognize the value of diverse perspectives and experiences in driving innovation and performance.

When trying to access or navigate the web, people with disabilities—such as those that affect sight, hearing, or mobility—frequently encounter major challenges. This is where artificial intelligence (AI) comes in like a superhero, striving to increase internet accessibility and make sure that everyone, regardless of physical ability, can access, explore, and utilize the wealth of materials available online. It's revolutionary because it creates an inclusive online environment and levels the playing field for digital competition. According to accessibility standards for UX/UI design, AI, for instance, can modify text sizes, color palettes, and navigation options. AI for disability promotes a more inclusive environment by customizing the interface to each user's needs, guaranteeing that all users can participate fully in digital goods and services.

Another illustration is AI-assisted closed captioning and subtitling, which improves the accessibility of multimedia content for people with visual or auditory impairments by using machine learning algorithms to produce more accurate captions and translations. AI may also be used to produce audio descriptions for pictures and films, giving visually challenged persons more context. This is achieved by examining the image or video's content and producing a description that highlights its salient characteristics. The content is then made more inclusive and accessible by incorporating these descriptions into the audio version.

6.2.5 Data-Driven Decision Making

The future of industrial relations will increasingly rely on data-driven insights. AI systems can analyze vast amounts of employee data to identify trends, predict outcomes, and inform decision-making processes. This capability allows organizations to make more informed choices regarding talent management, employee engagement, and organizational development. As a result, companies will be better equipped to respond to the evolving needs of their workforce. Analytics and AI tools are used in data-driven decision-making to inform and direct corporate choices. Data-driven decision-making uses empirical data and sophisticated algorithms to produce actionable insights, in contrast to traditional decision-making approaches that mostly rely on intuition and prior experience. By using objective proof instead of subjective assessment, this method ensures that decisions are more accurate. Large volumes of data can be analyzed by AI systems to find hidden correlations and patterns that human analysts would miss. Organizations can make more precise and well-informed decisions because to this capabilities. AI, for example, may forecast consumer behavior, economic conditions, and operational inefficiencies, enabling companies to proactively handle possible problems and seize opportunity. Systems for making decisions driven by AI are scalable enough to manage complicated decision-making procedures and massive data sets. For businesses aiming to grow or into emerging markets, this scalability is crucial. By automating regular decisions and using AI to supplement human decision-making, businesses may more effectively and efficiently manage development. Businesses can improve their strategy and maintain their competitiveness in a fast evolving environment by using an iterative, information-driven decision-making method. Data analytics are used by a large streaming video service to guide some parts of its content production and growth in the market.

6.2.6 Evolving Skill Requirements

As AI continues to reshape job roles and responsibilities, there will be a significant shift in the skills required for various positions. Jobs with high AI exposure will demand a greater emphasis on management and business process skills, as employees will need to work alongside AI systems and leverage their capabilities effectively.

6.2.7 Balancing Automation and Human Touch

While AI has the potential to automate many tasks, the future of industrial relations will require a careful balance between automation and the human touch. Even if AI is capable of handling repetitive jobs and offering prompt solutions, it still lacks the personal touch that clients require. Maintaining empathy in customer encounters is crucial for long-term success, loyalty, and trust as firms incorporate more technology into their operations. Let's examine why empathy is still so crucial in today's technologically advanced society. Organizations will need to ensure that while AI enhances efficiency, it does not diminish the value of human interaction and emotional intelligence in the workplace. This balance will be crucial for maintaining employee morale and fostering a positive organizational culture.

Humans are special in their capacity for understanding, empathy, and connection. Emotional intelligence is essential in customer connections, teamwork, and leadership that AI cannot replace. A more encouraging, cooperative, and responsive work environment is fostered by human compassion and understanding. Deep insights into consumer behavior and preferences can be obtained through AI and data analytics. By using this data, human agents can then customize their interactions and provide solutions that are specific to the needs of the client. Instead of taking the role of empathy, AI could be utilized as a tool to increase it. The ability to exercise ethical judgment is more crucial than ever in a world where human actions might be greatly impacted by AI decisions. AI, constrained by its programming, is unable to think about moral and ethical issues the way humans can. This human oversight guarantees that AI applications conform to ethical norms and societal values. Humans will always require relationships, empathy, and compassion, regardless of how sophisticated our technologies get. Businesses may provide a seamless client experience that satisfies a range of demands and fosters enduring loyalty by skillfully blending the two.

6.2.8 Focus on Employee Well-Being

In addition to creating a healthy working culture, putting employee well-being first is essential for establishing trust and guaranteeing the successful integration of AI technologies. AI technologies are also being leveraged to enhance employee well-being. By analyzing data related to employee engagement and satisfaction, organizations can identify areas for improvement and implement targeted interventions. When it comes to employee experience, managers are vital. People who put their well-being first encourage candid communication, offer guidance, and provide support when things go tough. This proactive approach to employee well-being is expected to become a standard practice, as companies recognize the link between employee satisfaction and overall productivity.

AI can provide recommendations based on the requirements and interests of workers to produce a personalized and interesting work environment. By appealing to each person's objectives and driving forces, customization promotes more engagement. The capacity of AI and machine learning to evaluate vast volumes of data and provide tailored recommendations is a significant benefit for employee wellbeing. AI can sort through health data, preferences, and habits to develop personalized wellness programs using algorithms and predictive modeling.

Early health risk detection is a strong suit for AI and machine learning. They can spot trends or anomalies in your employees' health data using sophisticated data analysis, allowing for early intervention and the avoidance of potentially dangerous health problems. Wearable technology with an AI-powered remote ECG, for instance, may track biometric information such as heart rate, sleep habits, and activity levels and identify any anomalies that can point to underlying medical issues. The welfare of workers must be given top priority as a guiding principle as businesses negotiate the challenges of implementing AI. Organizations that prioritize people not only foster a great work environment but also develop trust and resistance to technological disruption. Employers may foster cultures where workers flourish, develop, and contribute to the organization's long-term success by using AI to augment human abilities rather than substitute them.

The future of AI-driven industrial relations is poised for significant transformation, characterized by enhanced communication, improved accessibility, data-driven decision-making, evolving skill requirements, and a focus on employee well-being. As organizations navigate these changes, the successful integration of AI will depend on their ability to balance technological advancements with the essential human elements of work. This synergy will ultimately lead to more adaptive, inclusive, and productive workplaces.

6.3 Current and Emerging Trends in AI for Business

AI has become a crucial element of the business environment [11–13], transforming sectors and fostering creativity. As companies examine both current advancements and future developments, it is clear that AI will keep progressing and influencing how businesses function. Let's explore seven trends in AI for business and the effects it will have on the organization.

6.3.1 Enhanced Natural Language Processing

Advancements in recent years have greatly improved Natural Language Processing (NLP) and one can anticipate further enhanced capabilities in the future. AI-driven chatbots and virtual assistants are expected to enhance their conversational abilities, detecting context and intent more accurately in the future. This will allow companies to deliver customized user experiences and optimize customer service processes.

6.3.2 *Reinforcement Learning and Autonomous Systems*

One kind of machine learning procedure that concentrates on autonomous agents' decision-making is called reinforcement learning (RL). Any system that is capable of making judgments and responding to its surroundings without direct human user direction is considered an autonomous agent. Also it can be thought of as a part of AI that allows machines to learn by trial and error, is rapidly becoming more popular. Machines and technology that can function without constant human supervision are referred to as autonomous systems. They analyze information, make choices, and carry out activities by combining sensors, AI algorithms, and machine learning. Advanced autonomous systems like self-driving cars and robotic process automation will increase in complexity and dependability. This will result in improved productivity, lower expenses, and more secure procedures in sectors such as transportation, logistics, and manufacturing. AI and ML in autonomous systems appear to have a bright future. Robots, drones, and self-driving cars will proliferate. AI-driven autonomous systems will also play a major role in the development of smart cities.

6.3.3 *Explainable AI*

With the increasing prevalence of AI, there will be a greater demand for transparency and accountability. Explainable AI methods will become more popular, enabling businesses to comprehend and explain the decisions made by AI systems. This will be especially important in industries such as finance, healthcare, and legal, where regulatory compliance and ethical concerns are extremely important. The ability to articulate the reasoning behind an AI system's choice, suggestion, or forecast is known as explainability. Gaining this capacity necessitates knowing the workings of the AI model and the kinds of data that are used to train it.

Explainability may be required to comply with regulatory requirements, assist developers in making sure the system is operating as intended, or be crucial in enabling anyone impacted by a decision to contest or alter the result. Machine learning operations teams tasked with overseeing AI systems can monitor and manage AI systems more effectively if they use techniques that provide explainability, which can more rapidly highlight mistakes or opportunities for development. Concerns with explainability have varying effects on different AI techniques, and different techniques or tools can offer various kinds of explanation. Some AI systems are difficult to explain but can be implemented without any issues; other situations call for the application of explainable AI techniques, which must be backed by broader systems to guarantee accountability throughout the entire analytics process, from data collection to decision-making. Building trust also requires explainability. Consumers, authorities, and the general public must all have faith that the AI models making important choices are doing so fairly and accurately.

6.3.4 Edge Computing and AI

In order to collect and analyze data in real time without continuously depending on cloud infrastructure, edge artificial intelligence refers to the direct implementation of AI techniques and models on local edge devices, such as sensors or Internet of Things (IoT) gadgets. Edge computing, where data is processed closer to its origin instead of depending on cloud infrastructure, will become increasingly common. The demand for making quick decisions in real-time and minimizing delays will push this trend forward. AI algorithms at the edge will provide quicker insights and actions, which will be advantageous for areas such as autonomous cars, IoT gadgets, and remote surveillance systems. Assuring prompt decisions, data protection, efficient infrastructure, and continuous functioning, including computer vision, edge AI provides real-time responsiveness, privacy compliance, cost effectiveness, and edge autonomy. Camera-equipped edge devices can use AI at the edge to detect anomalies, segment images, and detect objects.

Since edge AI algorithms can process data closer to the device's location, data is processed in milliseconds, giving real-time feedback whether or not an internet connection is available. Since sensitive data never leaves the edge, this procedure may be more data-secure. At the frontline of an organization's user contact are edge AI devices. Real-time edge device monitoring via cloud platforms allows automatic upkeep and spots possible problems before they affect performance. Furthermore, cloud systems provide elastic resources for an organization that manages a fleet of devices and may scale as required.

6.3.5 AI-Powered Cybersecurity

As cyber threats become more advanced, artificial intelligence will be essential for strengthening cybersecurity defenses. AI algorithms will be utilized for detecting abnormalities, recognizing trends, and taking proactive measures against potential threats. This will enable organizations to stay one step ahead of cybercriminals and safeguard sensitive data, ensuring continuity of business operations and maintaining customer trust. Artificial intelligence-powered cybersecurity protection will never completely replace security experts because the workplace will always require innovative problem-solving techniques and more difficult problems. Because AI-powered cybersecurity automation is based on proven use cases in a variety of commercial contexts, it is safe. AI is used, for instance, by information technology (IT) and human resources (HR) teams to onboard new hires and give them the tools and right amount of access they need to perform their jobs well.

AI also has the ability to revolutionize penetration testing by purposefully examining software and network security to find vulnerabilities. By using artificial intelligence (AI) tools to target their own technology, companies will be better equipped to spot flaws before hackers can take advantage of them. AI is particularly good at spotting dangers that humans would otherwise miss. Conventional security technologies could miss irregularities or have trouble identifying zero-day attacks. On the other hand, AI-powered systems identify anomalous activity that can point to an assault by using pattern recognition and anomaly detection.

AI plays a crucial role in automating the management process after a danger is identified. By prioritizing vulnerabilities according to their possible impact, AI helps organizations prioritize priority concerns and expedite patch administration. This entails ranking threats according to risk levels and choosing the best course of action. AI can assist in real-time reaction coordination, reducing the harm that an assault can do.

6.3.6 Personalized Marketing and Recommendation Systems

AI-driven recommendation systems are expected to develop further, allowing companies to provide extremely customized marketing interactions. Through the analysis of extensive customer data, artificial intelligence algorithms will create personalized suggestions, offers, and ads. This will boost customer interaction, increase sales, and enhance overall marketing efficiency.

6.3.7 AI Ethics and Responsible AI

As artificial intelligence becomes more widespread, ethical concerns will become more significant. Businesses will concentrate on creating and executing structures for responsible utilization of AI. This involves recognizing prejudices in AI algorithms, guaranteeing equity and diversity, and setting standards for AI regulation. Companies that focus on ethical and responsible AI practices will not only decrease risks but also establish trust with customers and stakeholders. Establishing confidence in AI solutions that have an opportunity to empower companies and their stakeholders is made possible by a set of principles known as "responsible artificial intelligence" (AI). AI models ought to be developed with specific objectives that center on developing a model in a manner that is secure, reliable, and moral. The process of creating and utilizing AI systems in a way that maximizes positive social effects while lowering the possibility of unfavorable outcomes is known as responsible AI. The goal is to develop AI technologies that not only improve human capabilities but also solve moral issues, especially those pertaining to bias, privacy, and transparency. From improved natural language processing and autonomous systems to AI that can be explained and personalized marketing, these trends in AI will transform industries and open up new possibilities.

A complete goal to reflect society's moral fabric in the field of artificial intelligence is represented by responsible AI. Governments, organizations, and businesses around the world must exemplify these principles in order to shape ethical AI, making sure that their quest for innovation is coupled with moral accountability. AI needs to be transparent in order for stakeholders to have faith in it. Tech businesses need to be transparent about who trains their AI systems, what data was utilized for that training, and—above all—what went into the suggested modifications of their algorithm.

6.3.8 Enhanced Intelligence

The emergence of AI should be a welcome development for people who are still concerned about AI consuming their jobs. By combining the greatest qualities of people and technology, it enables businesses to raise employee productivity and performance. According to Gartner, 40% of big enterprise operations and infrastructure teams will employ AI-augmented automation by 2023, increasing efficiency. Augmented reality has already found applications in the travel, retail, and healthcare sectors. As a result, the number of augmented reality apps will rise in tandem with this AI trend.

Nevertheless, businesses must responsibly embrace these technologies, taking into account ethical concerns and guaranteeing transparency. Organizations can achieve a competitive advantage, foster innovation, and prosper in the AI-driven future by adopting these present and upcoming trends.

6.4 AI Transforming Industries: A Widespread Overview of Its Various Applications

Artificial Intelligence (AI) is advancing greatly in different sectors, fundamentally changing how industries function [14–16] and improving human capabilities. Here is a thorough examination of its various uses.

6.4.1 Healthcare

Artificial intelligence (AI) has revolutionized healthcare by changing how we identify, treat, and keep track of patients. By enabling more individualized treatments and generating more accurate diagnoses, this technology is significantly enhancing healthcare research and results. AI is transforming the healthcare industry with technologies like predictive analytics, personalized medicine, and robotic surgery. Machine learning algorithms examine extensive medical information to anticipate patient results and help with diagnosing, resulting in enhanced patient care and operational effectiveness.

For instance, AI systems could convert a patient's complete medical history into a single number that indicates a likely diagnosis. AI's strength is in its capacity to learn and identify patterns and relationships from vast multidimensional and multimodal datasets. Both prognostication and diagnostic decision-support systems are being developed using machine learning. Medical images, including X-rays, CT, PET, and ultrasound scans, are being read using computer vision and deep learning models. AI-based tools are being used to find tumors early. In order to increase efficiency in sectors like hospital bed management and insurance claim processing, machine learning (ML) procedures are being developed. ML is being used to increase the efficiency of a few online platforms that help with finding a doctor, keeping medical records, or obtaining medication. Others are finding doctors, scheduling appointments, and automating the initial evaluation of symptoms. The manner in which healthcare practitioners give care is changing as a result of AI's ability to evaluate the medical history of a person and produce better, faster results. This allows them to spend more time and money on their patients.

Medical personnel can save time, cut expenses, and enhance medical records administration by employing artificial intelligence in healthcare to make better judgments based on more accurate information. AI in healthcare has the potential to revolutionize everything from finding novel cancer treatments to enhancing patient experiences, paving the path for a time when patients will receive high-quality care and treatment more quickly and precisely than in the past.

6.4.2 *Finance*

In the finance sector, AI enhances risk assessment, fraud detection, and customer service. Algorithms analyze transaction patterns to identify anomalies, while chatbots provide 24/7 customer support, streamlining operations and improving user experience. AI algorithms use real-time market data to conduct trades with previously unheard-of speed and accuracy, revealing deeper insights and determining where investments should be placed. Financial firms can enhance risk management, including security, fraud, anti-money laundering (AML), know your customer (KYC), and compliance operations, by using AI technologies to analyze complex patterns in transaction data sets. Data input, data gathering, data verification, consolidation, and reporting are examples of financial procedures that have historically relied significantly on human labor. The finance function is often expensive, time-consuming, and sluggish to change as a result of all these manual tasks. However, a lot of financial procedures are standardized and clearly defined, which makes them perfect candidates for AI automation. By anticipating consumer behavior and comprehending their purchase preferences, artificial intelligence is also transforming how financial institutions interact with their clientele. More individualized interactions, quicker and more precise customer service, improved credit scoring, and cutting-edge goods and services are all made possible by this.

6.4.3 Manufacturing

The intentional incorporation of AI technology into different facets of the manufacturing process is known as AI for manufacturing. Production, supply chain management, quality assurance, and predictive maintenance are all included in this. AI technologies, including robotics and predictive maintenance, are reshaping manufacturing processes. Smart factories utilize AI to optimize production schedules, reduce downtime, and enhance quality control, resulting in increased efficiency and reduced costs. Predictive maintenance is one of AI's most significant uses. Artificial intelligence (AI) systems evaluate sensor data from equipment to predict faults before they happen, lowering maintenance expenses and unplanned downtime. Computer vision systems that use AI to detect flaws in goods in real time are another example of advanced quality control. Manufacturers are beginning to use "cobots" on their shop floors after decades of using robots. Cobots securely work alongside humans, doing a variety of tasks like picking parts, running machines, and even conducting quality inspections to increase overall production and efficiency, whereas traditional robots need to be kept apart. Cobots are incredibly adaptable and can do a wide range of jobs, from picking and packaging produced goods to gluing, welding, and lubricating automotive components. AI is revolutionizing quality control and testing. Automatically identifying product flaws and equipment damage is possible with image recognition. AI models that have been trained on pictures of both good and bad products, for instance, may determine whether an item needs to be recycled, trashed, or reworked.

6.4.4 Retail

The retail industry benefits from AI through personalized shopping experiences, inventory management, and targeted marketing. AI-driven analytics enable retailers to understand consumer behavior, optimize stock levels, and tailor marketing strategies to individual preferences. Both online and physical retailers use AI-powered retail solutions, which have an impact on everything from pricing and product recommendations to inventory control and customer support. The retail industry has seen a gradual transformation in recent years due to developments in generative AI technologies, which have created new prospects for content creation and natural language real-time customer interaction.

Retailers may increase the likelihood that customers would want to make a purchase by utilizing AI to analyze purchase history data and present relevant cross-selling offers and personalized recommendations. They can receive an email with a promotional offer for a product they've already purchased or be presented with individualized product recommendations when they visit an online store. Retailers can utilize AI to optimize operational efficiencies in warehouse storage and distribution, inventory transit, and retail locations, as well as to monitor, automate, and optimize the intelligent supply chain and assist customers throughout their purchasing experience. Retailers can manage promotions and increase profitability by adjusting prices in real time with the use of AI-enabled dynamic pricing. Demand, stock levels, and what rivals are charging can all affect prices. Additionally, they could change based on the season or past purchasing patterns. Retailers are looking for ways to make their relationship with customers "frictionless," which includes creating more avenues for customers to make purchases, improving functionality, and expanding communications for relationship-building and interactive involvement. In order to expedite encounters and receive individualized attention, customers desire omnichannel search and purchase flexibility. AI in retail can help consumers with problem-solving, brand engagement, and customer service concerns, which will ultimately increase customer loyalty. AI business intelligence systems foresee industry developments and make proactive adjustments to a company's marketing, merchandising, and business strategies by mining insights from consumer, competitor, and marketplace data. AI-powered route planning lowers transportation expenses and speeds up delivery for retailers. Retailers can reduce fuel use and deliver goods to customers more quickly by optimizing their routes. In order to ensure that goods arrive on schedule, logistics staff can also adjust to shifting traffic conditions with the aid of intelligent route planning tools.

6.4.5 Agriculture

Artificial Intelligence (AI) incorporation is not just a novel idea but also an essential in today's agricultural environment. AI in agriculture allows for smarter, more effective operations, marking a major departure from conventional farming approaches. Insufficient land holdings, workforce shortages, climate change, environmental problems, and declining soil fertility are just a few of the challenges that are pushing the modern agricultural scene to alter and go in different creative directions. AI applications in agriculture include precision farming, crop monitoring, and yield prediction. By analyzing data from sensors and drones, farmers can make informed decisions about planting, watering, and harvesting, leading to increased productivity and sustainability.

AI-powered precision farming enables farmers to make well-informed crop management decisions. AI-powered solutions optimize pest control, fertilization, and irrigation by analyzing data from sensors, drones, and satellite photography. For example, real-time crop health issue detection is made possible by drone-assisted aerial surveillance, which is outfitted with sophisticated computer vision. By precisely applying pesticides or nutrients to areas that require attention, these drones reduce waste and their negative effects on the environment. Furthermore, AI's predictive powers include foreseeing possible crop illnesses, pest invasions, and weather patterns. Farmers can proactively protect their crops thanks to this foresight, which improves yield protection. In India, crop diseases have been a significant contributor to production loss, but artificial intelligence is starting to shift the game. Neural networks have a 95% success rate in identifying diseases like apple scabs, according to a study published in Computers and Electronics in Agriculture. In a similar vein, yellow rot in wheat crops has been detected using machine learning algorithms, allowing for prompt interventions. In order to ensure healthy harvests, AI-based pest surveillance systems, such as the National Pest Surveillance System, are also assisting Indian farmers in mitigating climate change-related losses. AI is transforming agriculture, especially in the areas of crop health monitoring and pest identification, providing a clear illustration of how technology is improving farming's precision and sustainability. AI-powered agricultural solutions use cutting-edge methods such as satellite thermal imagery analysis. This novel technique enables the early detection of possible agricultural illnesses or insect infestations.

6.4.6 Education

AI in education enables tailored learning experiences and streamlines administrative processes. Adaptive learning systems utilize artificial intelligence to customize educational materials for each student, while automation simplifies administrative duties like grading and organizing schedules. AI's impact goes beyond individual uses; it is transforming entire sectors by facilitating fresh business strategies and improving operational efficiency. The combination of AI with technologies such as IoT and big data analytics is expanding the limits of what can be achieved, resulting in more intelligent and effective systems. As artificial intelligence advances, its ability to foster creativity and enhance the standard of living across different industries remains vast. Continued advancements in AI technologies offer the potential to unlock more applications and continue transforming industries globally.

6.5 Opportunities for Collaboration Between Humans and Machines in Industrial Settings

During the era of automation, traditional labor relations encounter unparalleled difficulties. Jobs are vanishing, algorithms are determining who gets hired, and the ethical issues related to AI usage are becoming more important [17].

6.5.1 Critical Thinking and Problem-Solving

Evaluate intricate situations related to automation and AI, and create original methods for overseeing a changed workforce. Negotiation and conflict resolution: Connect humans and machines through effective communication to resolve conflicts stemming from technological changes. Strategic foresight and planning: Predict upcoming trends and proactively create plans for adjusting to the constantly changing workplace.

6.5.2 Ethical Concerns and Use of AI Responsibly

Ensure ethical and responsible AI deployment, protecting worker rights and well-being. The incorporation of advanced technologies in industrial environments has created many chances for cooperation between humans and machines. This collaboration is not just boosting efficiency but also advancing safety and creativity in the work environment. This is a summary of the evolving collaboration and its advantages.

6.5.3 Efficiency and Productivity

AI-powered equipment with advanced sensors, motors, and actuators can identify individuals and objects, enabling them to work alongside humans safely in factories. This feature facilitates a smooth workflow where machines manage repetitive and laborious tasks, allowing human workers to concentrate on more intricate and innovative aspects of their tasks. In places such as Amazon's fulfillment centers, robots support employees by handling inventory and moving items, leading to a marked increase in productivity. Additionally, by working together, humans and machines improve safety in the workplace. Industries can lower the chance of accidents related to manual handling and repetitive tasks by using collaborative robots (cobots). Cobots are created to operate near human employees, guaranteeing safety measures are followed while also enabling a more interactive work setting. This collaboration promotes worker safety and well-being and also encourages a culture of safety. Sharing real-time data is a key benefit of human-machine teamwork. This ability enables employees to make educated choices using the most up-to-date information. For instance, machines have the capability to offer observations on operational effectiveness, warning human operators about possible problems before they worsen. This proactive method improves decision-making procedures and aids in creating more efficient operations.

6.5.4 *Innovation and Creativity*

With machines handling routine tasks, human workers have more time to focus on innovation and problem-solving. The partnership promotes an innovative atmosphere in which humans and machines work together to explore and create novel solutions. This collaboration may result in the creation of new and inventive products and methods that would not have been achievable without the strengths of both parties. The rise of Industry 5.0 highlights the significance of synergy between humans and machines, with a focus on sustainability and improving human dignity in the workplace. This new way of thinking encourages industries to embrace methods that honor human input and utilize machine capacities. Creating a cooperative atmosphere within companies enables them to enhance manufacturing procedures and enhance working conditions, ultimately driving toward a more sustainable future. The partnership between humans and machines in industrial environments offers numerous chances to improve efficiency, safety, and innovation. As industries increasingly adopt these technologies, the opportunity for enhanced productivity and a more involved workforce will expand, leading toward a future where humans and machines collaborate seamlessly.

6.6 Approach and Asses AI Adoption in HR

AI will impact the HR function's work throughout the employee life cycle. This influence involves HR activities and providing services, recruitment, education and training, and managing talents (see Fig. 6.1). Initially, AI will generate different employee requirements regarding their interactions with HR and HR technologies [18].

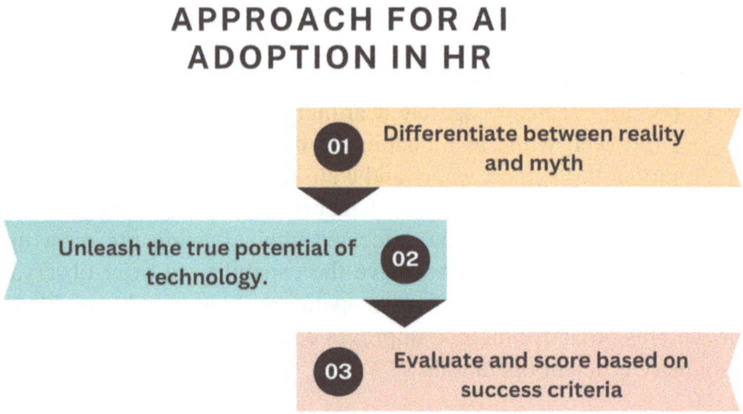

Fig. 6.1 Approach for AI adoption in HR

A recent study suggests that by 2024, 80% of Global 2000 companies will use algorithmic managers for hiring, firing, and training workers. The Future of Work survey by Eightfold AI indicates that HR departments are increasingly deploying AI across a range of functions, such as employee records management, payroll and benefits administration, recruitment, performance management, and onboarding. As AI redefines HR roles, professionals must acquire new competencies to stay relevant and contribute to business value. Here are some key areas where AI is making an impact in HR.

(i) AI-powered Recruitment and Hiring: AI is streamlining the recruitment process, from sourcing candidates to conducting initial screenings, reviewing resumes, and setting equitable salary offers.
(ii) AI-driven Onboarding and Off-boarding: AI-driven platforms are enhancing employee onboarding by streamlining form completion, policy dissemination, and training schedules. AI also supports efficient offboarding, managing exit surveys, company asset returns, and access revocation with ease.
(iii) Workforce Planning: With AI, HR analytics can shift through vast data sets to identify trends, forecast turnover, and detect skills shortages, enabling proactive training and succession planning.
(iv) HR Chatbots and Virtual Assistants: Chatbots are revolutionizing HR by providing round-the-clock responses to queries on leave policies, benefits, and more, improving the employee experience and freeing HR professionals for more complex tasks.
(v) AI-enabled Learning and Development: AI facilitates tailored learning journeys, adjusting educational content to match an individual's progress and preferences. As AI entrenches itself within HR, adept professionals capable of melding technological advancements with human-centric approaches will become increasingly vital. They are the pioneers guiding companies toward a new, more efficient, unbiased, and profound era of HR operations.

6.6.1 Current Trends in AI Adoption in Various Industries

The global AI market was valued at USD 638.23 billion in 2024 and is expected to increase at a rate of 19.1% from 2024 to 2034, reaching over USD 3680.47 billion. In 2023, the artificial intelligence (AI) market in North America was valued at USD 198.57 billion. By 2023, the market for AI technology was valued at over $200 billion, and by 2030, it is expected to have grown to over 1.8 trillion dollars. AI is no longer considered futuristic; rather, it is currently a crucial component of many industries, including manufacturing, retail, healthcare, banking and finance, and information technology [19]. In order to create a more intelligent and effective economy, artificial intelligence is transforming operations, user interfaces, and product design. It is now clear that artificial intelligence (AI) offers a wide range of uses in corporate expansion and strategic direction determination. The Top 5

Industries have been examined in this infographic. Leading AI adoption is anticipated in 2024: AI is being used by the banking and financial sector to automate procedures, lowering individualization and insecurity.

Furthermore, information technology is undergoing rapid advancements through the application of artificial intelligence in cyber security and data management, and medicine and health care are ready for the use of AI in illness diagnosis and customized treatment programs (see Fig. 6.2). Smart factories and predictive maintenance are bringing significant benefits to the manufacturing sector, while the use of AI in retail is facilitating better customer interactions and company advancements.

AI utilization in manufacturing is growing by 12%, smart production is becoming more common, and automation is significantly improving production process efficiency. With only 4% of AI adoption in professional and personal service and civil construction industries in their later stage, there has been a significant trend towards AI adoption.

The trends that were examined focus more on practical applications rather than futuristic concepts, and they can be beneficial for small and medium-sized businesses. Consider MobiDev if a team is needed to integrate AI into the product or improve company's processes. The vast internal knowledge in software engineering and AI enables companies to identify efficient solutions for particular business requirements and integrate AI technology to align with the product's unique characteristics. Various AI adaptation trends have been examined in this section.

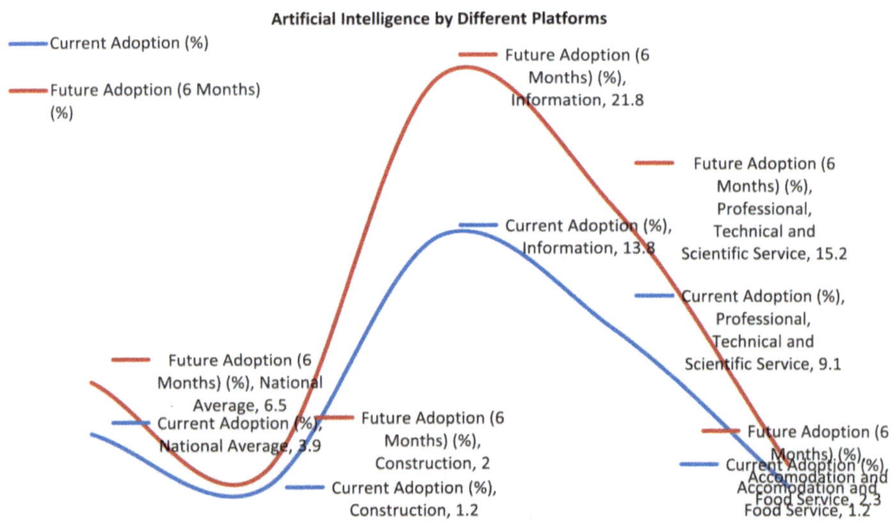

Fig. 6.2 Artificial intelligence by different platforms

6.6.1.1 Generative AI Dominates Market

It is forecasted that in 2024, the growth of generative artificial intelligence will persist, leading to a revolutionary shift in the worldwide economic scene as companies acknowledge its vast possibilities. As per Bloomberg Intelligence (BI) research, the generative AI market is expected to significantly increase, reaching $1.3 trillion in the next decade from its current size of $40 billion in 2022 [20]. Different methods and models, such as diffusion models for creating images and transformer-based models for generating text, are utilized by Generative AI. LLMs also utilize transformer structures. These techniques allow the system to gain knowledge from current data and generate new data that mirrors the original information. Sophisticated generative algorithms will reach new levels of ability, ease of use, and expandability across different fields, leading to increased adoption by organizations.

Generative AI has shown its benefits in different fields like demand estimation, supply chain improvement, and product creation. Its ability to examine large amounts of data, identify trends, and provide useful information has resulted in enhanced decision-making and more streamlined operations. For instance, Generative Adversarial Networks (GANs) are dominating the market by mainly functioning as tools for entertainment. Two famous instances include FaceApp, created for the Western market, and ZAO, customized for the Eastern market.

Furthermore, the use of generative AI in the healthcare industry has resulted in notable enhancements in patient care and operational effectiveness, especially in fields such as managing medical supplies and monitoring medical devices. The same idea applies to customer service as well. Using Natural Language Processing technology (NLP) can enhance customer satisfaction through online searches, spell-checking, and voice assistants.

6.6.1.2 Generative AI for Software Development

Generative AI is essential in developing code solutions for website creators and platforms that do not require coding. Automated code generation simplifies the development process, making it possible for a broader audience to create advanced AI solutions without requiring in-depth coding knowledge. Generative AI solutions come equipped with pre-made algorithms and AI website creators, making the process of AI development more accessible and user-friendly [21]. Site builders can range from basic options with automated content and personalized designs to more advanced AI tools tailored for specific objectives.

No-code AI platforms are needed when customization of the created products is not a top priority. Companies frequently utilize these choices in computer programs to detect and categorize images, objects, poses, sounds, and additional elements. Google Cloud Auto ML, Google ML Kit, Runaway AI, CreateML, and MakeML are some of the most widely used platforms. The plan provided will assist in getting ready to utilize no-code AI platforms for company.

Generative AI plays a crucial role in promoting the connection of API endpoints, enabling the creation of advanced applications for developers. It is predicted that in 2024, software developers will have access to improved software development kits and APIs to enhance existing AI models with AI microservices such as RAG as a service. This tailorization will enable businesses to make full use of AI's efficiency, integrating smart assistants and summarization tools for accessing up-to-date financial data [21, 22].

6.6.1.3 LLMs Power Up Virtual Assistants and Chatbots

ChatGPT has boosted both LLMs and AI in the media and everyday conversations. A lot of people are already using ChatGPT in our daily routines as required. Utilizing Large Language Models (LLMs) strategically within business environments offers a multitude of advantages such as handling customer inquiries, analyzing sentiments, aiding human agents, and recognizing customer trends [23].

LLMs are commonly used as digital assistants and are frequently the first interaction people have with AI technology. The unique aspect of these AI solutions is their capacity to engage with users personally. For example, a chatbot powered by AI surpasses basic pre-programmed instructions. The focus is on understanding customer intentions and actions. These tools help with communication in a way that closely mimics human-to-human interaction, making sure important information is conveyed in a way that customers find comfortable. The adoption of chatbots is growing in sectors like healthcare, finance, marketing, sales, travel, and hospitality, leading to a significant decrease in the requirement for human manpower [24, 25]. For instance, a medical chatbot can efficiently assist in booking a patient's appointment, answering common queries, and sending reminders for medication and exercise.

In various industries, chatbots are essential for organizing and guiding customer questions, sending customized messages, and providing personalized help. In the field of education, chatbots have become essential tools that are easily accessible to help strengthen understanding at a time that suits the learner. According to Business Insider, it is expected that the chatbot market will reach a value of USD $9.4 billion by 2024 [26]. The rapid pace of modern life makes it easy to understand why AI-powered virtual assistants are so popular. Engaging with conversational AI assistants allows individuals to access essential information while still carrying out their daily tasks. In the end, improvements in Natural Language Processing (NLP) and speech recognition have significantly enhanced the functionality of tailored automated systems. An illustration can be seen in the video of how the NLP-powered system for generating questions avoids mistakes during the secure authentication procedure.

6.6.1.4 Narrow-Tailored AI Solutions Promote the Adoption of Artificial Intelligence

Narrow AI is used to describe AI systems created for specific, clearly defined purposes or uses. These systems are excellent at carrying out particular tasks within a limited area, encouraging the implementation of AI across various levels in business. Despite being adaptable in nature, general AI is more suited for specific business objectives and simpler to create within a constrained budget. It is expected to see an increase in specialized AI solutions in 2024. Though ChatGPT functions well as a general AI assistant, it may not always be the most suitable option for every task. Therefore, it is anticipated that in 2024 there will be AI platforms customized for researchers, writing generation tools created for journalists, and rendering platforms made specifically for designers, as well as other specialized applications. AI solutions will be enhanced to address particular use cases, either by using a unique foundational model or by creating a specialized workflow tailored to it [27]. Businesses can take the chance to lead the upcoming technological age by dominating a specific category and then diversifying their products. In this situation, a more targeted and specific starting product is probably going to have more success.

6.6.1.5 AI Enhances Security and Surveillance

The advancement of fresh artificial intelligence technologies enables the attainment of a higher level of quality in security systems. Video surveillance can now integrate biometric authentication through face and voice recognition, human pose estimation, and automated image analysis. AI-powered security and monitoring systems enable businesses and customers to operate with more precise configurations and accurately detect objects that require action when they are detected. Video capture and analysis software aids in securing vast public and private spaces in crowded areas by identifying possible threats. Automated identification of violent behavior and theft can quickly alert authorities, potentially preventing loss of life [27]. AI-powered applications now have improved voice recognition abilities that can determine a person's age, gender, and emotions. Furthermore, biometric facial recognition is crucial for upholding security in general. It's essential to note that there are many technologies available to potential attackers and fraudulent users. Instances of spoofing attacks, in which a person impersonates another individual for illegal benefits, are fairly common. They could use harmful software, doctored images, or illegally obtained personal information for these intentions. Because numerous Internet protocols do not have methods to verify the origin of a request is essential. This is the reason why software needs to include strong and secure identity verification features to guarantee the authenticity and safety of user interactions. Therefore, the need for a variety of advanced anti-spoofing techniques will continue to be high in 2024. Using biometrics for "who you are" authentication allows the confirmation of a person's identity through unique traits such as fingerprints, iris patterns, voice, and facial characteristics [27–29].

The strategy of Edge AI entails installing and operating biometric AI applications on the user's peripheral device, removing the need for a constant internet connection and cloud service. The information is processed independently on the user's portable, and possibly wearable, device. Using edge biometrics for office security is a frequent occurrence. This kind of solution has emerged as a hopeful field in AI-driven advancements to enhance security and surveillance.

6.6.1.6 AI Boosts Real-Time Video Processing

The live-streaming industry has grown substantially in the past few years due to the widespread internet access, advancements in video-streaming tech, popularity of smartphones, and the rise of social media. The CMI Team's market research predicts a 28% compound annual growth rate for the global Live Streaming Market between 2023 and 2032. It is projected that the valuation will reach USD $256.56 billion by 2032 [30]. It is vital to guarantee precise data transmission and reduce video processing latency for the effective management of real-time video streams. Artificial intelligence is essential in the key aspects of this process, specifically in data pipeline processing. The modern system for processing live video incorporates a pre-trained neural network model, algorithms for implementing user scenarios, and cloud infrastructure. This merging is crucial in attaining the speed of live streaming. Algorithm improvements and parallel processing can achieve speed up in video processing. The pipeline architecture is the best option for quick and top-notch video processing, with the added advantage of integrating features such as face recognition and blurring [31]. AI technology is used to separate the person in a frame from the background in real-time video by developing a model. This project is dependent on a neural network. To run, there are options to select from available models like BodyPix, MediaPipe, or PixelLib. Afterward, the selected model with the appropriate framework and structure the best performance procedure utilizing WebAssembly, WebGL, or WebGPU should be combined.

6.6.2 *AI Trends Winning the Market Across Industries*

The next chapter will explore how artificial intelligence is changing within different industries. Let's analyze how AI developments are impacting different sectors by looking at the progress, uses, and consequences specific to each industry.

6.6.2.1 AI Improves Diagnostic Accuracy in Healthcare

The most recent advancements in AI technology have been causing significant changes in the development of healthcare applications. In the field of healthcare, the latest tendencies emphasize these encouraging AI development areas: Personal health advisors are provided by both wearable and non-wearable health devices that track vital health indicators in real-time and provide tailored feedback for individuals. Incorporating AI into the automation and personalization of drug and vaccine development research and trials, including the use of digital twins. Progress in AI-driven technology for Internet of Medical Things (IoMT), enhancing capabilities of medical equipment, and the creation of "Software as a Medical Device" (SaMD) to optimize the effectiveness of medical devices [31].

Utilizing AI in segmenting medical images like MRI and CT scans to improve the efficiency of analyzing anatomical data. Another potential application of AI in the healthcare sector is related to diagnosing medical conditions. Experts in research and healthcare have applied AI technology in various medical conditions, such as identifying cancer, diabetic retinopathy, and EKG abnormalities, as well as forecasting risk factors for cardiovascular diseases. For instance, consider the research carried out in South Korea that compared diagnoses of breast cancer between radiologists and artificial intelligence. The AI diagnosis was 12% more sensitive in detecting breast cancer masses compared to radiologists, with a 90% accuracy vs. 78% accuracy. Additionally, AI outperformed radiologists by detecting early breast cancer at a rate of 91%, compared to the radiologists' rate of 74%. Dementia poses a healthcare challenge due to the inconsistency of its symptoms and the struggle to identify them. The problem is being tackled using speech processing models, with help from artificial intelligence. These models help to identify communicative and logical problems that signal the likelihood of developing this illness [31, 32].

Utilizing AI in dementia diagnosis involves the use of three specific areas of artificial intelligence: Natural Language Processing (NLP), Machine Learning (ML), and Neural Networks. It can be applied for early detection and tracking the advancement of the condition. Neuropsychological evaluations can be conducted via telephone recordings to diagnose early, while classification models aid in tracking changes in the patient's state. The integration of new AI technologies has greatly helped in the development of fresh approaches to diagnosing cancer using AI, offering medical professionals comprehensive and detailed information. Specialists require a significant amount of time and effort to manually examine the vast amount of unstructured data in whole slide imaging (WSI) [33]. The issue of manual examination can be tackled effectively with the use of AI. People should know how AI is used in the fields of fitness and rehabilitation. In these regions, it is connected to human pose estimation (HPE) [34]. Human Pose Estimation (HPE) is a computer vision challenge focused on recognizing and accurately following specific points on the human body. Recognizing motion patterns, determining specific joint positions, or analyzing the overall pose is highly dependent on these key points. HPE can be utilized for a range of functions like body motion sensing, posture improvement aids, workout monitoring, and AI-driven fitness guidance. Human pose estimation and natural language processing algorithms enable users to navigate various exercises and provide and receive immediate feedback.

6.6.2.2 AI-Driven Visual Inspection in Manufacturing

AI-powered visual inspection in manufacturing is an innovative development that utilizes AI technologies to improve quality control and inspection procedures in manufacturing settings. This method combines computer vision, machine learning, and other AI methods to automate and improve the examination of products, components, or procedures [35].

AI-based visual inspection is utilized to check the appropriateness of components for car assembly, as well as for detecting defects on the conveyor. The next step in enhancing the identification of flaws in manufacturing companies will concentrate on automating analysis and decision-making processes. AI software has the ability to identify the type of imperfections in components or final goods using information from cameras and IoT sensors. Utilizing AI-powered computer vision enables the seamless detection and removal of faulty items, meeting manufacturing needs, and maintaining high-quality criteria. This ensures manufacturing processes run smoothly with minimal interruptions.

6.6.2.3 AI Advancements in Retail

AI data analytics streamlines decision-making for business owners, increasing effectiveness, efficiency, and saving time. AI-driven demand forecasting provides businesses with enhanced predictions, quicker decision-making, improved marketing planning, optimized supply chain operations, and increased customer satisfaction, ultimately leading to improved operational performance and competitiveness in the market. McKinsey research shows that companies who implement artificial intelligence for supply chain management before others experience a 15% decrease in logistics costs, a 35% drop in inventory levels, and a 65% rise in service levels compared to those who adopt AI later [36–38].

In the retail sector, there have been many examples of AI-driven changes in the past few years. The introduction of self-checkout technology in supermarkets, which automates cash registers using computer vision, can help to reduce traditional bottlenecks and improve customer satisfaction by saving time. Utilizing the most advanced artificial intelligence technologies allows for enhancing retail through various automation solutions, ranging from partial modular automation like vending machines to a completely automated "grab-and-go" store [37].

Another notable trend to highlight is the growth and widespread adoption of virtual fitting room technology within the retail industry. With the use of artificial intelligence, image processing, and machine learning, this advanced virtual fitting technology accurately replicates how clothing fits and looks on users of varying body shapes. This advancement lets customers virtually test out clothes at home, helping them see how the items will look before buying them. Methods implemented in retail can be effectively applied to the catering industry as well [38]. Innovations target key steps of online shopping, such as identifying the buyer, tracking their actions, recognizing products, verifying purchases, and processing payments.

6.6.2.4 AI Trends in Marketing

The improvement in the caliber of content produced by Artificial Intelligence is a significant example of advancements in the field, a subject discussed in this article. Research and development in this field are classified as part of Generative AI. In particular, Natural Language Processing (NLP) focuses on developing algorithms for generating text. This branch of AI concentrates on making models that improve search engine functions, produce text for business uses, and aid in chatbot advancement [39].

Another trend is linked to AI product suggestions and AI intelligent search functions. By utilizing AI to examine past data, it is feasible to anticipate future performance by considering a range of factors. Analyzing users' preferences can be valuable in recommending products they may enjoy. Additionally, AI can assist companies in customizing website search outcomes for an individual customer by analyzing their previous search history, in-platform actions, and product characteristics. AI is also enhancing the automation of marketing tasks. It encompasses a wide range of tasks, such as automated email sending and social media updates. This development could enable faster changes, the implementation of additional micro-campaigns, the effective targeting of smaller segments, and more possibilities. The increased use of AI-driven marketing automation could transform audience expectations [39, 40]. People may start expecting campaigns that are more timely, segmentation that is more refined, and content that is even more personalized on a hyper-individualized level.

6.6.2.5 AI Trends in Fintech

The emergence of various significant trends, influenced by the integration of AI in the Fintech industry, has transformed the sector's overall landscape. AI in Fintech enables financial institutions to enhance security measures and deter fraud. AI algorithms, powered by artificial intelligence, improve fraud detection by analyzing transactions in real-time to prevent and detect suspicious activities. This enhances security protocols in the financial industry as a whole and simplifies decision-making for various management levels. AI-supported biometric authentication is becoming increasingly common in the Fintech industry to ensure secure user verification. Facial recognition, fingerprint scanning, and voice authentication improve the level of security for financial transactions [41–43].

AI algorithms are revolutionizing the credit scoring and underwriting processes through intelligent document processing. AI assists in making more precise lending decisions by examining a wider range of data, such as non-traditional sources, leading to improved risk assessment. AI aids in managing large amounts of documentation more efficiently. Financial regulators have to handle numerous compliance documents manually in order to enforce regulatory changes, and this task also necessitates eligible staff from various business units. The OCR technology can make these processes much easier by automating document management for client onboarding, payments, and receipt recognition. Plus, AI is utilized to streamline regulatory compliance processes and reporting in the Fintech sector [42]. Automated systems ensure adherence to complex financial regulations, reducing errors and enhancing efficiency.

Fintech firms are more and more using AI-powered chatbots and virtual assistants to improve customer engagement. These tools offer customized help, simplify customer support, and give information about financial questions. Additionally, AI can assist in making individual financial choices. AI-driven financial apps provide solutions for financial planning. Through examining how users manage their money and what they hope to achieve financially, these resources offer personalized guidance, help with budgeting, and suggestions for investing. AI algorithms are heavily utilized in algorithmic trading to quickly make investment decisions based on data analysis. These algorithms study market trends, news, and different data points in order to make trades at the best times. AI-driven smart advisors provide automated investment guidance based on algorithms [42, 43]. These instruments evaluate market patterns, investor choices, and risk profiles in order to offer tailor-made and budget-friendly investment plans.

6.7 Conclusions

The fast progress of AI brings challenges and chances for industrial relations. Organizations need to adjust to the impact of AI-induced technological disruptions, which can change job responsibilities and necessitate acquiring new abilities. Ongoing communication between employers and employees will be required for this adjustment to ensure a seamless transition. In conclusion, the future of AI-driven industrial relations involves increased employee empowerment, HR practices alignment, and the importance of adaptive leadership. AI advancements will greatly impact workplace interactions, transforming organizational structures to be more creative and adaptable. AI has the ability to promote inclusivity and responsiveness in workplaces, in line with the needs of contemporary employees seeking transparency and participation. In the future, industrial relations will be more closely tied to business strategies through AI insights, enhancing the role of human resource management. Organizations have the ability to use AI for examining workforce data, forecasting trends, and making well-informed decisions that are in line with their overall business objectives. This strategic approach has the potential to enhance organizational performance and increase employee satisfaction.

References

1. West, D. M. (2018). *The future of work: Robots, AI, and automation*. Brookings Institution Press.
2. Oosthuizen, R. M. (2022). The fourth industrial revolution–smart technology, artificial intelligence, robotics and algorithms: Industrial psychologists in future workplaces. *Frontiers in Artificial Intelligence, 5*, 913168.
3. Böhmer, N., & Schinnenburg, H. (2023). Critical exploration of AI-driven HRM to build up organizational capabilities. *Employee Relations: The International Journal, 45*(5), 1057–1082.
4. Cooke, F. L., Xu, J., & Bian, H. (2019). The prospect of decent work, decent industrial relations and decent social relations in China: Towards a multi-level and multi-disciplinary approach. *The International Journal of Human Resource Management, 30*(1), 122–155.
5. De Stefano, V., & Doellgast, V. (2023). Introduction to the Transfer special issue. Regulating AI at work: Labour relations, automation, and algorithmic management. *Transfer: European Review of Labour and Research, 29*(1), 9–20.
6. Chukwuka, E. J., & Dibie, K. E. (2024). Strategic role of artificial intelligence (AI) on human resource management (HR) employee performance evaluation function. *International Journal of Entrepreneurship and Business Innovation, 7*(2), 269–282.
7. Khandelwal, K., Upadhyay, A. K., & Rukadikar, A. (2024). The synergy of human resource development (HRD) and artificial intelligence (AI) in today's workplace. *Human Resource Development International, 27*(4), 622–639.
8. Sinha, E. (2023). Integrating human and artificial intelligence within organizations: A conceptual framework based on artistry and scientific HR elements. In *Managing technology integration for human resources in industry 5.0* (pp. 48–67). IGI Global.
9. Vrontis, D., Christofi, M., Pereira, V., Tarba, S., Makrides, A., & Trichina, E. (2023). Artificial intelligence, robotics, advanced technologies and human resource management: A systematic review. In *Artificial intelligence and international HRM* (pp. 172–201). Routledge.
10. Tambe, P., Cappelli, P., & Yakubovich, V. (2019). Artificial intelligence in human resources management: Challenges and a path forward. *California Management Review, 61*(4), 15–42.
11. Ruiz-Real, J. L., Uribe-Toril, J., Torres, J. A., & De Pablo, J. (2021). Artificial intelligence in business and economics research: Trends and future. *Journal of Business Economics and Management, 22*(1), 98–117.
12. Garg, V., Aggarwal, S., Tiwari, P., & Chatterjee, P. (Eds.). (2021). *Applications of artificial intelligence in business and finance: Modern trends*. CRC Press.
13. Lee, J., Suh, T., Roy, D., & Baucus, M. (2019). Emerging technology and business model innovation: The case of artificial intelligence. *Journal of Open Innovation: Technology, Market, and Complexity, 5*(3), 44.
14. Rashid, A. B., & Kausik, A. K. (2024). AI revolutionizing industries worldwide: A comprehensive overview of its diverse applications. *Hybrid Advances, 7*, 100277.
15. Javaid, M., Haleem, A., Singh, R. P., & Suman, R. (2022). Artificial intelligence applications for industry 4.0: A literature-based study. *Journal of Industrial Integration and Management, 7*(01), 83–111.
16. Kuhar, N., Kumria, P., & Rani, S. (2024). Overview of applications of artificial intelligence (AI) in diverse fields. In *Application of artificial intelligence in wastewater treatment* (pp. 41–83). Cham.
17. Pizoń, J., & Gola, A. (2023). Human–machine relationship—perspective and future roadmap for industry 5.0 solutions. *Machines, 11*(2), 203.
18. Hmoud, B. I., & Várallyai, L. (2020). Artificial intelligence in human resources information systems: Investigating its trust and adoption determinants. *International Journal of Engineering and Management Sciences, 5*(1), 749–765.
19. Gündüzyeli, B. (2024). Artificial intelligence in digital marketing within the framework of sustainable management. *Sustainability, 16*(23), 10511.
20. Kumar, V. (2023). The economic value of digital disruption. *Management for Professionals*. https://doi.org/10.1007/978-981-19-8148-7

21. Rajbhoj, A., Somase, A., Kulkarni, P., & Kulkarni, V. (2024). Accelerating software development using generative AI: ChatGPT case study. In *Proceedings of the 17th innovations in software engineering conference* (pp. 1–11). IEEE.
22. Ebert, C., & Louridas, P. (2023). Generative AI for software practitioners. *IEEE Software, 40*(4), 30–38.
23. Singh, V. (2023). *Exploring the role of large language model (LLM)-based chatbots for human resources* (Doctoral dissertation).
24. Raj, K., Priya, K., Senthilkumar, K., Natarajan, S., Arun, R., & Thoti, K. K. (2024). The role of Chatbots and virtual assistants in enhancing customer service and engagement: A stacked BiLSTM and A-GRU technique. *In 2024 international conference on integrated intelligence and communication systems (ICIICS)* (pp. 1–6). IEEE.
25. Casheekar, A., Lahiri, A., Rath, K., Prabhakar, K. S., & Srinivasan, K. (2024). A contemporary review on chatbots, AI-powered virtual conversational agents, ChatGPT: Applications, open challenges and future research directions. *Computer Science Review, 52*, 100632.
26. Raihan, A., Mia, M. R., Tafsirun, U., Naher, K., Islam, N., Rashid, F., & Rahman, S. (n.d). *Financial risk and management reviews.*
27. Bertolini, A. (2020). A functional approach to the regulation of AI. In *AI-Enabled health care: From decision support to autonomous robots* (Vol. 39, pp. 285–296). Gruppo Nazionale di Bioingegneria.
28. Srivastava, S., Bisht, A., & Narayan, N. (2017). Safety and security in smart cities using artificial intelligence—A review. In *2017 7th international conference on cloud computing, data science & engineering-confluence* (pp. 130–133). IEEE.
29. Vashishth, T. K., Sharma, V., Kumar, B., Sharma, K. K., Chaudhary, S., & Panwar, R. (2024). Enhancing surveillance systems through mathematical models and artificial intelligence: An image processing approach. In *Mathematical models using artificial intelligence for surveillance systems* (pp. 91–120). Wiley.
30. Oyeniyi, J., & Oluwaseyi, P. (2024). Emerging trends in AI-powered medical imaging: Enhancing diagnostic accuracy and treatment decisions. *International Journal of Enhanced Research in Science Technology & Engineering, 13*, 2319–7463.
31. Zeb, S., Nizamullah, F. N. U., Abbasi, N., & Fahad, M. (2024). AI in healthcare: Revolutionizing diagnosis and therapy. *International Journal of Multidisciplinary Sciences and Arts, 3*(3), 118–128.
32. Khanna, N. N., Maindarkar, M. A., Viswanathan, V., Fernandes, J. F. E., Paul, S., Bhagawati, M., et al. (2022). Economics of artificial intelligence in healthcare: Diagnosis vs. treatment. *Healthcare, 10*(12), 2493.
33. Rodriguez, J. P. M., Rodriguez, R., Silva, V. W. K., Kitamura, F. C., Corradi, G. C. A., de Marchi, A. C. B., & Rieder, R. (2022). Artificial intelligence as a tool for diagnosis in digital pathology whole slide images: A systematic review. *Journal of Pathology Informatics, 13*, 100138.
34. Zheng, C., Wu, W., Chen, C., Yang, T., Zhu, S., Shen, J., et al. (2023). Deep learning-based human pose estimation: A survey. *ACM Computing Surveys, 56*(1), 1–37.
35. Arora, M. (2023). AI-driven industry 4.0: Advancing quality control through cutting-edge image processing for automated defect detection. *International Journal of Computer Science and Mobile Computing, 12*(8), 16–32.
36. Viswanathan, J. (2024). Artificial intelligence: Transforming the future of retail. *International Journal of Science and Research, 13*(9), 5.
37. Joshi, N. K., Kulshreshtha, K., & Jain, U. (2024). The role of AI in enhancing customer service in the retail sector. *Journal of Data Acquisition and Processing, 39*(1), 1270–1277.
38. Muthukalyani, A. R. (2023). Analyzing the adoption and influence of AI in retail supply chain operations. *International Journal of Artificial Intelligence Research Development, 1*(01), 43–51.
39. Kopalle, P. K., Gangwar, M., Kaplan, A., Ramachandran, D., Reinartz, W., & Rindfleisch, A. (2022). Examining artificial intelligence (AI) technologies in marketing via a global

lens: Current trends and future research opportunities. *International Journal of Research in Marketing, 39*(2), 522–540.

40. Pradeep, A. K., Appel, A., & Sthanunathan, S. (2018). *AI for marketing and product innovation: Powerful new tools for predicting trends, connecting with customers, and closing sales*. John Wiley & Sons.
41. Gupta, R., Kukreja, G., Gupta, A., & Tyagi, L. (2021). Artificial intelligence fostering fintech: Emerging trends and use cases. In *Cybersecurity in emerging digital era: First international conference, ICCEDE 2020, Greater Noida, India, October 9–10, 2020, Revised Selected Papers 1* (pp. 61–73). Springer.
42. Saiyed, A. (2025). AI-driven innovations in Fintech: Applications, challenges, and future trends. *International Journal of Electrical and Computer Engineering Research, 5*(1), 8–15.
43. Jain, R., Prajapati, D., & Dangi, A. (2023). *Transforming the financial sector: A review of recent advancements in FinTech*. https://ssrn.com/abstract=4380348

Chapter 7
Case Studies and Success Stories

7.1 Introduction

The incorporation of artificial intelligence in labor and industrial relations signifies a fundamental change in our approach to work, employment, and employer-employee dynamics. Throughout this essay, we have examined the significant potential of AI to increase productivity, enhance decision-making, and revolutionize work interactions. AI has the potential to revolutionize various aspects of labor relations, from improving recruitment processes to enhancing workforce planning and streamlining collective bargaining. Despite its benefits, implementing AI in this field presents its own set of hurdles. Concerns such as job disruption, privacy issues, bias in algorithms, and the possible worsening of current disparities need to be addressed. The case studies we investigated highlight the potential and challenges of AI integration, emphasizing the importance of careful, ethical, and inclusive strategies for utilizing these technologies [1]. Ethical guidelines and governance structures are urgently needed to guarantee the responsible development and deployment of AI in the workplace.

Engaging stakeholders is crucial for the successful implementation of AI, necessitating continuous communication and cooperation among employers, employees, labor unions, policymakers, and AI developers. Skills development is essential in preparing the workforce for a future driven by AI, requiring substantial investments in education and training that focus on skills that work alongside AI capabilities. Regulatory evolution refers to legal and regulatory systems that must change to confront the distinct challenges presented by AI in the workplace, harmonizing creativity with safeguarding workers. Designing AI systems should prioritize diversity and inclusion, aiming to prevent and mitigate biases [2]. Increasing transparency and explainability in AI systems is crucial for building trust and accountability. Focus on humans means AI should aim to increase human abilities and enhance working conditions in labor relations rather than just substituting for human

S. Majumder, B. Misra, *AI-Empowered Industrial Relations*, Studies in Computational Intelligence 1254, https://doi.org/10.1007/978-3-032-14557-4_7

employees. Manufacturing is undergoing significant changes due to artificial intelligence, which can identify inefficiencies in production and streamline processes. Its capacity to handle vast quantities of data, whether from machines or human sources, has revolutionized operations and delivered consistently high-quality outcomes that comply with sector regulations. Moreover, AI has helped progress production design, a crucial factor in promoting innovation in manufacturing. PwC's study suggested that reinforcement learning, a branch of AI, can transform the production of electronic devices in smart manufacturing [3]. This technology optimizes production processes by dynamically adjusting machine parameters. The system maintains a competitive advantage and increases profits by continuously learning and adapting to maximize production, minimize errors, and optimize resource utilization. In general, AI has revolutionized manufacturing by promoting creativity, cutting expenses, and improving operational effectiveness. Let us examine primary AI uses in manufacturing for understanding.

7.1.1 Amazon

AI-powered manufacturing needs cobots to improve production by helping human workers. They help with packing and choosing items at fulfillment centers, among other tasks. These collaborative robots utilize AI algorithms to identify objects and move through intricate spaces while operating alongside human employees. For example, Amazon uses cobots powered by machine learning to speed up order processing, improve logistics, and enhance operational procedures [4]. These robots, which are enhanced with AI technology, demonstrate accuracy and flexibility when completing intricate tasks. They manage complex assembly processes and quality control checks while working closely with human colleagues. This collaborative approach ensures the peak performance of equipment, reduces maintenance expenses, and decreases downtime. Collaborative robots, also known as cobots, play a critical role in AI-powered manufacturing by increasing productivity through supporting human workers. They help with packing, selecting, and other duties while employed in fulfilment centers.

In 2014, Amazon created a recruiting tool using AI technology to automate the process of screening resumes. Nevertheless, the company determined that the system was biased toward female candidates, especially those in technical positions. The AI was trained on historical hiring data that mirrored previous gender biases in the technology sector [5]. The advantages of this approach include the opportunity for improved efficiency in reviewing resumes and the ability to handle a high volume of applications rapidly efficiently. On the other hand, obstacles such as algorithmic bias mirror and magnify past instances of discrimination, the absence of clarity in the decision-making process of AI, and adverse effects on diversity and inclusion initiatives.

7.1.2 Foxconn

The integration of AI in manufacturing is increasing precision and consistency, revolutionizing quality control methods [6]. Manufacturers utilize AI technology to analyse images or videos of products and parts through computer vision algorithms. These algorithms outperform humans in identifying defects, abnormalities, and deviations from quality standards with unparalleled precision.

Foxconn, a famous electronics producer, offers a clear example of the impact of AI on manufacturing quality control. Foxconn has enhanced its operations quality control processes by integrating AI and computer vision technology into its production lines. Artificial intelligence (AI) uses image and video analysis to rapidly and accurately detect flaws in electronic components, ensuring adherence to stringent quality standards. This implementation of AI improves efficiency and precision in production, allowing companies such as Foxconn to produce high-quality products on a large scale in the ever-changing electronics industry. AI trends in manufacturing are also observed in the field of predictive quality assurance. By analysing historical and current sensor information, machine learning algorithms can detect patterns and trends that could indicate potential quality issues [7]. Proactive producers can predict issues and address them before they impact the final product's quality.

7.1.3 General Electric

Optimizing manufacturing performance is crucial, with artificial intelligence (AI) sparking significant innovation in the industry. Artificial intelligence (AI) systems analyse historical and real-time data to identify trends, pinpoint irregularities, and develop data-based predictions. This enables manufacturers to increase equipment efficiency and optimize operations while decreasing downtime. General Electric (GE) provides a real-life demonstration of how AI improves factory performance optimization. GE integrates AI algorithms into industrial operations to analyse large volumes of data collected from sensors and historical data. This enables the GE to recognize patterns, forecast issues with equipment, and improve operational efficiency [8]. This forward-thinking approach enhances manufacturing productivity, reduces equipment downtime, and enhances overall equipment performance. Factories connected through AI showcase the incorporation of artificial intelligence into production processes, forming smart, interconnected ecosystems. Artificial intelligence in manufacturing processes real-time data from machines, predicts maintenance requirements, and optimizes operations with the use of IoT sensors. This interconnected system promotes effective communication between machines, allowing for quick adaptations to production schedules based on fluctuations in demand. Predictive analytics improve decision-making and ensure smooth operations.

General Electric (GE) utilizes AI-driven connected factories on its Predix platform. GE uses artificial intelligence in conjunction with the Internet of Things to monitor equipment health, predict maintenance needs, and improve production methods. The Predix platform utilizes data analysis and machine learning to minimize downtime and enhance efficiency within GE factories.

General Electric (GE) provides a real-life demonstration of how AI improves factory performance optimization. By integrating AI algorithms into its industrial processes, GE examines vast quantities of data from sensors and historical records. This enables the GE to recognize patterns, predict issues with equipment, and enhance operations. This proactive approach enhances manufacturing efficiency, reduces equipment downtime, and enhances overall equipment effectiveness [9]. Connected factories demonstrate the incorporation of artificial intelligence into production processes, forming intelligent, interconnected ecosystems. AI in manufacturing processes real-time data from machines, predicts maintenance requirements and enhances operations with IoT sensors. This interconnected system allows for effective communication between machines, enabling quick adjustments to production schedules based on fluctuations in demand. Predictive analytics improve decision-making, guaranteeing smooth operations. General Electric (GE) utilizes AI-powered connected factories via its Predix platform. By combining artificial intelligence with the Internet of Things (IoT), GE oversees the health of equipment, forecasts maintenance requirements, and maximizes efficiency in production lines. By analysing data and using machine learning, the Predix platform reduces downtime and improves efficiency in GE factories.

7.1.4 Whirlpool

The utilization of AI and machine learning in industry is prominently seen in robotic process automation (RPA), specifically in automating paperwork tasks. Manufacturing procedures often require extensive documentation, including invoices, purchase orders, and quality control reports. These manual processes require considerable labor and are prone to errors, resulting in delays and inefficiency. The implementation of conversational AI in manufacturing streamlines these paperwork processes [10]. Smart bots with AI functions effortlessly retrieve data from documents, organize content, and enter it into appropriate systems. For example, Whirlpool utilizes RPA for automating manufacturing tasks, especially in assembly line and material handling operations. RPA robots manage repetitive and rule-based duties, maintaining precision and efficiency in the manufacturing procedure. Furthermore, Whirlpool utilizes these robots for quality control checks, utilizing automation to improve consistency and precision in evaluating final products. The whirlpool upholds high product quality standards by optimizing operations and implementing automated quality assurance procedures.

7.1.5 IBM

IBM has produced a HR platform named Watson Career Coach, which uses artificial intelligence to offer customized career guidance to workers. The system evaluates an employee's abilities, background, and aspirations and recommends possible career trajectories within the organization. IBM utilized its AI technology, Watson, to improve employee involvement and efficiency. Watson Workspace uses artificial intelligence to examine communication patterns and offer insights into team dynamics. The result was a 25% boost in project efficiency and increased employee satisfaction, fostering a more collaborative work environment. IBM's method highlights how AI can promote a cooperative and productive workplace setting. It also suggests appropriate training courses and employment opportunities. These advantages are similar to tailored professional growth opportunities for staff members and an enhanced ability to keep and move talented individuals within the company, insights based on data for planning workforces [11]. The obstacles are similar to difficulties. This ensures that the AI system's suggestions are unbiased, ensuring the privacy and security of employee information, and achieving a balance between AI-powered guidance and human discernment in career choices.

7.1.6 Unilever

Unilever has put in place an AI-powered hiring process for junior roles. Applicants engage in games rooted in neuroscience to evaluate their skills, provide video interviews reviewed by AI for both language and facial cues, and obtain continuous feedback during the entire procedure. The following benefits are as follows. Decreased time taken to fill a position and expenses associated with hiring expanded varieties in the pool of candidates. Enhanced applicant experience through fast response times [12]. The challenges are such as securing the fairness and accuracy of AI-powered evaluations, dealing with privacy and data usage issues in video analysis, and equilibrium between AI evaluations and human judgment in making ultimate hiring choices. Unilever, a large multinational company in the consumer goods industry transformed its hiring procedure through the use of artificial intelligence. By utilizing a candidate assessment platform powered by AI, Unilever achieved a substantial decrease in hiring expenses and time. The outcomes were impressive: a 50% reduction in hiring time, a 75% decrease in recruiting costs, and a significant increase in candidate variety. This case study demonstrates how AI can remove biases and make the recruitment process more efficient [13].

7.1.7 Siemens

Siemens has created an AI system named "Futuresight" to help with workforce planning. The system uses both internal and external data to forecast future needs for skills, pinpoint possible gaps in skills, and suggest approaches for improving the workforce. The advantages are as follows: anticipate future skill requirements, utilize data to make informed decisions in strategic staffing planning, and enhance the matching of employee skills with company objectives [14].

The challenges lie ahead, guarantee that AI predictions are precise and dependable, deal with employees' possible worries about job stability, and strike a balance between AI suggestions and human wisdom in strategic planning.

7.1.8 UNI Global Union

The UNI Global Union, a worldwide labor unions, has created principles for the moral application of AI in work settings. These guidelines cover topics such as transparency, accountability, and the effects of AI on employment and working conditions. These advantages include the active involvement of labor unions in influencing AI regulations, a focus on safeguarding employee rights in the era of artificial intelligence, and a structure for conversation between employers and workers about AI integration. The challenges lie ahead, i.e., Ensuring that guidelines are widely adopted and enforced, staying up to date with quickly changing AI technologies, and finding a balance between promoting innovation and ensuring worker protection [15]. These examples demonstrate the intricate balance between advantages and obstacles when using AI for labor and industrial relations. They emphasize the importance of thorough planning, ethical deliberations, and continuous communication among all parties for the effective integration of AI in the workplace.

7.1.9 Bosch

Bosch uses big data and machine learning technology to enhance product quality through optimizing manufacturing processes in its facilities. The company claims that its data collection and analysis methods have been revolutionized by recent developments. Advanced deep learning techniques have led to considerable advancements in automated optical inspection, anomaly detection, root cause analysis, and production scheduling. To strengthen its position further, the company runs the Bosch Center for Artificial Intelligence, which concentrates on developing and integrating advanced AI technology and services in different sectors. This dedicated research and development endeavor includes exploring and integrating deep learning, natural language processing, probabilistic modeling, and reinforcement learning [16, 17].

7.1.10 Schneider Electric

Schneider Electric has openly stated its dedication to implementing digital transformation throughout the entire organization. One recent instance is its implementation of Jo-ChatGPT. In contrast to ChatGPT, which is available to the public, this internal tool sets employees up for success by securely granting them access to the capabilities of OpenAI. Consequently, the data remain within the company's boundaries, a crucial aspect mentioned by the Chief AI Officer for business success. AI is changing industrial systems, providing organizations with the chance to access value, efficiency, and more independence [18]. Labour shortages, plants running at full capacity, and growing demands for quality products have made it a key focus for operations, IT, and engineering leaders. The Schneider Electric Artificial Intelligence Hub employs AI technologies to revolutionize energy management and automation in various industries, enabling sustainability and efficiency while ushering in a digitized, electric future. Specializing in energy management and automation worldwide, they offer a distinctive range of interconnected technologies: connected products, edge control and apps, analytics, and services.

7.1.11 Rockwell Automation

The manufacturer from Wisconsin gained attention by introducing a new AI tool called the asset risk predictor (ARP), which enables users to analyze maintenance data via AI to identify anomalies, increase OEE, and schedule maintenance more accurately. This advancement uses AI sensor data, machine recipes, and operational environments to predict problems, helping customers avoid failure and downtime. Furthermore, Rockwell stated that the incorporation of ARP into a production setting can yield outcomes within a few days. Rockwell Automation plans to enhance Emulate3D by integrating NVIDIA Omniverse Cloud APIs, offering users data compatibility, real-time collaboration, and realistic visualization for creating, constructing, and running digital twins of large-scale production systems. A new study conducted by Rockwell Automation revealed that artificial intelligence is considered the most important feature by manufacturers for achieving significant business results. Indeed, 83% of manufacturers plan to integrate GenAI into their operations by 2024. Through this partnership, NVIDIA has become an official member of the Rockwell Automation PartnerNetwork™, allowing Rockwell customers to utilize NVIDIA applications to increase the resilience, flexibility, and sustainability of their operations [19].

7.1.12 Cisco

By introducing the network intuitively, Cisco is transforming the way networking is understood. Cisco uses machine learning to analyse large amounts of network data for detecting abnormalities and selecting optimal network settings. Ultimately, Cisco will enable networks to operate on the basis of intent, be autonomous, and self-repair. The network will autonomously redirect traffic and bounce back from outside threats such as cyberattacks and internal issues such as device malfunctions [20]. By utilizing a centralized management application, machine learning software examines configuration, telemetry, and traffic patterns to recommend optimization and security actions, which ultimately simplifies wide-area network deployments and improves performance. Machine learning is utilized to analyse network data for detecting activities that indicate threats such as ransomware, cryptomining, and advanced persistent threats in encrypted traffic flows.

Moreover, Cisco utilizes AI and ML to aid in complete, automated, coordinated reactions among different security elements to safeguard organizations in an ever-changing threat environment. Machine intelligence is used to detect harmful domains, IP addresses, and URLs proactively, safeguarding cloud access for businesses in multicloud settings. Once a malicious agent is discovered on one network, it is immediately added to the blacklist on all customer networks. Machine learning is applied to detect abnormal activity in IT environments by dynamically studying user behavior, safeguarding the utilization of SaaS applications. Machine learning is utilized for safeguarding Infrastructure-as-a-Service instances through the detection of malicious communications and sophisticated threats [21].

7.1.13 Electrolux

In recent times the multinational home appliance manufacturer Electrolux Group experienced a talent shortage. According to their Global Talent Acquisition Director, AnjaUllrich, "it is essential to stay ahead of talent market trends during times of labor shortage." The TA team realized that they needed to improve the experiences of candidates, employees, recruiters, and hiring managers by digitizing processes to maintain a competitive edge. They also aimed to decrease hiring time and expenses while increasing internal mobility [22]. They needed an AI-powered platform that could keep up with their plans to revamp nearly every aspect of their hiring process. Their recruiters are empowered to nurture leads by sending pertinent content that is tailored to a candidate's stated preferences, career goals, and interests owing to the potent combination of an external career site that is highly personalized, an internal talent marketplace, an active talent community, a talent CRM, and automated campaign functionality. The platform's AI-driven fit scoring, candidate matching, and one-way interviews can help recruiters and hiring managers improve the screening and selection process to find better fits faster. Automated AI scheduling removes unnecessary back-and-forth communication, expediting the process and enhancing the overall experience for applicants who apply and meet the interview criteria. Since implementing this comprehensive AI-driven platform, Electrolux has seen an 84% increase in applications under review, a 51% decrease in incomplete applications, a 9% reduction in hiring time, a 20% decrease in time spent on one-way interviews during hiring, and a 78% increase in time saved owing to AI scheduling [23].

7.1.14 Brother International Corporation

Brother International Corporation, the top provider of office and home supplies, needed a better plan to attract talent and boost its brand. They thus embarked on the use of AI for advertising their brand and attracting potential candidates. They needed a professional website to showcase their authentic employer brand, provide personalized job suggestions to candidates, and feature a chatbot for a friendly first interaction with visitors. They utilized AI-based talent analytics to automatically utilize data insights to enhance application choices for candidates, and they introduced a new CRM system to assist in evaluating passive candidates and obtaining potential leads following the launch of their upgraded website. Without this AI recruiting platform, Brother's recruiters would not be able to collect any leads from the chatbot, similar job subscriptions, or partial applications. Darius Smith, Brother's director of talent marketing and employee engagement, declared that this type of efficiency is extremely advantageous, especially for sales and marketing roles with higher levels of output. After only 3 weeks of rebranding their career site and implementing new AI recruiting tools, Brother experienced a 140% rise in completed applications, a 45% surge in total page views, 40% growth in job seekers, a 15% increase in returning job seekers, and a 25% decrease in application completion time. "The reality is that 99% of applicants will leave without being hired for a single position," Smith stated [24].

7.1.15 Mastercard

Mastercards and Phenom collaborated to implement their vision with advanced automations, ethical AI, and timely data to enhance the experience of staff and job seekers. They know that they need a partner dedicated to enhancing the user experience and maintaining the efficiency and consistency of our internal processes. Kerry Royer, SVP and Global Talent Acquisition Leader at Mastercard, mentioned the importance of integrating the career site with the application process and CRM to gain insights into the entire candidate experience. Mastercard and Phenom introduced various solutions, including a new career site, Talent CRM, campaigns, Talent Analytics, and automated interview scheduling. Additionally, they established dedicated teams for recruitment marketing and direct sourcing to discover numerous potential leads and create a personalized, interactive candidate experience. By implementing targeted, multichannel recruitment marketing efforts, Mastercard's continuous hiring strategy attracts individuals interested in joining their talent network for current and future roles. To meet their business needs quickly, they can maintain a steady flow of qualified workers. Their proactive approach helps them with their high hiring volume, especially after incorporating phenom automated interview scheduling to streamline the previously time-consuming, mostly manual process [25]. In both the near and distant future, the team has profited from attracting, involving, and converting a greater amount of talent. Owing to the new, internationally applicable job platform, individuals looking for work spend more time on the Mastercard's career site and submit applications more often than before, when two-thirds of visitors leave the job search page. Increasing the number of leads in talent scout allows us to build a higher-quality team. Moreover, enhancing our communication with potential candidates will help us stay in touch with them, building a strong group of potential candidates for the future. Matthias Leitzmann, Global Talent Discovery Head at Mastercard, stated that the use of this method has allowed them to expand their investment towards achieving long-term success. Automated interview scheduling has been a significant improvement for both Mastercard's internal team and prospective candidates. Over 5000 interviews were scheduled, with 88% of them being arranged within 24 h of the request. Leitzmann reported that the interview scheduling time has been reduced by more than 85%. This increased efficiency allows us to attract top talent more efficiently by simplifying internal procedures, minimizing administrative tasks, and enhancing the candidate's overall experience.

After a year of collaboration, Mastercard's talent community grew from having fewer than 100,000 lifetime profiles to having more than one million profiles. As a result, the number of influenced hires (from sourcing and recruitment marketing campaigns) increased from less than 200 in 2021 to almost 2000 in 2023 [26]. Additionally, they streamlined and combined more than 75 local career sites into one, which noticeably increased website visitor retention (~60%) and loyalty rates (~27%).

7.1.16 Panasonic

Businesses can better understand what motivates employee engagement at work via AI-based tools. Employers can create a better, more inclusive workplace by using AI-powered surveys to gather employee data. AI technologies also enable businesses to pinpoint areas in need of development and suggest solutions that will benefit the entire group. Panasonic North America revolutionized its HR management by implementing the Visier people insight platform. Previously, the organization struggled to retrieve accurate information to direct its human resources strategies toward achieving successful business outcomes [27]. Panasonic currently utilizes the Visier People's Organization to combine data, analytics, and instant insights in a smart platform. According to Lydia Wu, the director of HR strategy and technology, this has increased employee satisfaction and shown employees that integrating their work can increase productivity.

7.1.17 Health Enterprises Manipal

According to a case study, Manipal Health Enterprises, also known as Manipal Hospitals, sought to transition from transactional to strategic HR by implementing a system that could provide doctors, nurses, and other staff members with round-the-clock responses to their HR-related inquiries. The healthcare company developed MiPAL, a virtual assistant that proactively answers employee questions about holiday calendars, taxes, paystubs, leave time, and related topics via desktop or mobile devices, using Leena AI's service delivery and engagement platform [28]. This led to more than 60,000 h saved for the HR staff and workers, a 5% yearly reduction in new recruit attrition, and a reduction in the average time needed to resolve employee cases from 2 days to 24 h.

7.1.18 Goggle DeepMind

Google DeepMind created the AI model AlphaFold, which was trained on enormous databases of known protein structures. It outperforms current techniques in terms of speed and accuracy by evaluating the angles and distances between amino acids to forecast how a protein will fold. This discovery marks a significant development in computational biology. It significantly speeds up the process of finding new drugs and understanding diseases. Additionally, it established a new standard for biological computational techniques. AlphaFold2 is a multi-component artificial intelligence (AI) system that predicts the three-dimensional structure of proteins based on their primary amino acid sequence using machine learning. One example of an artificial neural network is AlphaFold2. It consists of an assembly of simulated nodes connected by mutable connections. These networks are capable of machine learning. AlphaFold's network is called a "deep learning" approach because it has several layers of nodes. AlphaFold is a preview of the future and what could be achievable in biology with the use of AI and computational techniques [29]. Though incredibly complex and emergent, biology may be seen at its most basic level as an information processing system.

7.1.19 *Zara: Using AI to Shape the Future of Retail*

Success in the fast-paced fashion sector depends on accurately forecasting trends and effectively managing inventory. Zara has to meet customer demand and avoid overstock while swiftly adjusting to shifting fashion trends. Zara uses artificial intelligence (AI) algorithms to examine sales data, consumer preferences, and fashion trends. Additionally, the AI system helps with inventory management by making sure that popular items are swiftly supplied and that stores aren't overloaded with unsold merchandise. Production and distribution are both optimized with this method [30].

7.1.20 *Netflix: Using AI to Customize Entertainment*

Even though we might not be aware of it, the streaming market has grown much more competitive. One of the greatest strategies to keep current clients is probably to provide them with personalized entertainment. AI enters the picture here. Netflix created a sophisticated AI-powered recommendation system that examines user preferences, ratings, and viewing patterns. Because they are more likely to discover information that piques their interest, consumers are kept interested by this tailored approach, which also improves their entire watching experience. As more people join the site, subscription fees rise [31]. It results in increased user involvement as a result of customized preferences.

7.1.21 *Salesforce*

In March 2023, Salesforce, a cloud-based software provider with a focus on CRM goods and services, introduced Einstein GPT. OpenAI is coupled with generic AI software to create personalized marketing content, generate emails, assist with basic customer care, and compile and update knowledge articles. To assist staff in evaluating their present tactics, Einstein GPT offers data insights on topics including marketing trends, customer interaction, and industry trends in addition to integrating with Salesforce's CRM platforms. Einstein GPT is a fantastic illustration of how AI can be included into CRM software and meet the demands of employees across multiple departments, despite the fact that the product is new to the market and is still being enhanced [32].

7.1.22 *Adidas*

Adidas, a well-known seller of sports goods, uses generative AI because of its vast data storage capacity. Engineers may utilize the company's information store using an interactive interface and get responses to both generalized and hyper-specific questions by using an AI data management tool. The integration of AI into their database has relieved them of a significant administrative burden, enabling them to concentrate on the essential elements of their LLM projects, as stated by Daniel Eichten, Vice President of Enterprise Architecture. In addition to database maintenance, the AI product provides safe data storage, which cuts down on the time required for data coding [33].

7.1.23 *Canon*

Since its initial release, Canon's digital mailroom system has led the way in robotic process automation (RPA). All incoming mail can be automatically recorded, recognized, verified, and sent to the appropriate systems or individuals with pertinent index data thanks to a digital mailroom. The intelligent mailroom, according to Canon, is the next stage of automation. Integrating digital and paper-based data into reliable, efficient, and effective procedures will be the main problem of the future. As a result, businesses require more sophisticated digital mailroom solutions that facilitate data collection through all channels [34]. The Multichannel Advanced Capture is one instance of an intelligent mailroom. First, automated credit and identity checks are performed. A second human check can be performed if all of the first checks are successful.

7.1.24 *American Express*

In the financial industry, credit card fraud is a serious problem that erodes consumer confidence and causes large losses. American Express required a quick and effective method to identify and stop fraudulent transactions. American Express analyzes transaction data using machine learning algorithms. These models spot odd trends and actions that point to fraud. The system gets better at identifying fraudulent activity, sending out real-time notifications, and stopping illegal transactions by continuously learning from improved data. Financial losses are minimized as a result of fewer fraudulent operations. It also uses improved customer security and trust in financial transactions [35].

7.2 Conclusions

Artificial intelligence (AI) has become a disruptive force in many facets of the economy and society in the quickly changing twenty-first century. It has the potential to completely transform labor and industrial relations, presenting both difficult problems and previously unheard-of opportunities. This study examines the complex ways in which AI influences labor negotiations, the nature of work in the future, and the greater dynamics of industrial relations. Governments have a significant influence on how AI is developed and used, and they have quickly adapted to recognize the significance of technology for science, economics, and self-governance. However, government institutions are still lagging behind, and it will take consistent time and money to meet the challenges presented by quickly changing technology. Governments must control not only the most significant societal effects of AI applications but also the future to guarantee the development of knowledgeable communities. Over the last 5 years, artificial intelligence has advanced remarkably and is now influencing people, organizations, and culture in the real world. This chapter covers several AI implementation strategies in various business organizations. It is anticipated that the majority of jobs will be moved to a different industry, primarily the service sector and that new service models, such as the gig economy and the sharing economy, will be developed.

References

1. Cao, Z. (2022). Online dispute resolution mechanism in China: Principle of proceedings and impact of technologies. *China and WTO Review, 8*(1).
2. Lindquist, D. H., & Dautaj, Y. (2021). AI in international arbitration: Need for the human touch. *Journal of Dispute Resolution, 1*, 39.
3. Singh, B. (2023). Unleashing alternative dispute resolution (ADR) in resolving complex legal-technical issues arising in cyberspace lensing e-commerce and intellectual property: Proliferation of e-commerce digital economy. *Revista Brasileira de Alternative Dispute Resolution-Brazilian Journal of Alternative Dispute Resolution, 5*(10), 81–105.
4. Farooq, N., Rafique, Z., Merchant, A., & Narejo, K. R. (2025). Investigating how artificial intelligence AI systems powered by emotional recognition technologies can assist in conflict resolution by understanding human emotions and behavior. *Review of Applied Management and Social Sciences, 8*(1), 193–205.
5. Zafar, A. (2024). Balancing the scale: navigating ethical and practical challenges of artificial intelligence (AI) integration in legal practices. *Discover Artificial Intelligence, 4*(1), 27.
6. Ford, M., Gillan, M., & Ward, K. (2021). Authoritarian innovations in labor governance: The case of Cambodia. *Governance, 34*(4), 1255–1271.
7. Woodcock, J., & Cant, C. (2022). Platform worker organising at Deliveroo in the UK: From wildcat strikes to building power. *Journal of Labor and Society, 25*(2), 220–236.
8. Lofaso, A. M., & Stephens, A. M. (2022). Alternatives to mainstream alternative dispute resolution: Eliminating forced arbitration agreements as a condition of employment. *Utah Law Review, 2022*(5), 1015.
9. Rizzo, A. (2023). The changing landscape of worker rights in the 21st century workplace. *New York University Annual Survey of American Law, 79*, 221.

10. Jolley, S. (2022). Home run or strike out: Can baseball arbitration solve America's medical debt crisis? *Journal of Dispute Resolution, 169*, 172.
11. Cherkaoui, M. D. (2023). Small states' pursuit of impact at the UN Security Council: The case of Tunisia 2020–2021. *International Peacekeeping, 30*(3), 380–409.
12. Majumder, S. (2022). The moderating role of employee commitment and its impact on employee involvement and organizational productivity. In *Proceeding of 4th virtual international conference path to a Knowledge Society-Managing Risks and Innovation, PaKSoM 2022* (pp. 465–470)
13. Obadara, O. E. (2016). Effectiveness of collective bargaining as a tool for industrial disputes resolution. *SIU Journal of Management, 6*(2), 2229–0044.
14. Budlender, D. (2013). Informal workers and collective bargaining: Five case studies. *WIEGO Organizing Brief, 9*, 1.
15. Ukokhe, E. S., & Florah, O. M. (2022). Effect of collective bargaining on industrial disputes management. *European Scientific Journal, 7*, 585–585.
16. Ibietan, J. (2013). Collective bargaining and conflict resolution in Nigeria's public sector. *IFE PsychologIA: An International Journal, 21*(2), 220–231.
17. Comboh, M. A. (2014). Examine conflicts in industrial relations & collective bargaining context and its impact on workers & organization performance. *Academy of Contemporary Research Journal, 3*(1), 14–25.
18. Gahan, P., Pekarek, A., & Nicholson, D. (2018). Unions and collective bargaining in Australia in 2017. *Journal of Industrial Relations, 60*(3), 337–357.
19. Araujo, S., Safradin, B., & Brito, L. (2019). *Comparative report on labour conflicts and access to justice: the impact of alternative dispute resolution*. Framework Programme of the European Union.
20. Majumder, S., & Dey, N. (2022). Knowledge management in various sectors. In *AI-empowered knowledge management* (pp. 37–61). Springer Singapore.
21. Ibsen, C. L. (2021). Conciliation, mediation and arbitration in collective bargaining in Western Europe: In search of control. *European Journal of Industrial Relations, 27*(1), 23–39.
22. Asamu, F., Asaleye, A. J., Arisukwu, O. C., & Rasak, B. (2019). Industrial conflict and collective bargaining: evidence from north central region of Nigeria. *International Journal of Mechanical Engineering and Technology, 10*(3), 120–128.
23. Katsaroumpas, I., & Koukiadaki, A. (2019). Greece: 'Contesting' collective bargaining. In T. Müller, K. Vandaele, & J. Waddington (Eds.), *Collective bargaining in Europe: Towards an endgame* (Vol. 2, pp. 267–293).
24. Majumder, S., & Dey, N. (2023). Artificial intelligence: The future of people management. In *The Vogue of managing people in workplace* (pp. 83–102). Springer Nature Singapore.
25. Radogno, C. (2022). Reconceptualizing the international health regulations in the wake of COIVD-19: An analysis of formal dispute settlement mechanisms and global health diplomacy. *Yale Journal of Health Policy, Law, and Ethics, 21*, 90.
26. Chatterjee, M., & Majumder, S. (2024). Industrial relation climate and provision of labour welfare measures in manufacturing sector. *Journal of Management, 23*(1), 26.
27. Ige-Olaobaju, A. (2017). Alternative dispute resolution and collective conciliation in Nigeria: A review of contemporary literature. *International Journal of Business and Management, 12*(8), 261–273.
28. Grubesic, I. (2023). Collective labour disputes: Between judicial and peaceful dispute resolution. *Annals Fac LU Zenica, 33*, 285.
29. Powles, J., & Hodson, H. (2017). Google DeepMind and healthcare in an age of algorithms. *Health Technology, 7*(4), 351–367.
30. Purawat, S. (2024). Digital marketing in ZARA. In *Designing tomorrow: AI, ethics, and society's next steps* (p. 144). Paper2Publish.
31. Raghavapuram, S. (2024). *Custom AI Chatbot as an advanced user search system: AI enhancing the user watching experience for Netflix films*.

32. Kaliuta, K. (2023). Personalizing the user experience in Salesforce using AI technologies. *Computer-Integrated Technologies: Education, Science, Production, 52*, 48–53.
33. Jiang, R. X. (2023). Research on the digital marketing strategy of Adidas. *Advances in Economics, Management and Political Sciences, 54*, 306–312.
34. Overman, D. (2022). *Canon launches new US products at RSNA show*. AXIS Imaging News.
35. Giglio, G., Michalcova, S., & Yates, C. (2007). Instilling a culture of winning at American express. *Organization Development Journal, 25*(4), 33.

Chapter 8
Conclusions

Currently, much research is being conducted on theory, frameworks, and tools for explainable AI (XAI), and it might be difficult to articulate problems and goals coherently. There are now at least two strands that occasionally overlap and complement one another. First, practical strategies for improving the transparency of prediction models that are automatically learned—for example, through deep or reinforcement learning—were developed. The second seeks to foresee the detrimental effects of opaque models to regulate or control significant repercussions of inaccurate forecasts, particularly in delicate fields such as law and medicine. The development of techniques to enhance the building of predictive models with domain expertise can help in creating explanations for forecasts that are comprehensible to humans. This is occurring concurrently with AI legal issues such as the General Data Protection Regulation (GDPR) of the European Union, which establishes guidelines for the generation of explanations from automated or semiautomatic decision-making. We should remember that explainability is one of the oldest areas in computer science, even if there is a growing recognition of its importance due to the research activity around it. In reality, early artificial intelligence was interpretable and retraceable, making it clear to people how it works. The main objectives of this research are to identify the overarching concepts and their significance in furthering the creation of XAI systems, to recognize their historical foundations, and to highlight the most significant obstacles to progress. Artificial intelligence (AI) has applications in labour and industrial relations for workforce management, negotiations, dispute resolution, and policymaking. It may be used for everything from delivering advanced analytics for strategic decision-making to automating administrative duties. The goal of artificial intelligence development is to integrate human thought with mechanical systems. The purpose of this event is to decrease the need for human involvement in mechanical work and enhance productivity. Automation is utilized in various areas, such as industrial electronic services and personal devices, to enhance tasks and replace human abilities. In instances

S. Majumder, B. Misra, *AI-Empowered Industrial Relations*, Studies in Computational Intelligence 1254, https://doi.org/10.1007/978-3-032-14557-4_8

where human errors can occur in the work process, robotic involvement in a factory can effectively eliminate these errors. Hence, the adoption rate of Air increased over this period, as it is built with powerful algorithms and can perform complex tasks without any errors. The adoption of automation in industries and businesses is progressing at a rapid pace, implying digital transformation and technological advancements in the business environment. Moreover, Industry 4.0 has accelerated the digitalization process and provided data and information for commercial and non-profit activities. AI can process, manage and use data, making it well suited for implementation in business environments.

Predicting business-relevant data is a supplementary method for making intelligent AI decisions in the business world. It can also serve customers 24 h a day, 7 days a week without the need for intermediaries. Using AI to manage operations benefits businesses and has led to the rise of AI. Automated technologies in production processes reduce labor costs and improve efficiency. AI devices can work around the clock without human assistance, scaling business capabilities and reducing operational costs. The reliability and efficiency of AI help reduce business costs and increase profitability. The data analysis capabilities of AI offer valuable insights and lower analysis expenses. AI-powered technologies are not only efficient at creating goods and services on time but also have minimal mistakes.

The elimination of human error in the production process ensures high-quality products and reduces labor costs, which impacts the unit production cost and increases the company's profits. Moreover, these technologies are effective in producing products in large quantities, as they can provide services to business organizations 24/7. Another advantage of implementing AI technology is that it is characterized by a low error rate, as there is no human intervention in its operation. Highly accurate processes are effective when a company operates at a large scale and provide an opportunity to increase not only profits but also business expansion. Organizations that implement AI-based technologies have the opportunity to build consumer loyalty through automated communications such as web graphics, calls, emails, etc. Hence, AI proves to be efficient in engaging with numerous customers simultaneously and providing responses to each of them, thus bolstering trust in the company. Business operation functions have been linked to the traditional labor force since the dawn of the first industrial revolution.

Nevertheless, during the fourth industrial revolution, automation has transformed the traditional work setting, with most tasks now being executed by automated technologies that need less human involvement. AI technologies such as robots and automatic cat treatment devices demand expertise in technology advancements. The collaboration of employers has impacted the technical advancements in commercial organizations. Companies using AI require less staff, leading to lower labor expenses but diminishing the pool of human resources available. Essentially, the implementation of AI systems in businesses will result in higher rates of layoffs and joblessness. Nevertheless, additional positions are generated as part of this transition, resulting in a change in the employment demographic from less skilled workers to more skilled workers. Technological advancements influence the actual workspace, connecting pay directly to abilities. Real-time data are pushing the new work environment for sales organizations. The data offer improved insights into market and other business factors that the traditional workforce cannot provide as accurately. The low-skilled labor force may be more prone to making mistakes in their work, leading to negative impacts on the business. Nevertheless, automated technology operates with great precision. This is beneficial for corporations. Furthermore, these technologies are capable of functioning autonomously and in the absence of human involvement. Hence, automation technology is beneficial for companies, with AI technology becoming more crucial in terms of human resources and labor relations. Essentially, the implementation of AI systems in businesses will result in higher rates of layoffs and joblessness. Nevertheless, additional positions are generated as part of this transition, resulting in a change in the employment demographic from less skilled workers to more skilled workers. Technological advancements influence the actual workspace, connecting pay directly to abilities. Real-time data are pushing the new work environment for sales organizations. The data offer improved insights into market and other business factors that the traditional workforce cannot provide as accurately. The low-skilled labor force may be more prone to making mistakes in their work, leading to negative impacts on the business. Nevertheless, automated technology operates with great precision. This is beneficial for corporations. Furthermore, these technologies are capable of functioning autonomously and in the absence of human involvement. Hence, automation technology is beneficial for companies, with AI technology becoming more crucial in terms of human resources and labor relations. AI also supports continuous learning by providing updates and information on the basis of the latest HR research and developments.

AI is considered one of the most transformative technologies of the current era and is able to completely overhaul industries and sectors. AI has the ability to streamline tasks, enhance human abilities, and produce fresh perspectives and possibilities. However, what implications does this have for the future of employment and human resources? We delve into the myths and realities of AI's influence on employment and how HR leaders can prepare themselves for upcoming changes. One of the main concerns people have about AI is that it will take over jobs currently done by humans and lead to high levels of joblessness. Nevertheless, this misunderstanding fails to acknowledge the ever-changing aspects of work and the supporting function of AI. A recent study by Gartner states that by 2025, AI will generate more employment opportunities than it displaces while also improving the quality and efficiency of current jobs. AI will not take over human jobs but instead will change the tasks and abilities that humans engage in. In the retail industry, AI can assist with tasks such as inventory management and customer service, allowing humans to concentrate on merchandising, marketing, and building relationships. AI can assist with quality control, predictive maintenance, and design optimization within manufacturing, allowing humans to concentrate on innovation, collaboration, and problem-solving.

Rather than perceiving AI as a danger, everyone should recognize it as a resource that can improve human abilities and achievements. AI can streamline monotonous, mundane, and unprofitable tasks, allowing individuals to dedicate their time and resources toward more imaginative, intricate, and valuable tasks. AI can enhance human decision-making by offering insights, suggestions, and forecasts through the use of vast amounts of data and advanced analytics. AI can assist humans in problem-solving, acquiring new skills, and improving collaboration. AI in finance can assist in identifying fraud, evaluating risks, and optimizing portfolios, whereas humans can offer tailored guidance, establish trust, and guarantee adherence to regulations. In the field of healthcare, AI can assist in diagnosing illnesses, suggesting treatments, and keeping track of patients, whereas humans can offer empathy, compassion, and ethical decision-making.

In the field of education, artificial intelligence can support individualized learning, evaluate advancement, and offer feedback, whereas humans can offer encouragement, direction, and interpersonal connections. Science fiction has long featured the idea of AI taking over the planet. There are several tales of artificial intelligence programs that take over governments and break into the world's most guarded networks. Under no circumstances is this feasible. First, since AI programs are only utilized as tools, they cannot be granted such national security privileges. Without human assistance, they will be unable to make such decisions.

Algorithms used in artificial intelligence are just algorithms. They are merely a complicated collection of instructions that a computer must obey; they are not at all like the functioning of the human brain. Although they are inspired by the structure of the human brain, contemporary AI innovations such as neural networks remain unable to think like people do. At least in the context of AI as it exists today, a computer program cannot reproduce many cognitive processes. Furthermore, because there are still many unidentified factors at play, it is very challenging to fully replicate a human brain in software.

The idea that more data inevitably leads to stronger AI is another misconception. First, the quality of AI depends on the data it consumes. The majority of the advantages of training the AI are lost if the data are erroneous or improperly formatted. This is because AI merely searches through the data to identify the best answer; it does not enhance the data that are provided. This implies that for AI to be genuinely effective, any data it receives must be in a machine-readable format, necessitating human labeling. Labeling the vast volumes of data that they gather is a challenge for even enormous corporations.

Despite the promise of AI to improve human performance, its implementation will determine its success. The capacity of AI to enhance human performance frequently depends on the caliber and volume of data it can access as well as how well it is incorporated into processes. AI will not function successfully without a rigorous and tried-and-true implementation, particularly in an enterprise setting. The best outcomes are achieved via a well-rounded approach that combines advanced AI capabilities, high-quality data, workflow linkages, and human judgment. AI is transforming the job market by changing job functions and the essence of work. This encompasses the rise of technological unemployment, in which some jobs are rendered redundant because of automation, along with the development of new positions that necessitate varied skill sets. The growth of AI has resulted in greater implementation of algorithmic management in work environments, which can improve efficiency but may also trigger worries about employee autonomy and job satisfaction. This approach to management frequently depends on making decisions based on data, which can result in a work environment that is more regulated and supervised. With the rise of AI technologies, there is an urgent requirement for proper regulation to tackle concerns like data privacy, market competition, and the ethical consequences of AI in the work environment. The book probably stresses the significance of creating policies that harmonize innovation with safeguarding workers' rights. The implementation of AI could worsen income inequality, since the advantages of heightened productivity and efficiency might not be shared fairly among all workers. Workers with high skills might experience wage growth, whereas those with low skills may encounter job loss. The book likely addresses the idea of the "future of work," emphasizing how AI will require a transformation in workforce training and education. Employees must adjust to emerging technologies and develop skills that enhance AI systems. AI is impacting global trade and industrial relations by transforming the production and distribution of goods. This change might result in alterations in competitive advantages across countries and sectors. "AI in Industrial Relations" likely indicates that while AI offers considerable prospects for boosting productivity and efficiency, it also introduces challenges that necessitate careful attention to regulatory structures, workforce adjustment, and the socioeconomic effects of these technological innovations.

MIX
Papier aus verantwortungsvollen Quellen
Paper from responsible sources
FSC® C105338

If you have any concerns about our products,
you can contact us on
ProductSafety@springernature.com

In case Publisher is established outside the EU,
the EU authorized representative is:
Springer Nature Customer Service Center GmbH
Europaplatz 3, 69115 Heidelberg, Germany

Printed by Libri Plureos GmbH
in Hamburg, Germany